More Praise for *Radical Marketing*

"Great premise. Fabulous case studies. Startlingly original. Exactly right for the times."
—Tom Peters

"This book is revealing, refreshing, and readable—a practical mind-stretching guide to nurturing a brand."
—Rosabeth Moss Kanter, Harvard Business School,
author of *Rosabeth Moss Kanter on the Frontiers of Management*

"Radical marketers follow a different set of rules in serving their markets. The real value of this book will be to traditional marketers, who need either to learn from radical marketers or lose market to them."
—Philip Kotler, Professor of International Marketing,
J. L. Kellogg Graduate School of Management, Northwestern University

"Today's marketplace is all about cutting through the clutter and breaking new ground. After reading the case studies of the major players in this book, the concept of *Radical Marketing* won't seem so radical. These days, every mainstream marketer needs to consider this type of strategy."
—Stuart Layne, Executive Vice President of Marketing and Sales, The Boston Celtics

"Radical marketing, in today's media-cluttered, image-cluttered, consumer environment, may be the only kind of marketing that gets anyone's attention. Now, more than ever, the old school thinking about marketing in business practice should be thrown out the window. If results are what you want, then a little radical mo-jo in your marketing mix is what you need."
—Angel Martinez, CEO, The Rockport Company

"My advice to CEOs: Read this book before you sign off on the marketing budget. (And my advice for the ones that create the marketing budget: Read this book before your boss does)."
—Ray Lane, Chief Operating Officer, Oracle

"Vibrant, fun, and illuminating, *Radical Marketing* makes other marketing books look tired. If you're only going to read one marketing book this year, make it this one."
—Nancy Austin, co-author of *A Passion for Excellence*

"Relevant, realistic, and radical ideas based on vigorous, powerful, and deep thinking, presented in an exciting, engaging, and readable style!"
—Benson P. Shapiro, former Malcolm P. McNaire
Professor of Marketing, Harvard Business School

"Ten fascinating stories of creative firms using radical means to build brand and customer relationships show the path to success in the new media age."
—David Aaker, author of *Building Strong Brands*,
Professor of Marketing Strategy, University of California, Berkeley

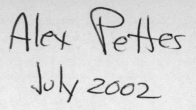

RADICAL MARKETING

RADICAL

FROM HARVARD TO HARLEY, LESSONS FROM TEN THAT BROKE THE RULES AND MADE IT BIG

MARKETING

Sam Hill and Glenn Rifkin

A HarperBusiness Book
from HarperPerennial

A hardcover edition of this book was published in 1999 by HarperBusiness, an imprint of HarperCollins Publishers.

First HarperPerennial edition published 2000.

Designed by Christine Weathersbee

Library of Congress Cataloging-in-Publication Data
Hill, Sam.
    Radical marketing: from Harvard to Harley, lessons from ten that broke the rules and made it big/Sam Hill, Glenn Rifkin—1st ed.
        p. cm.
    Includes index.
    ISBN 0-88730-905-4
    1. Marketing—Management. 2. Marketing research. 3. Marketing—Planning. I. Rifkin, Glenn. II. Title.
HF5415.13.H547 1999
658.8—dc21   98-31064

ISBN 0-088730-979-8 (pbk.)
00 01 02 03 04 ❖/ RRD 9 8 7 6 5 4 3 2

To John Diamond, who taught me marketing
SH

To my son, Benjamin, my greatest inspiration
GR

Contents

CONTENTS

Preface

The Story Behind the Book

I am a professionally trained traditional marketer.

I have a very strong vested interest in the marketing status quo. So it may seem somewhat out of character for me to write a book about radical marketing and to comment on the extraordinary successes achieved by a bunch of unorthodox marketers, many of whom openly challenge guys like me and question the very formulas we have long thought of as *immutable*. Nonetheless, I now find myself coauthoring just such a book.

My epiphany came in 1996 in a trendy, white-tablecloth New York restaurant. As chief marketing officer of Booz-Allen & Hamilton, the well-known management consulting firm, one of my duties was to lunch with journalists and try to flag stories that featured the firm in a good light. It was an inherently frustrating task for both sides. Journalists don't really care about our ideas, breakthrough or not, nor do they appreciate being manipulated into doing free advertising for consulting firms. What they really want is to get some juicy dirt on our clients. We, in turn, are absolutely, positively committed to not giving away any secrets. The net result is a level of mutual frustration on a par with that of teenagers slow-dancing.

In this particular interview, we had already exhausted all of my carefully planned topics and all of his questions, and our entrées hadn't arrived yet. The journalist sat bored, examining his fingernails. I was making little roads in the tablecloth with my fork. Sweat was beading up on my PR guy's forehead as he sat watching us, disconnected and distracted. Finally, in desperation, I blurted out, "Well, you could do a story on our Marketing Hall of Fame, the list of the world's best marketers."

He looked up, curious. Encouraged, I went on. "Nike, P&G, Madonna, Iams, Harley-Davidson, NBA, Providian, the Grateful Dead."

"Why," he asked, "are the Grateful Dead on the same list with P&G? That's radical."

At that moment, I didn't have a well-rehearsed answer, but I knew, however radical, that the Grateful Dead and Harley-Davidson belonged on any list of great marketers. So he went back to his nails. There was no story. And I went back to work.

But I continued to think about the list. I became obsessed with the question of how and why my list of best marketers could contain both an obscure pet food company in Dayton, Ohio, run by a former purchasing agent, and mighty Procter & Gamble, inarguably the best marketing company the world has ever known. I began to understand how great brands emerge from unexpected—indeed, radical—places, just as they do from conventional marketers like P&G. I used the list at conferences, debated it with my colleagues, added names, then deleted them, built files on the contenders. I began examining every company I encountered for radicalness.

I continued to play with the list whenever I met with journalists. Indeed, it might have remained just a list if not for Joel Kurtzman, editor of *Strategy & Business,* and Hank Gilman, assistant managing editor of *Fortune.* It was Kurtzman who first commissioned the veteran business writer Glenn Rifkin to write a case study of the Grateful Dead's approach to marketing, and Gilman who assigned a reporter, Erin Davies, to do a feature on the broader list.

The reaction from readers was remarkable. The Dead piece was picked up by several newspapers and inspired a big feature article in the *Financial Times* in London. Kurtzman received calls from marketing professionals across the country applauding *Strategy & Business* for its cutting-edge insight. The enthusiasm for the piece was so great that Kurtzman commissioned a series of case studies for the magazine on radical marketers.

But what really convinced me that this was more than just an interesting story was a phone call from Davies. She rang me in Hong Kong the week before her article went to press. I answered the telephone groggily.

"Where did you get this list of companies?" she demanded. "Do you realize that every single one is growing like crazy and is absurdly profitable?"

I sat straight up in bed. Obviously, radical marketing was more than just lunch conversation. My own research and the series of articles Rifkin was writing for *Strategy & Business* had already begun to validate my initial theory. *Fortune's* analysis added more support to the argument. Clearly, there was more to the concept than I had realized.

However, I knew that I would have neither the time nor the particular journalistic talent to explore the topic thoroughly on my own. I was fortunate that Glenn Rifkin, who had been doing the case studies for *Strategy & Business*, was now equally obsessed. We agreed that we both wanted to really dig in and understand this phenomenon of radicalness. We wanted to get inside these marketers and understand *how* they did it. Thus began a yearlong research and writing effort during which we conducted hundreds of interviews, across the United States and the United Kingdom, and reviewed mountains of existing work in order to identify and investigate a list of radical marketers. The result of that effort is this book. We hope you find these cases as insightful and enjoyable as we have.

—Sam Hill
Chicago, November 1998

Introduction

What Is Radical Marketing?

Why is Madonna a radical marketer and the Spice Girls are not? Why the Grateful Dead and not Kiss or Milli Vanilli? Why Amazon.com instead of Microsoft? Nike rather than Reebok? Why include organizations that many don't think of as marketers at all, like the Harvard Business School? And if so, why Harvard and not Northwestern? How can frumpy Budweiser be a closet radical and Miller be secretly traditional despite the wild, youthful tone of its latest advertising?

Why not Gucci with its fifty-foot-high G-string billboard in Manhattan? Why does Ralph Lauren, who was one of the first designers to figure out a way to sell upscale shirts and sheets side by side, have a radical bent? Why not Michael Levey, the father of infomercials? Why not Du Pont, which invented the concept of branded ingredients like Teflon well before 3M, Nutrasweet, and Intel? Why not, for that matter, Procter & Gamble? Surely any company that invented brand management and soap operas and is single-handedly trying to eliminate the coupon industry must qualify as radical. Indeed, these are all extremely innovative and successful marketers. All broke the rules in some way, shape, or form, yet in our judgment none are radical. What, then, does it take to be radical?

Being a radical marketer goes beyond being innovative or successful or even wild and crazy. Radical marketers differ from traditional marketers both in how they view the market and in the techniques and approaches they use (or don't use): they are deeply skeptical of most market research; CEOs lead the marketing function; they have tiny marketing departments composed of passionate missionaries and a marketing plan based primarily on grassroots communication; and they use advertising in an extremely selective way that militarists would call a "surgical strike capability"—short, highly targeted, and very intense.

In contrast, traditional marketers tend to rely heavily on market research, professional marketing departments, and marketing plans based primarily on advertising. P&G, despite its brilliance, is still a traditional marketer. Bob Herbold, formerly head of marketing at P&G and now COO of Microsoft, told the *Financial Times* that in consumer marketing, "marketing comes down to one thing: communicating an image of the product via television."

In all, as we shall see in Chapter 2, there are ten major differences in the approaches radical marketers use. These differences are profound and striking. But one set of differences is even greater than those of technique. The technical differences are, for the most part, simply the natural outgrowth of something much deeper—that is, the difference in how radical marketers view the market and themselves. Words like *vision* and *values* and *passion* have been used so much and so broadly in the business literature of late that we hesitate to employ them here. Nevertheless, the truth is that we left our meetings with traditional marketers feeling impressed and intellectually challenged. We left our interviews with radical marketers humbled by their achievements and envious of their passion. When we boil these impressions down, we come up with three essential ingredients.

First, radical marketers relate differently to their customers than do traditional marketers. There is none of the patronizing cynicism that all too often creeps into discussions in traditional marketing departments. Instead, there is a warmth and respect that translates directly into a visceral connection with the consumer. It would be easy to dismiss this as warm and fuzzy new-age folderol were it not for its breathtaking implications. Because radical marketers understand their markets so well, this intimate connection makes it possible for them to gain superior marketing and product development insights without employing huge marketing departments and allocating multimillion-dollar market research budgets.

Second, radical marketers are in it for the long haul. Their long view influences not only short-term, day-to-day budgeting decisions but also spills over into far more fundamental areas—like the caring tone of their customer communications and their fierce commitment to product quality. There is much less of a tendency to hype today if you know you'll have to face the same consumer tomorrow.

Third, most radical marketers are resource-constrained. At first blush, this certainly doesn't seem like much of an advantage. But in fact, the tremendous drive created by confidence in the consumer and a commitment to stick it out for the long term, while at the same time constrained by a lack of resources, results in something magical— breakthrough innovation. While not all radical marketers are small— quite the contrary, in fact—a surprisingly large number experienced some type of resource constraint in their history, forcing innovation at a pivotal point in their development.

Based on our in-depth research of radical marketers, we believe that the secret of their success lies somewhere in these three lessons— a visceral connection to the customer, a long-term commitment to the cause, and a willingness to work with and make the best of what's at hand.

—— How to Use This Book ——

Very few things have been overmarketed as much as marketing. One-to-one marketing, stealth marketing, inside-out marketing, relationship marketing, targeted marketing, direct, indirect, guerrilla, gorilla marketing—the shelves groan under the weight of books offering up marketing solutions. Many are good, some less so. In writing this book, we have tried to learn from all of them.

We have tried to be rigorous and intellectually honest in our assessments of radical marketers. While all have experienced admirable, sometimes remarkable success, radical marketers are still subject to the vagaries of business cycles and shifting markets, the unwanted attentions of giant competitors, and even poorly executed management decisions that have resulted in stumbles along the way. Indeed, as we put the finishing touches on this manuscript, several of our case study organizations were grappling with difficult business pressures: the NBA, for example, had initiated a lockout over player salaries.

Radical marketers tend to take nothing for granted and are thus less susceptible to dramatic falls. We have, however, avoided trying to shape their stories to meet our hypotheses or to portray them in a more flattering light. We have tried to present each case in as balanced a way as possible.

We have also tried to make this book useful, both to the general reader, and to senior managers and professional marketers, by including detailed case studies of the most salient best practices of radical marketers and discussing their application to large, complex marketing organizations. We hope this book will be read by senior-level executives who have not participated as actively as they could have (and should have) in their organization's marketing effort. We hope that excited executives will be crowding into conference rooms for the next marketing planning meeting. Professionals at all organizational levels should find this book useful as well. After all, each of us is, at the very least, our own brand manager. In today's hypercompetitive and dynamic world, we must market ourselves each day. As individuals, most of us need to be radical marketers, since we typically have more enthusiasm than professional training or resources to promote ourselves. But most of all, we hope this book is encouraging and useful to the next generation of radical marketers.

In Chapter 1, we make the case for radical marketing and contrast it with more traditional professional marketing. In Chapter 2, we present the ten rules of radical marketing—the charter that our radical marketers have followed and made their own. Though we have studiously avoided making this a how-to guide, we believe the lessons of radical marketing are succinct, purposeful, and adaptable to any organization with the will to succeed. And if there is a blueprint to be drawn, these rules provide a solid starting point. In Chapters 3 through 12, we present case studies of each of the radical marketers we have selected for analysis. And finally, in Chapter 13, we introduce the "trad/rad," the traditional marketers who have successfully adopted radical marketing techniques. It can be done!

RADICAL MARKETING

1

Getting to Radical

In 1982 Clyde Fessler was asked to start a club.

At the time, Fessler was the advertising and sales promotion manager at Harley-Davidson Motorcycle Company, which was teetering on the edge of bankruptcy. Just recently repurchased from its parent company, AMF, by a die-hard group of thirteen Harley executives, the Milwaukee-based motorcycle company was on life support, barely breathing after a decade-long onslaught by the Japanese motorcycle makers and a continuing string of poor management decisions by AMF.

The Harley brand, once synonymous with freedom, rebellion, and red-blooded American individualism, had been tattered by years of poor quality, fierce competition, and a dwindling market. The last of what was once a group of more than two hundred American motorcycle manufacturers, Harley was clearly at its final reckoning. The company had just one more chance to grow from survival mode into a new era of prosperity.

Fessler was a member of the company's marketing strategy team. An outspoken iconoclast and a risk taker, he was very much like the other members of Harley's new management team. With minimal resources and amid harsh economic conditions, the team had taken on the daunting task of resuscitating the Harley brand.

Among other responsibilities, Fessler was asked by then chief executive, Vaughn Beals, to start a factory-sponsored club for Harley owners. What might have seemed a low-priority item for a struggling company was to become a critical marketing weapon for Harley.

Fessler understood the reasons why. In addition to being a Harley manager, he was also a Harley customer, a bearded, leather-clad biker who rode with packs of Harley lovers and understood intimately the emotional attachments Harley owners felt to their bikes.

Even in the company's blackest days, a Harley-Davidson was more than a motorcycle—it was a way of life for its owner. And Harley had effectively transcended its 1950s image as the bike of choice for outlaw riders like the Hell's Angels. Harley riders might like beer and black leather jackets and boots, but they were honest, hardworking, law-abiding citizens. Fessler, of course, understood that Harley riders liked to gather, to ride, to rally and meet and swap tales about their bikes and their lives. This club would be an important link in reestablishing the bond between the company and its customers. More important, it would provide a community for the Harley nation.

Fessler foresaw a club that would be different. It would offer members perks like the ability to rent a Harley in any city where they might be traveling. It would have dozens of chapters so that customers all over the country could join a regional branch. It would join forces with a major charitable foundation and sponsor rallies around the country. And it would be called the Harley Owners Group, or HOG, a play on the popular name for Harleys. "Hog" had always had a negative connotation—a loud, obnoxious, road-hogging bike ridden by outlaw motorcycle gangs. But Fessler believed he could turn that negative into a positive by providing club members with an authentic identity they could proudly own.

HOG was officially introduced in 1983. Fessler met with the Harley dealers and designated a single dealership in each city or region as the host of the local HOG chapter. Newsletters and later a club magazine were used to communicate the few rules at the outset. In the spring of 1984, Fessler and Beals attended the first HOG rally in Gardenia, California; Fessler swallowed hard when only twenty-eight people showed up. He had hoped to build an organization of three hundred clubs across the United States that would boast 100,000 members. This was a humbling start. But despite its financial woes, Harley stayed with the club. Beals and the other Harley executives never faltered in supporting the club, and Fessler believed deeply in the "Field of Dreams" theory: "If you build it, they will come."

And come they did. Obviously, the club was just one factor in a series of strategic and radical decisions that fueled the company's remarkable rebirth. But as Harley-Davidson emerged from its brush with oblivion, stronger and more successful than ever, the club flourished beyond Fessler's richest fantasies.

Without an elaborate and expensive advertising campaign, Harley promoted the club through its dealer network with newsletters, posters, and word of mouth. Today HOG has more than 350,000 members and nearly 1,000 chapters around the world. The club sponsors hundreds of rallies each year, providing the structure and foundation for a worshipful and loyal Harley customer base. Every five years, HOG sponsors a massive birthday party for Harley-Davidson, an event entirely run and organized by employees inside Harley and volunteers from among HOG's members.

HOG is just one example of Harley's remarkable and decidedly nontraditional marketing prowess. And Harley is just one example of what we call "radical marketing." Simply stated, radical marketers are those who have achieved extraordinary success without the modern machinery of professional marketing. To be sure, Harley-Davidson today is a highly profitable corporation with a sophisticated marketing department and advertising know-how. In 1984, however, Harley-Davidson's limited resources were stretched as far as they could go. The company would reach this pinnacle by eschewing the traditional marketing formulas of giant brand-driven marketers like Procter & Gamble, Coca-Cola, and Walt Disney. Though most radical marketers lack the deep pockets and vast resources of the traditional marketing behemoths, their success is no accident.

Some of the techniques they use—tight brand control, for instance, and highly efficient customer loyalty programs—are those of classic marketing. But how they apply those strategies is radically different.

—— **The Essence of Radical** ——

In the hunt for radical marketers, we found an eclectic group of professionals—engineers, rock stars, lawyers, academics, consultants, technologists—whose résumés hardly resemble that of a professional marketer. If there was a single trait common to all the individuals identified, it was an exceptional level of intelligence. Another striking characteristic: most had no formal marketing background at all. Each in a sense invented the principles of marketing for himself or herself. Perhaps this is more than coincidence—with no formal marketing training, they drove their organizations to great success and achievement by ignoring academic marketing theories and bucking conventional wisdom.

Though they were all rebels with a cause, they became radical marketers because they had no choice. Driven by a dream that borders on obsession, hindered by limited financial resources, and inspired by a belief in their product, radical marketers bring a trump card to a game whose table stakes would otherwise keep them from playing.

Clyde Fessler, for example, may not have had a multimillion-dollar advertising budget or reams of research data on customer demographics. But he had something more powerful: a deep and visceral understanding of the soul of the Harley customer. Fessler says the company, battered by relentless Japanese competition, knew back in the early 1980s that it could not survive by playing the competition's game. "We decided very clearly, if the competition turns right, we'll turn left," Fessler says. "That became our strategy in everything we did and still do."

Eschewing massive advertising campaigns and expensive marketing and promotions, Harley-Davidson painstakingly carved out a decidedly nontraditional path back to profitability. By focusing on quality, tradition, and the powerful emotional bond between Harley owners and the product, Fessler and the Harley management team took the company from the brink of bankruptcy to a continuous

stream of record sales and earnings and a demand for Harley motorcycles that far outstrips supply. Harley's turnaround was indeed fueled
by turning left when the competition turned right.

By our definition, Clyde Fessler is a radical marketer. So are Shailesh
Mehta at Providian Financial, Richard Branson at Virgin Atlantic, Clay
Mathile at Iams Company, David Stern of the National Basketball
Association, Jim Koch of Boston Beer, the members of the Grateful
Dead, and the others in this book whose ability to market their product
successfully and build their brand in a nontraditional manner is proven
by any measure: market share, stock price, profit margins, fame, and
glory. These are not the usual suspects in professional marketing circles.

Mention the concept of radical marketing to anyone, and a candi-
date debate will erupt. How about Ben & Jerry's or Dell Computer or
L. L. Bean? Or Ty with its ubiquitous Beanie Babies? In fact, in the
pantheon of great American brands, there is a hall of fame's worth of
brilliant marketers, from Nike's Phil Knight to Apple's Steven Jobs,
from Oprah Winfrey to Madonna, who are not alumni of the Procter
& Gamble marketing department, who hold no MBAs in marketing,
and who began on their road to success with little money, no clout,
and nothing more than a deep belief in their product and the impossi-
bility of failure. They all turned left when conventional wisdom urged
them to go right—or worse, go home.

All worthy, no doubt. And like other halls of fame, this one is
exclusive but hardly finite:

The Grateful Dead
Providian Financial
Harley-Davidson
The Iams Company
The National Basketball Association
Snap-on Tools
Virgin Atlantic Airways
EMC Corporation
Harvard Business School
Boston Beer Company

—— Beyond Serendipity ——

It is tempting for those of us with more formal marketing credentials to dismiss these radical marketers for succeeding through serendipity or perhaps we begrudgingly attribute their success to stumbling on to a good strategy and having nothing more than the wisdom to recognize their good fortune. This would be a mistake. And indeed, the best of the traditional marketers recognize this. Top marketers from Detroit and New York have trekked to Milwaukee to learn more about Harley-Davidson's approach; financial services giants covet Providian's technology-driven marketing prowess; Anheuser-Busch has sincerely flattered Boston Beer by imitating its brand message about quality; and the best marketers at Procter & Gamble and elsewhere openly admire the brand-building capabilities of the Dead.

The Grateful Dead, for example, created a highly successful brand over a thirty-year span by offering a consistent, recognizable musical repertoire, by embracing a phenomenal fan base—known as Deadheads—and by exploiting the best aspects of that intensely personal relationship. Perhaps no one in the group could explain why the Deadhead nation—which continues to expand—emerged, why these fanatical legions literally followed the band around the world when it toured, but the band understood its value, embraced it with a series of inspired marketing decisions, and built a $100 million annual business around it. More improbable, but equally compelling, is the fact that the Grateful Dead brand lives on in highly profitable merchandise sales even though the band split up in 1995 when Jerry Garcia died.

Radical marketers tend to succeed by finding a consumer base they understand and sticking with it for the long term. Madonna, a legendary radical marketer, owes no small part of her success to her uncanny ability to reinvent herself and her career every few years. This ability is, in fact, based on a deep understanding of her loyal fan base and a wonderful ability to anticipate the changes her fans are about to experience in their own lives. From the saucy disco dancer turned singer to the material girl to *Evita* to her latest incarnation as a spiritual, yoga-loving, first-time unwed mother, Madonna has, by design, redefined herself while retaining her loyal fans and simultaneously winning new ones with each new persona. Each time she has reinforced a career that might have easily left her a one-hit wonder and emerged as nothing less than an international pop icon and enduring brand.

Oprah Winfrey rose from obscurity as an overweight black female morning-talk-show host in Chicago to one of America's wealthiest and most powerful media moguls by connecting with her customers, her viewers, in a visceral, honest, and personal way previously unknown in talk-show circles. Beyond Winfrey's multiple talents as an actress, producer, and businessperson, she understands the power of the bond with her customer base, a bond she has transformed into a brand. Dial Harpo Productions, Winfrey's Chicago-based company, and Oprah herself provides the friendly, welcoming voice message that instructs callers through the options. And while other show-business types remain hidden behind makeup and publicity agents, Winfrey turned her own lifelong weight problem into an ongoing theme on her show, thus creating widespread empathy among the women who make up her target audience and simultaneously discovering new business opportunities in diet and fitness markets.

—— Traditional Versus Radical ——

While classic, traditional marketers can appreciate the achievements of radical marketers, often there is no obvious way to apply these lessons to their own needs. In fact, to understand what radical marketing is, it is important to understand what it is not. Traditional marketing is:

- *Big.* As practiced by the likes of P&G, Philip Morris, General Motors, Coca-Cola, and Walt Disney, marketing is a powerful and highly evolved art form; in many ways, it's the engine that drives not only commerce but our nation's very culture. In order to do that, these organizations think in massive terms: big ideas, big advertising budgets, big audiences. The top fifty advertisers in the United States, for example, spent nearly $28 billion on advertising in 1997. Procter & Gamble spent nearly $2 billion alone! Anheuser-Busch agreed to pay a stunning $2 million for each thirty-second commercial during the 1999 Super Bowl, nearly double the record amount from the previous Super Bowl. And when Pepsi Cola wanted to change the color of its soda cans and bottles to a striking blue, the company, in late 1997, launched a $500 million marketing campaign and advertising blitz in the United States, after a similar $500 million international marketing effort in 1996. Pepsi did extensive test-marketing in New Orleans, Des Moines, and all over Europe before settling on the right look. All this just for a new design on a soda can!

- *Complex.* The cola war between Coke and Pepsi epitomizes traditional marketing. Pitting each company's vast marketing machine against each other, using basic academic marketing techniques— all aimed at teasing out consumer insights—it represents the best and worst of traditional marketing, with armies of young foot soldiers in multilayered marketing departments, often battling each other for corporate resources. It is a market-share war, a battle of demographics, skillful media buying, deep and plentiful research data, and clever but wildly expensive advertising.

- *Aimed at the center of a large "mass" market.* For many traditional marketers, brand management, advertising, and research are the ingredients of a blitzkrieg mentality. Conventional giant marketers don't think of marketing in terms of narrow niche channels but approach media buying as a set of demographics: six minutes on *Seinfeld* to target white twenty-five to forty-year-old males, in order to deliver twenty-five million households on Thursday night. Media buying, in fact, has become a commodity business, akin to buying pork belly or soybean futures on the Chicago Mercantile Exchange. Even in the midst of a dramatic shift to technology-driven mass customization, personalized direct mail, business on the Internet, and one-to-one selling in the marketplace, professional marketers continue to pay huge amounts of money for great quantities of data, load it into a big cannon, fire, and hope they hit something. As John Wanamaker once said, "I know half of my advertising is wasted; I just don't know which half."

- *Separated from the consumer.* The bigger the marketing organization, the more the marketers are separated by layers of bureaucracy from the consumer. When a powerful brand like Crest toothpaste starts to lose market share, the methodical bureaucracy within Procter & Gamble makes it difficult to respond not only to the more nimble competitors but to the media that inform the consumer. When the *New York Times* requested an interview about Crest for a 1997 article, P&G took two weeks to decide *not* to make an executive available for a comment. Big corporations often create vast marketing departments around individual brands, entrusting valuable corporate assets to groups of young marketers who might be six or seven layers removed from the core customer base. "Brands are valuable assets which have a massive impact on the way you run your business," said Raymond Perrier, brand evaluation director for Interbrand, a brand consulting firm, in an interview with the *Financial Times*. "No one would hand a $20 billion asset to a twenty-three-year-old in the marketing department—but many companies that aspire to global reach do just that with their brands."

- *Formulaic.* As long as there have been marketers, there has been a search for a marketing formula. All MBAs can rattle off McCarthy's four Ps—promotion, price, product, and place—the marketing guru's simple way of dividing the marketing world into neat bundles. More sophisticated marketers trained in the big marketing factories in Cincinnati and New York use more sophisticated formulas, but they are formulas nonetheless. The most common is the one used by consumer goods marketers. The vast majority of all marketing plans are built around this simple (though seldom written-out) formula: SOM = NPD + Promo + Adspend + ACV. (SOM stands for *share of market*; NPD is *new product development*, also called *product delta* in some marketing departments; and ACV stands for *all commodity volume*, a weighted distribution number tracked by the A. C. Neilsen Company.) It works something like this. The end objective of all marketing must be share of market. Market share comes from four things: frequent new product introductions, intense promotion (such as coupons, buy-two-get-one-free, and so forth), heavy advertising, and ubiquitous distribution. On the face of it, there's nothing wrong with this marketing plan, but as we will see, radical marketers break this formula in every way possible and are very successful using no formulas at all.

As a result of these characteristics, traditional marketing can often be useless or wasteful or both. Which isn't to say that traditional marketing cannot succeed. Practiced with academic clarity and precision, traditional marketing can be highly effective.

Philip Kotler, the author of *Marketing Management,* a preferred marketing textbook in graduate schools of business, writes:

> Authentic marketing is not the art of selling what you make but knowing what to make! It is the art of identifying and understanding customer needs and creating solutions that deliver satisfaction to the customers, profits to the producers, and benefits for the stakeholders. Market innovation is gained by creating customer satisfaction through product innovation, product quality, and customer service. If these are absent, no amount of advertising, sales promotion, or salesmanship can compensate.

The best traditional marketers understand their "art" this way and practice it with great success. It is no coincidence that Coke is the most recognized brand in the world and that generations of small children have embraced Mickey Mouse as a cherished friend. Marketing powerhouses like Coca-Cola and Disney are characterized precisely by the attributes cited in Kotler's definition of marketing: an ability to identify and understand customer needs and to create solutions that deliver satisfaction to customers as well as mountains of profits to corporations.

Radical marketers, it turns out, are driven by Kotler's tenets as well—identifying a customer's needs and delivering quality solutions that meet those needs. But radical marketers achieve similar or even greater marketing success with far fewer resources at far less cost.

Radical marketers often enjoy a remarkably tight connection to their customer base and are usually driven by a charismatic, visionary leader and a determined workforce built in that leader's image. Indeed, some radical marketers evolve into traditional marketers when sales and earnings start to skyrocket. Some, like Apple, forget their radical marketing roots and even go so far as to hire professional marketers (like Pepsi's John Sculley) to lead them. Others, like Nike, find a way to keep the connection to their radical roots and exploit those precepts using traditional marketing methods. There are lessons to be learned from each model.

As we noted in the preface, radical marketing has three key differentiating characteristics:

1. *Radical marketers have very strong visceral ties with a specific target audience.* Because of this visceral bond, they understand that single segment extremely well—so thoroughly, in fact, that they are often able to cut several complex and expensive steps, such as market research and the brand management superstructure, out of the marketing process.

For example, Clay Mathile, chief executive of the premium pet food maker Iams Company, decided early on that the Iams customer was the dog and the cat, not the pet owner. A healthier animal, a shinier coat, brighter eyes, and a longer life would sell the product far better than any advertising campaign. If you got the breeders, the kennel operators, and the veterinarians to see the results, he ventured, the word would spread. So Mathile spent thirty weekends a year traveling to dog shows and plying the breeders and show-dog owners with free samples of Iams when he first joined the company in 1970. He had his family, including his small children, hand-pack the free samples of the food to give out at the shows.

Mathile responded to the inferior, soy-based dry food the giant pet food suppliers were offering on the market by institutionalizing quality both in the product and into the Iams culture. He also knew intuitively that pet owners would pay a higher price for a better product. "Our primary customer is always the dog and cat," Mathile says. "Our products must live up to the highest quality standards in the industry." Under Mathile, Iams has grown from $16 million in 1982 to more than $500 million in 1997.

For most of its seventy-eight-year history, Snap-on Tools eschewed advertising completely, relying instead on the bond established with its core customer base, the auto mechanic, by the thousands of Snap-on dealers who arrived at the garages and service stations like clockwork every week in their familiar Snap-on vans. In 1994, however, Snap-on, today a highly profitable $1.7 billion company, quietly launched its first consumer advertising campaign, spending $2 million specifically to pay tribute to its oft-maligned customers. (Though Anheuser-Busch spent the same amount for a single thirty-second commercial during the Super Bowl, such spending at Snap-on represented a major commitment for an entire campaign.)

Realizing that auto mechanics had long been painted as unscrupulous and disreputable by Hollywood and the media, Snap-on decided to counter that image by running a series of print ads that cast mechanics in a highly favorable light, as professionals who take pride in what they do. "It takes a lot to be an auto technician" was the tag line in a series of ads that have run now for the past three years in popular magazines and trade publications. Snap-on was already the tool of choice for the 1.1 million auto mechanics in the United States. But the campaign touched a chord, providing a measure of status and pride that further cemented the company's relationship with its customers. Now Snap-on dealers report seeing framed copies of the ads hanging in the garages, service stations, and service departments of auto dealers.

In fact, radical marketers have a visceral view of the market because *they look like the market.* Rather than being trained in marketing techniques, radical marketers are trained in the market itself, a crucial difference. Indeed, what has happened in recent years is that traditional marketers have grown further and further away from their customers and the market. It is not at all unusual to attend a meeting in New Jersey where a thirty-year-old white male who makes $125,000 a year and grew up in an affluent American suburb stands in front of a room and proposes a communication strategy for incontinence products aimed at a seventy-year-old lower-income African American woman in Miami. His only understanding of the target audience comes from some highly amalgamated, quantitative attitudinal research and a few focus groups. This example may sound ridiculous, but it is very real.

Traditional marketers inside brand-driven corporations generally apply an intellectual rather than an emotional understanding of the market, relying too heavily on focus groups, research, and advertising campaigns. Shailesh Mehta, chief executive of Providian Financial, says that consumers in focus groups may say one thing but inevitably behave quite differently once they are buying in the real world. Coke learned that lesson dramatically when it unveiled "New Coke" in the mid-1980s. Consumers in focus groups and in taste tests told the company that they preferred—and would buy—New Coke. They didn't. That expensive disaster testifies to the danger of allowing research data to come between you and your target customer.

Brand managers whose hearts and minds are set on a fast career track—or as Pepsi's Roger Enrico dubbed it, "the Manager of the Month Club"—often seek to become general managers and have little emotional investment in a product they might be associated with for just two or three years. Furthermore, as large companies merge and consolidate, there is more and more bureaucratic separation between the marketers and the end user. Innovation and innovative thinking get bogged down as corporations have often become a gauntlet rather than a conduit for big ideas.

Indeed, in the history of marketing, thousands of techniques have been developed, all of them aimed at identifying and exploiting certain consumer behaviors and insights. Unlike traditional marketers, radical marketers don't have to tease out these insights because they live them. Ask Clyde Fessler of Harley-Davidson, or listen to Jim Koch, founder of Boston Beer Company, in an interview with *Inc.* magazine:

"I'm not knocking marketing people as individuals," said Koch, whose Samuel Adams Boston Lager has become the top-selling craft beer in the country since he founded the company in 1984.

> Many of them are warm, intelligent and creative. They're some of the business world's best and brightest. I only wish they'd get out and try to sell some of the product they're hyping. See, to the consumer—and I'm talking about the person sitting at the bar choosing a beer—markets don't exist. Market niches don't exist. These are concepts that exist only in the minds of people with a vested interest in promoting them. To me, the only reality is beer and people drinking beer. And to that guy sitting at

the bar, the bartender's word is more powerful than all the advertising he's ever seen. If the bartender says, "Want my advice? Try a Sam Adams—it's a helluva good beer," that's more powerful than $500 million worth of advertising.

2. *Radical marketers tend to focus on growth and expansion rather than on profit-taking.* They enter a market with a natural optimism that they will be able to grow and build and create more value. Failure is not an option.

Marketing plans are traditionally driven by research, demographics, and statistical analysis, and by slicing and dicing market segments in order to define target audiences. Often this research is done by outside consulting firms that fail to put the numbers into a relevant context, leaving more—not less—distance between the product and the customer. Radical marketers like Jim Koch and Clay Mathile believe so strongly in their products—that Samuel Adams is a better-tasting, higher-quality beer, that Iams really is a healthier food for your dog and cat—that the idea of failure is not part of the equation. These entrepreneurs, often starting out with little more than an idea, quickly realize that building a business takes time and that growth is more important than profits initially. Koch says that the best advice he ever received was "Jim, nothing good happens fast." That bit of wisdom, in fact, was whispered in his ear by a high school girlfriend. But, Koch says, "when you are building a company, it is not bad counsel."

In 1984 Koch literally carried bottles of Sam Adams beer from bar to bar trying to interest bartenders in the new brew. His goal was to sell five thousand barrels in three to five years, little more than an hour's worth of brewing for Anheuser-Busch. He had a long-term plan and the determination to stick it out.

This is not an argument against analysis. Indeed, some of our radical marketers are hyper-analytical. Providian's Mehta pioneered the use of individual behavioral data to develop one-to-one marketing programs. But it is an argument against using superficial statistics about an ill-defined market in lieu of genuine understanding of who your customers are and why they will buy your product.

Radical marketers will stick with an idea far longer than traditional marketers because the pressures to succeed, while just as great, are measured in dramatically different ways. Today professional marketers are more aware than ever that they must "get the message right" or it will be zapped in the first five seconds. They are finding that the holy grail of market-share gain is suddenly fleeting or temporary, that customers are more often attracted by price cuts and promotions than motivated by any long-standing loyalty or deep-seated belief in a particular brand.

But radical marketers understand the nature of their product in a way that would elude a professional brand manager whose emotional tie to a product is limited. At the National Basketball Association, for example, David Stern remains unruffled by the varied perturbations of the game, the antics of a Dennis Rodman, the violence of a Latrell Sprewell, or the retirement of stars like Larry Bird and Magic Johnson and even Michael Jordan. The product, he realizes, is the game itself, and that is a dynamic force, ever-changing, always subject to the idiosyncrasies and talents of the players. The NBA invests in the long-term vision of the game itself rather than in any one player or situation, and around the globe growth continues to be dramatic.

Such long-term commitment is usually coupled with an uncompromising focus on quality and customer service. To land a new account, EMC Corporation will install its million-dollar computer storage systems for free for several months and send dozens of field technicians to the customer's site to make sure the system is working. When a Virgin Atlantic Airways flight arrives several hours late at Heathrow Airport in London, there is a good chance that Richard Branson himself, the company's dynamic chairman, will be waiting at the gate to apologize personally for the inconvenience and to hand out tickets for future flights or gift certificates to a Virgin Megastore.

3. *Radical marketers tend to be very resource-constrained and are forced to make do with marketing budgets that are far smaller than average.* Such resource constraints tend to keep them very focused and promotes a willingness to try new, innovative ideas and "out of the box" marketing concepts. Classical marketers find this state of mind difficult to emulate; there is a tendency toward the jaded and cynical in the widespread mass markets, and bureaucratic corporate structures lack the flexibility to encourage creative thinking and entrepreneurial behavior. Despite the hype around "demassification," classic marketers

still emphasize quantity over quality. Traditional marketing organizations think big. A single brand group inside a giant consumer goods company might have a dozen people in it, all charged with touting a single toothpaste or potato chip. A manager several levels down in the organization might have a $75 million advertising budget under her jurisdiction alone.

When Koch introduced Samuel Adams beer, for example, he couldn't afford an advertising budget. For ten years, in fact, he had no marketing department at all. Instead, he marketed the beer through direct selling and grassroots public relations, going bar to bar himself proselytizing, cajoling, and pleading for a spot on the beer menu. While large corporations often spend millions of dollars on market research and consulting in order to name a product, Koch printed mock beer bottle labels and personally polled beer drinkers at bars and restaurants before choosing the name Samuel Adams.

Realizing that he could not compete with the advertising might of giant competitors, he relied on clever public relations efforts to land stories about his company in dozens of newspapers and magazines. With no advertising budget, Koch invested all the money he could in inexpensive but clever point-of-sale promotions to create awareness. Boston Beer, for example, introduced customized menu stands to bars and restaurants. Restaurants send their menus or beverage lists to Boston Beer, which produces tent cards and menu stands with the Samuel Adams logo on them. The company today produces more than two million menu cards a year.

Even when resources become available, radical marketers tend to think and act differently than the marketing powerhouses. In 1996 Harley-Davidson, though highly profitable, spent exactly zero dollars on advertising. Harley's rationale: the demand for its motorcycles was so high that every bike the factory could make was already spoken for. Why spend money on advertising Harley management concluded. Instead, the company funneled as much money as it could into increasing production, believing that the brand was strong enough to sustain itself in the marketplace for the short term without expensive ad campaigns.

Radical marketing is not about displacing traditional marketing— far from it. An admonition to simply "break all the rules" is silly hype.

Nike, which began life as a radical marketer but today spends more than $150 million in the United States annually on advertising, manages to retain the spirit and response of a radical marketer. Nike's advertising, beginning in the 1980s with the highly successful Michael Jordan campaign, played off CEO Phil Knight's deep understanding of and commitment to setting an emotional agenda for sports in the United States. "Just Do It" was not only a brilliant advertising campaign but a testament to Knight's belief in his product, which extended back to the company's earliest days when his "marketing" staff was made up of distance runners and he paid thirty-five dollars to have the famous "swoosh" logo designed. Even with a massive advertising budget, Nike managed to build its brand for two decades without eliminating its visceral connection to its customers.

Radical marketing, as our case studies demonstrate, is about more than just breaking rules. It is about creating an entirely new game in which you can write your own rules, sometimes on the very playing field of the existing game. Despite the vast differences in style and resources, radical marketing offers lessons that are universal, as relevant to marketing soup and shampoos as to promoting higher education and financial services. For the entrepreneur with little more than a dream and some early financing, or the small business owner in search of growth, the inherent value of the lessons in this book should be obvious. Our radical marketers have never forgotten the feeling of being in those shoes. Radical marketing techniques have proven equally effective for Fortune 500 companies such as Nike and Anheuser-Busch. There is much here to be learned by CEOs, senior-level executives, and marketing managers at large companies as well.

There is, after all, always something to be learned from the world's best, even if their strategies and styles evolved at an unlikely place—a Harley rally in Sturgis, South Dakota, or a beer hall in Boston—rather than in a conference room on Madison Avenue. Whatever stage of evolution your business may be in, these techniques should prove inspiring and invaluable to you as well.

2

The Nitty-Gritty of Radical Marketing

In introducing the concept of radical marketing, we began by describing radical marketers and the factors that are most important in their development—visceral connection to the consumer, long-term perspective, and a lack of resources. Descriptive analysis is useful in understanding how radical marketers became successful, but it is not terribly helpful for those trying to learn from these marketers and apply those lessons to their own situations. For that, what is needed is a more prescriptive set of guidelines that can be used to make pragmatic, day-to-day marketing decisions—what we call the "Rules of Radical Marketing."

We have stared hard at these case studies and examined them and discussed them again and again with many people in a range of industries and businesses. We have also spoken with the leaders of the organizations we profiled countless times, going back for more data, clarification, updates, additional details, and explanations. We pushed for an understanding of what made them radical and how they implemented and maintained these unique marketing techniques. Our conclusion is that there are many lessons to be learned from these stellar companies about radical marketing, but ten stand out.

—— The Ten Rules of Radical Marketing ——

1.
The CEO Must Own the Marketing Function

For today's CEO, the clamor for a piece of his or her time is unceasing. Leading business journals, from the *Harvard Business Review* to *Fortune* magazine, are constantly advising the CEO to personally take charge of any number of corporate domains, from employee communications to the strategic planning process to the year 2000 computing problem. To suggest that CEOs should personally lead the marketing effort may seem to be just another fruitless claim on executives' time. A claim it is, but far from a fruitless one.

For the CEOs of radical marketers, the one thing that is never, ever delegated is marketing. That's because radical marketers understand that corporations exist without shareholders and, in today's era of virtual companies, even without employees, but no business exists without customers.

Virtually all radical marketing organizations have CEOs involved in the marketing process at a level that would be unthinkable among most traditional marketers. Harley-Davidson's chairman, Richard Teerlink, and chief executive, Jeff Bleustein, actively ride with customers, attend rallies, solicit ideas, and turn them into marketing plans. Clay Mathile at Iams is so involved in the marketing process that he helped design the company's new corporate logo on a paper napkin over lunch. Shailesh Mehta, CEO at Providian Financial, shows up regularly at the company's back-office operations with boxes of cookies and milk and settles in with other senior managers to review customer files and plot new product and marketing ideas. Richard Branson arrives dressed in 1920s aviator garb to launch Virgin Atlantic Airways. In traditional marketing organizations, CEO involvement, if it exists at all, may be limited to a day or two a year reviewing a parade of dozens of brand plans.

For radical marketers, the chief executive officer is also the de facto chief marketing officer.

2.

Make Sure the Marketing Department Starts
Small and Flat and Stays Small and Flat

If CEOs are to stay actively involved with marketing, it is necessary to keep layers of people and bureaucracy from building up between them and the market. This is usually easier said than done. In most organizations and functions, layering is a natural process. Organizational pyramids seem to grow before our very eyes as vice presidents hire directors, directors hire managers, managers hire staffers, staffers hire assistants. In marketing, with its virtually inexhaustible stream of executional minutiae, pyramids seem to develop particularly rapidly.

Indeed, it is tempting to believe that it is possible to hand off the marketing function and stay fresh with customers by delegating down to a staff, who will then hire a market research firm to go talk to consumers and bring back useful insights. It is also tempting to believe that you can somehow stay in touch with consumers through reviewing the resulting market research.

It may be tempting, but it is unlikely to be true. Information is a dish best served warm. Filters are usually pretty subtle, and therefore all the more dangerous. Like the old party game "Telephone"—people sitting in a circle and each repeating a message to the person next to them, only to find it hilariously distorted when it makes its way back around—market data becomes distorted as it is handled. It is not at all unusual to see five or even ten layers of filtering between the consumer and the senior marketing decision makers in large professional marketing organizations. This filtering can fundamentally change the results.

That is why Jim Koch at Boston Beer refused to have a marketing department at all for the company's first ten years in business, and why Providian integrates marketing into all disciplines rather than treating it as a stand-alone department.

3.

Get Out of the Head Office and Face-to-Face
with the People Who Matter Most—the Customers

Even in a flat organization, it is possible to be distant from customers and to see them through secondhand market research and synthesized information. For radical marketers, customer proximity is an absolute essential. Radical marketers prefer data gathered directly to second-hand data. Rather than reading research reports, they read consumer letters. They listen to customers talk about their problems in their own words. They take this even further. They hunt down customers in the places where they live and shop.

In contrast, the closest many professional marketers get to customers is occasionally sitting in a comfortable chair behind a thick one-way mirror in a focus group facility watching "consumers" being carefully led through a structured discussion. (Often the focus group participants are not exactly the consumers the marketers had in mind when they first commissioned the research. As focus group usage has grown, it has become increasingly difficult to find qualified volunteers; often the people on the other side of the one-way mirror are paid semi-professionals.) Many senior marketers, unfortunately, don't even watch focus group discussions but rely on scanning the summary report.

This is not enough for radical marketers. Jim Koch of Boston Beer hangs out in bars. Every EMC executive, including Chairman Dick Egan and Chief Executive Mike Ruettgers, has a list of favored customers whom they call, visit, and actively court with books and other perks. They are constantly on the road, visiting customer sites and dining several nights a week with customers. Clay Mathile and Tom MacLeod of Iams spend weekends attending dog shows and visiting kennels. The Grateful Dead were legendary for spending more time on the road than any other band, and they paid close attention to all aspects of their live performances. David Stern sits in the stands at basketball games, not in the skyboxes. Great marketing is based on great insight. Insight can come only from understanding, and understanding only from proximity.

For radical marketers, "face-to-face" is a mantra.

4.
Use Market Research Cautiously

Constant proximity not only leads to better marketing, it removes the need for mountains of market research. In fact, the reaction of radical marketers to traditional market research varies from outright dismissal to cautious skepticism. Except for a few of the more radical of the radical marketers, like Jim Koch and Shailesh Mehta, few would argue that there is anything wrong with market research per se. Their opinion is that, like any tool, its value depends on how it is used. If used to supplement a well-grounded intuitive understanding of the market, most of our radical marketers feel it is a valuable help. If, however, it is used as a substitute for genuine consumer understanding, it becomes a dangerous distraction.

The problem with market research is simple—it deals with averages. It tells a marketer what an average consumer wants. But there are no average consumers. As the old saw goes, "Some people like iced tea and some like hot tea, but very few ask for lukewarm tea." Marketing history is replete with the failure of products and services like American Motors' Rambler automobile, which was designed to meet the needs of an average consumer. (And if you don't remember the Rambler, that's our point!)

Radical marketers use research differently from traditional marketers. Radical marketers go to consumers directly for ideas, and when they want to test those ideas, they ask consumers. Market research is used as a supplement to, not as a substitute for, consumer understanding.

5.
Hire Only Passionate Missionaries

One positive result of keeping a small marketing department is that each person can literally be hand-picked by the CEO more for attitude and raw talent than for marketing credentials. The companies we studied don't have marketers, they have missionaries. The organizations are often built in the image of their leaders. The NBA's front office is staffed with basketball zealots like Stern who love to promote the game. Boston Beer's first employee was Koch's ex-secretary, who was young enough to know the local bar scene and who shared her boss's enthusiasm for the product. Providian hires iconoclastic engineers and quantitative analysts who love mining data for business opportunities. None of them have anything remotely resembling significant marketing experience. All share a zealous passion for their customers and their products. When hiring the next generation of radical marketers, they search out not just skills but this same level of intensity and belief in what the company is trying to accomplish.

This question of zealotry is no small issue. It is extremely hard for even the most professional professionals to market something they really don't believe in.

We recall, for example, a meeting not long ago with an Australian automobile manufacturer to develop a new positioning for a struggling car brand. The car in question was losing sales and share each year, and despite pumping millions into product development and advertising, there had been no sign of improvement. At this crucial meeting, which bespoke the urgency of the situation, were the heads of marketing, sales, R&D, and the advertising agency, and even the division president.

After hearing everyone sing the predictable praises of the car and all the attendant marketing efforts, the finger was pointed at the customers for not realizing what a terrific driving experience awaited them in this great automobile. But just then the division president asked the sobering question, "Now tell me the truth: if you didn't work for this company, what would you drive?" One brave soul spoke up, then another, until all twenty people in the room had answered. Thirteen responded, "A BMW." Others said Ferrari or Saab or a variety of sport utility vehicles. Only one, the public relations manager, insisted he would buy one of the company's cars, but despite an ostentatious display of enthusiasm, he was far short of convincing. When pressed, each of the forty- or fifty-somethings admitted that they thought the car in question was for "old people," not really for them.

The marketing efforts have continued with little success. Sales are still dwindling. Our strong suspicion is that they will continue to do so until sooner or later the company finds and puts in charge people who really believe in the car and love the people who drive it. Until then, the passion is faked—and in marketing, as in love, it is almost impossible to fake passion.

6.
Love and Respect Your Customers

Iams' Clay Mathile once said in a *Forbes* interview, "I know who buys our dog food, it's people just like us." In the *New York Times,* Phil Lesh of the

Grateful Dead says of Deadheads, "We are them and they are us." Kim Clark, dean of Harvard Business School, says of the alumni, "They are our best salesmen." Throughout our research a consistent theme was the affection and respect with which radical marketers speak of their customers.

Further, all of the radical marketers in this book seem to respect customers as individuals. It is very easy to fall into the trap of describing customers in numerical terms and viewing them as a homogeneous mass. Despite the fact that Snap-on has over a million customers, the company views them as a million individuals. This view of customers as people, not statistics, is critical.

It is also easy to forget that even in the most ubiquitous of mass-market brands, a relatively small group of individuals is at the core of the success. Garth Hallberg, author of *All Consumers Are Not Created Equal,* has calculated that for a major yogurt brand that sells to more than one hundred million households, the most loyal one million households contribute more than one-half of the total profit. Radical marketers understand this and treat their customers accordingly.

When Snap-on runs a tribute campaign in trade publications saluting mechanics, it is more than a ploy to build share. It feels less like marketing and more like a sincere note from an old friend, and it's received accordingly. When the Dead allowed fans to tape their shows and even provided an advantageous area for them to do so, the rest of the record industry thought them mad for giving away sales. But by allowing fans to make tapes, and even to trade them with the agreement that they would not do so for commercial purposes, the Dead demonstrated a loyalty and a trust in the Deadheads that was returned many times over.

One of our ex-consulting colleagues summed it up well and eloquently. His simple view was that every call from a customer was "a gift from God." Any call, even a complaint, was to him a learning opportunity, a chance for honest feedback. Radical marketers take a similar view.

7.
Create a Community of Consumers

Radical marketers actively encourage their customers to think of themselves as a community, and of the brand as a unifier of that community. Few embody this concept better than Harley with its Harley Owners Group, the Grateful Dead with its Deadheads, and Snap-on Tools with its unique dealer network. The sense of community, like the passion, must be genuine. Mark O'Neil, head of marketing for the world's largest Harley dealership in Boston, calls his customers "family." He speaks of the importance of being there not just for the wealthiest customers who want to "buy an instant lifestyle" with a $20,000 purchase of a custom-designed motorcycle and all the attendant clothing and paraphernalia, but for the ones who "come in every week with their kids to buy a single chrome nut."

Community members signal their participation proudly, by wearing corporate logos on T-shirts, baseball caps, and class rings, and by displaying red toolboxes, bumper stickers, and even tattoos. Indeed, the "tattoo test" is an extreme but useful barometer of the successful community. Obviously, a tattoo is sufficiently painful and permanent that it makes a strong statement about commitment. Harley employees and customers sport tattoos. In fact, Harley devotes two full pages in its current annual report to discussing the importance of tattoos as a measure of brand equity. Nor are they the only customers this loyal to a product. Many Deadheads sport a red, white, and blue skull with a lightning flash or a grinning skull with a wreath of roses. There are Virgin V's and Nike swooshes. Even the more subdued brands have insignia that their customers proudly display.

Radical marketers like to hold events—concerts, festivals, motorcycle rallies, class reunions, seminars, neighborhood basketball clinics. These events range from a half-dozen people around a table in a pet store to fifty thousand motorcycles thundering down I-94 in Milwaukee. Such gatherings are an integral part of the creation of a community. Radical marketers also encourage and promote the clothing and bumper stickers and other badges of honor that identify the consumer as a member of a special group.

8.
Rethink the Marketing Mix

Of all the differences between radical marketing and traditional marketing, none stirs as much debate as the marketing mix—that is, how

much is spent and what percentage of marketing dollars go to advertising instead of other types of more highly targeted marketing communications.

Radical marketers market continuously and devote huge amounts
of money, effort, and time to communicating with their customers.
However, they seldom have huge advertising budgets. In fact, some,
like Providian, don't even have marketing budgets, reasoning that such
budgets act as "entitlements" and encourage spending when none is
needed—or, conversely, as ceilings, discouraging marketers from
spending more when they see an opportunity.

When radical marketers use advertising, they tend to do so in short,
sharp bursts, what we have called "surgical strike advertising." In contrast, traditional marketers typically use "adblast," huge and wildly
expensive amounts of continuous advertising. The ultimate example of
adblast, of course, is the Super Bowl, the commercials for which advertisers will pay $2 million for thirty seconds in 1999, and then wait for
the next morning's *USA Today* and *New York Times* to receive their
"grades" on how well their commercials were received. Such a strategy
may be exciting to the creative departments in ad agencies or to young
brand managers, but its effectiveness is suspect.

Radical marketers tend to use more one-to-one or targeted communications tools, ranging from direct mail to Web pages to local advertising
to sponsoring neighborhood basketball tournaments. The objective of
one-to-one marketing is dialogue. It is a lot more difficult for Jim Koch
to drive from bar to bar convincing bartenders to push Sam Adams than
to run a newspaper ad, but it is extremely effective.

This is not to say that traditional marketers use only advertising, or
that radical marketers don't. In practice, both radical and traditional
marketers use some combination of the two. Even the most outspoken
radical marketing critic of traditional advertising and marketing,
Samuel Adams beer, can be seen on network TV via a series of slickly
produced commercials. And traditional marketers are slowly shifting
away from large-scale, indiscriminate, mass market advertising and
toward highly targeted and personalized communication.

Kraft and TCI, for example, recently announced a deal to create
"sophisticated micro-marketing advertising vehicles that will reach con-

sumers with targeted messages on a household-by-household basis." Translated into English, that means households with teenagers will receive ads for pimple cream, and households with elderly members will get messages about in-home nursing. And who would believe that this quote in the *Wall Street Journal*—"We have got to rid ourselves of an obsession with television"—would have been uttered by someone like Keith Reinhard, who heads the giant advertising agency DDB Needham and is personally responsible for the McDonald's account. The marketing world is definitely changing.

Nonetheless, a huge gap remains. The basis of traditional marketing remains a belief in the effectiveness and economics of large-scale advertising. The two fundamentals of advertising are reach and frequency. Reach enough people often enough, and someone will buy the product. This fuels the view of consumers as targets, not individuals. A recent ad in media magazines shows a very graphic picture of a truck unloading consumers wrapped in brown paper with bull's-eyes painted on their sides.

This indiscriminate approach is fundamentally different from the radical approach. Radical marketers are not trying to reach huge segments of people in hopes that someone will find their message appealing and thus buy the product. They have defined a core group of loyal users around whom they have built their business and designed their marketing communication. They talk to that group. They define their market not in terms of demographics (for example, housewives between the ages of thirty-eight and fifty-two with one teenager living at home) but in terms of behaviors and needs (cat lovers or high-risk credit seekers, for example).

For traditional marketers, one-to-one marketing is a supplement to advertising. For radical marketers, advertising itself is the add-on.

9.
Celebrate Uncommon Sense

In a world of increasing fragmentation and what some have called the "demassified" market, it is not clear that it makes sense for any marketer to use these expensive solutions. But there is no question that for a smaller player to compete on those terms is folly. After all, David may have fought Goliath, but he certainly did not choose to wrestle him. The only way a smaller company with fewer resources can succeed against this type of might is to do something different. The best way to be sure that what you're doing is really different is to ask the experts. If they tell you it's impossible, you can be sure you're on the right track.

David Tait, head of Virgin Atlantic's U.S. operations, says, "If you really want to see Richard Branson's eyes light up, tell him something can't be done." All his business associates informed the brash Branson that the world simply didn't need another transatlantic airline. Sir Freddie Laker had already tried that and failed. On this and many other occasions, Branson simply turned the impossible into a highly profitable business.

For a young Jim Koch, already earning a lucrative six-figure salary as a manufacturing consultant with the prestigious Boston Consulting Group, jumping into the beer business could only be described as marketing madness. Hundreds and hundreds of small brewers had already proved that it was impossible to succeed, at least since the early 1970s, when Philip Morris bought Miller Brewing and started what J. M. Connor of Purdue has chronicled as the "beer wars." Philip Morris's strategy was to invest very heavily in advertising and quickly become the largest player, thus enabling itself to invest more heavily and therefore grow more, and so on ad infinitum. The net result was a dramatic rise in the price of participation in the brewing industry. The war was waged over the next two decades. Budweiser, one of the few competitors large enough to play by the new rules, responded immediately and forcefully. Others were less able. When the smoke cleared, more than three hundred small regional breweries had gone out of business. Koch jumped in anyway.

But Koch's decision was no more insane or impossible than Dick Egan and tiny EMC attacking IBM head-on. Or David Stern's challenge to turn around the moribund NBA. Or Clay Mathile trying to defeat the huge Ralston Purina marketing machine in St. Louis. Every single marketer in this book has at some point been labeled insane and told that what they were doing was impossible. Rather than being discouraged, they fed on it.

Indeed, radical marketers believe in uncommon sense, bucking traditional wisdom. Their eyes light up when they hear the words, "Well, everybody knows that the only way is to . . ." They refuse to apply the simplistic formulas of marketing.

They break the rules in every area—in advertising, in product development, in promotion, in pricing, and in distribution. For example, the distribution formula says that more is always better. Coca-Cola's Doug Ivester has been quoted as saying that his goal is for every human being on the planet to be within arm's length of a Coke. (One can only suppose he is saying this for effect.) For traditional marketers, it doesn't matter if there is a Coke machine across the street from the convenience store, in effect competing with itself. More is better.

However, radical marketers seldom follow this formula. Indeed, for the most part they deliberately limit distribution to create loyalty and commitment among their distributors. Iams, the Grateful Dead, Snap-on, Harvard Business School, Harley—all have eschewed putting their product into channels that would deliver more volume but didn't fit for one reason or another.

Perhaps it is because so many of our radical marketers lack formal marketing training that they are able to apply uncommon sense so well. For those who have been trained formally, it is much harder. Not too long ago, one of us received a call from a start-up technology company in San Francisco. The head of the small company had just written his marketing plan and was seeking some feedback before he put it before the board. It took almost an hour to work through the plan. It wasn't a bad plan, and at the end it was clearly better for the suggestions we'd made. However, while he was very polite and grateful, it was clear that he was still not satisfied with the conversation. In response to probing, he finally blurted out, "But what's the answer? Isn't there just a number I can plug in?" Like most managers trained in the analytics and rigor of MBA programs, he was looking for a simple formula.

There is, in fact, a simple formula employed by most professional marketers, and it often works: massive deployment of resources to simply overwhelm the problem, at substantial cost. Even when the formula works, the outlay is tremendous.

10.

Be True to the Brand

Radical marketers are obsessive about brand integrity, and they are fixated on quality. Iams almost went out of business rather than substitute cheaper ingredients in its dog food. The Dead truck and fly tons of gear and an army of technicians around the world rather than depend on rented sound equipment. While every other major rock 'n' roll act raised its ticket prices to astronomical levels, the Dead refused. Harley cuts its ad budget to zero and funnels its resources into increasing production and improving manufacturing quality. EMC builds automated sensors into its equipment that actually alert EMC engineers of impending failures; the company then sends an army of field service engineers to fix the problem. The customer doesn't even know that the incident transpired. Harvard Business School turns down a multimillion-dollar offer to run an executive education course for a company because the work does not enhance the knowledge and educational excellence of the school's faculty.

Every radical marketer would rather go out of business tomorrow than diminish quality today. It's easy to pay lip service to quality, to institute employee quality circles, to hire quality consultants, and to fill out applications for the Deming Prize. But radical marketers, each and every one, have at some point risked the business to maintain quality. They know that cutting corners on quality is like cheating on a diet— the results are cumulative and certain to show up sooner or later.

Nor is the radical marketing definition of brand integrity limited to product quality. More important, it is about remaining true to the brand. It is very common in traditional marketing to poll consumers and try to design a brand promise to reflect those needs and desires. This is called repositioning. However, if repositioning is unsuccessful, or if a new manager arrives with a different vision, it is common to see a brand's image change again and again, resulting in an identity crisis. Xerox, which used to be known as the "Copier Company," and then relabeled itself the "Document Company," is now trying to reposition itself as the "Knowledge Company." Brand extensions can exacerbate this. Chasing more and more customers, the brand becomes more and more banal, more accommodating, and less differentiated. Product lines that begin with very clear positionings, like Chevrolet trucks and GMC trucks, blur and overlap.

Marketing to existing customers is also good business. Rather than trying to develop brand or product extensions to attract new customers, radical marketers concentrate on developing new products to better serve the community they know so well. The Dead sells its community more than just live entertainment; it also sells CDs, clothes, and food. Virgin sells everything from records to travel. Traditional marketers tend to stay loyal to a product category and chase new customers. Radical marketers stay loyal to a customer group and chase new products.

What is most striking about our list of radical marketers is not how many things they do right. These are, after all, some of the most successful companies in the world. Rather, what is striking is how well the different elements work together strategically. It is easier to build community and remain true to the brand when you have zealots instead of marketing mercenaries. Hiring only passionate people and keeping the marketing department small obviates the need for market research. By avoiding market research, radical marketers have no option but to get out of the office and face-to-face with consumers. And on it goes.

The next ten chapters tell the stories of ten of the most remarkable brands we have encountered in over forty years of combined business experience. As you read, you will begin to see the rules in action, applied across a range of industries, company sizes, and competitive situations. We hope you will begin to understand how to think and market your product, service, or brand radically.

3

The Grateful Dead

Building a Rock 'n' Roll Brand

*"The relationship between the band and
the Deadheads needs to be nurtured because
they are us and we are them."*
—*Phil Lesh*

Radical marketing, by its very nature, can be applied by organizations both large and small across a wide diversity of industries. It often finds a champion in the most unlikely places. The Grateful Dead, for example, would seem a strange bedfellow in any collection of exemplary business organizations. A rock 'n' roll band, and a defunct one at that, seems hardly the place to find lessons in brand building and marketing.

Yet the Grateful Dead, over the course of a remarkable thirty-year run as a rock icon, employed a raft of nontraditional methods to build a brand that endures and continues to grow more than four years after the group disbanded. The 1995 death, of Jerry Garcia, the band's musical and spiritual leader, at the age of fifty-three, marked the end of an era as well as of the band. But if anything, the brand has actually thrived and grown stronger since Garcia's death, fueled by a broad and radical marketing plan by Grateful Dead Productions, the band's long-time corporate entity, and an insatiable desire on the part of Grateful Dead fans for the band to live on.

Because the lessons it offers are universal, as relevant to selling perfume or cars as they are to marketing music, the Grateful Dead is a radical marketer worthy of attention. As the group evolved from its early days in the psychedelic 1960s, it became much more than a set of talented musicians playing and recording a recognizable style of music. The Grateful Dead, through a series of both serendipitous circumstances and conscious best-practice business decisions, built a model that flew in the face of conventional music industry wisdom. What emerged was a highly successful, easily recognizable brand with the cachet of a Harley-Davidson and a vast following of fans known as Deadheads who were as devoted as a religious sect.

Today, despite the loss of revenues from concert ticket sales, the Grateful Dead brand does in fact live on. The Dead are, in many ways, in an enviable position. A highly profitable, debt-free, privately held thirty-four-year-old company like Grateful Dead Productions, still owned and run by the founders, is unusual in today's dynamic business environment. This fiscal serenity, along with the continuity of ownership and leadership, provides a prognosis for the future that is remarkably upbeat.

——— Keeping the Value Proposition ———

The remaining band members and their business advisers understand that the best brands can—and must—reinvent themselves again and again, like Madonna or the NBA, and that they flourish where others might simply close up shop and go home. Big traditional marketers like Pepsi and McDonald's spend hundreds of millions of dollars refreshing their brands, keeping them from getting stale. The Grateful Dead lost its musical center and guiding genius with the death of Jerry Garcia, but the value proposition for its customers never waned. In fact, quite the opposite occurred as the remaining band members and their organization found a way to reinvent the brand and make it flourish.

From its nondescript, 32,000-square-foot headquarters in Novato, California, Grateful Dead Productions has become the L. L. Bean of rock music, sending out its combination fan magazine and catalog to more than 150,000 fans who can choose from among more than 500 Grateful Dead items, from golf balls to CDs, and from baby clothes to toothbrushes. Employees wearing the group's trademark tie-dyed T-shirts ship more than 1,000 packages a day, and merchandise sales reached more than $8 million in 1998. That is just a fraction of the $60 million that all Grateful Dead items generate each year for the band, the record companies, and outside licensees. Grateful Dead Productions has revenues of more than $20 million from a combination of products that it makes and sells itself and royalties it receives from licensed items.

Because of its relentless touring schedule—the Dead played more than eighty concert dates each year for nearly thirty years—and its ability to hire and retain a highly talented road crew, the band developed unparalleled expertise in the marketing, promotion, and execution of musical events. Rather than laying off all these employees when the group disbanded, the band found new ways to draw on the expertise of these longtime loyal employees and create new revenue streams. Tapping these resources, Grateful Dead Productions created another business unit to sell its marketing services and expertise in concession sales, tour operations, and concert promotion to spin-off groups initiated by individual band members, as well to other artists like Bonnie Raitt, the Gipsy Kings, and Maxwell. The unit is even handling sports franchises, like the Oakland Raiders football team.

Grateful Dead Records, the band's longtime record label, continues to release CDs and videos from a vast archive of thousands of live recordings that the band created over the years. The unit has also branched out and is releasing CDs from other artists, such as the Allman Brothers and David Crosby and Graham Nash. Grateful Dead Productions handles all licensing for Jerry Garcia's estate, including the lucrative neckwear business he created in the years before he died.

In the works is a $60 million shrine to the Grateful Dead called Terrapin Station (named after a 1977 album). It will be located in San Francisco, where the group first came together. Though the *New York Times* called it "Disneyland for Deadheads," the remaining band members are adamant that Terrapin Station will not be a theme park or a Planet Hollywood look-alike. Rather, the 65,000-square-foot site will be a combination concert hall, museum, research center, amusement park, dance hall, and general gathering place for Deadheads, the largest such tribute location ever created for a single band. When the place opens, probably in the year 2000, more than one million visitors are expected annually. Like pilgrims to Mecca, Deadheads are likely to flock with religious fervor to this shrine.

Not bad for a group that no longer exists. And even more impressive for a band that never had a number-one hit single or album and whose appeal, though powerful, was narrowly focused.

The Grateful Dead represents the best of radical marketing because it focused on a simple value proposition that was built on a devotion to a unique but consistent style of music and a carefully established, long-term relationship with its customers. Unlike successful traditional marketers like Procter & Gamble, the Grateful Dead never used massive advertising or promotion; they simply went deep into a niche market. And in so doing, they won praise from even the most traditional of marketers.

"The Dead have an image, a brand equity, and trust from their customers," says Elizabeth Moore, corporate communications manager with Procter & Gamble in Cincinnati. "They met a genuine consumer need and never became a me-too product. There are very clear parallels to products we market." The parallels end, however, with the *way* they are marketed.

⎯⎯ A Clear Mission ⎯⎯

Like other great radical marketers, the Grateful Dead eschewed glitz and tricks and focused on sustained development against a single element, a marketing hallmark that is far too often ignored by even the biggest organizations. In essence, the Dead's story is a case study of substance over form in the context of niche marketing.

From the day the band came together, the group had a clear sense of what its "product" should be and who its audience was. But while the band members eventually started earning great sums of money and enjoying the lifestyles the money brought, they never put the money first and they never let the bottom line dictate what went out the factory door. The music was always the driver and the catalyst for all decisions and strategies.

Though they grew musically, the Grateful Dead remained consistent and true to their "brand." They picked a customer group, remained close to it, and didn't branch out. The Jefferson Airplane became the Jefferson Starship and went mainstream, recording pop songs in hopes of climbing the charts. In short order, the band faded into obscurity. The Dead never changed their music, on purpose and by design; they never went mainstream. But by never going mainstream, they earned larger sales and profits than many groups that went big-time.

Despite its roots in the antimaterialistic, counterculture era of "sex, drugs, and rock 'n' roll," several members of the band became astute businessmen, aware that there was revenue being generated around their popularity. The band incorporated in 1973 and, with the band members as co-CEOs and the board of directors, became a serious business venture. Each band member has an equal share of the profits and an equal vote in approving all merchandising and business decisions. The first crucial move was to agree that if a band member left or died, his shares would be brought back into the organization so that control remained central and they could carry out their mission without struggling with outsiders.

Though the bohemian Garcia was renowned for his disinterest in money, the band understood the power of its lure and the reach of its brand. All of them, Garcia included, came to appreciate the material rewards the band earned and understood that controlling all aspects of the business gave them more than just additional revenue streams; it gave them control over the quality of everything, from the music itself to ticket sales to the T-shirts sold at concerts. Most important, it strengthened the band's powerful relationship with its customers.

Indeed, the grungy, spontaneous image to some degree belies the genius of the band's business acumen. Decisions were made along the way—from instituting a ceiling on ticket prices to focusing on touring rather than recording—that flew in the face of conventional industry wisdom but had a profound impact on customer devotion and the extension of the brand.

—— Getting Radical ——

Radical marketers aren't always naturally savvy about business early in their careers, but they are quick studies. The Grateful Dead was just one of dozens of successful bands that emerged from the Bay Area in the mid-1960s. Their music, like that of the Jefferson Airplane, Janis Joplin's Big Brother and the Holding Company, and Creedence Clearwater Revival, became a focal point for the LSD-inspired experimentation that was burgeoning among a restless youth in America. It was also an enticing counterpoint to the slickly produced Beatles music that was dominating the pop charts of the day. Like Harley motorcycles, the Dead represented the radical fringe where freedom of expression was paramount and the rules did not apply. Perhaps nothing embodied the Summer of Love and the hippie movement like the Grateful Dead.

The Dead had little business sense starting out, but in those heady days of sixties acid rock, the entire industry was in a nascent stage and few rules or business tenets had emerged. It was an era of psychedelic drugs, sexual experimentation, and counterculture rhetoric. Agents and record producers in business suits were not necessarily welcome, and business discussions were rare. Early on, one unscrupulous manager stole $100,000 from the Dead, which was almost all they had in the bank. "Needless to say, for the first many years of our existence, we didn't run a very tight ship businesswise," said the band member Bob Weir in an interview in Robert Greenfield's 1996 book *Dark Star*. "God knows how much money got away from us."

Despite a record contract with Warner Brothers, throughout the late 1960s and early 1970s money was scarce and band members and crew all earned $125 per week. The focus was on creative freedom, an unconventional lifestyle, and experimental hallucinogenic drugs. It is not surprising that dozens of rock bands folded under these conditions, and the Dead's survival was a tribute to their musical devotion, their love of the customer, and their inherent marketing savvy. The band met regularly to plot its course, even if its "strategy" sessions were held in a grungy flat in San Francisco's Haight-Ashbury neighborhood. Like other radical marketers, the lack of financial resources simply fueled rather than hindered creativity and a deep belief in the product.

In the 1970s the Dead hired a New York attorney named Hal Kant to represent the band, and Kant convinced them, after much verbal wrangling, to copyright and protect not only their music but the accompanying artwork and other properties. Kant helped them form a corporation so that they owned the name, the goodwill, and the intellectual property. "They were a remarkably smart group of guys," Kant says. "They knew where their interests were, and none of them was passive. They talked things out until they got consensus, and if one didn't want to do something, they didn't do it."

But one thing never wavered: the care and devotion to the music. "All decisions were made on the integrity of the music," insists Dennis McNally, the band's publicist. "From those, many turned out to be great business decisions as well."

And spontaneity was the band's currency. Peter McQuaid, chief executive officer of Grateful Dead Productions, says that the Dead built its brand by creating "incredible trust" with its audience. "The group never packaged itself," McQuaid says. "What they did was for that night, for that moment."

One could argue, as McNally does, that the success of the band was simply the confluence of "one genius and five very good musicians who were sufficiently good enough to attract people and sufficiently sophisticated to keep themselves interested for thirty years." But a closer look reveals that the Dead, in fact, followed some key marketing principles: controlling the brand, creating a clear brand image, and having a well-defined value proposition. All of these principles are replicable, especially if you view the world as a radical marketer.

—— Making the Visceral Connection ——

A brand, most marketers agree, is more than a product—it is a relationship with consumers. Great brands have a single, clear, intuitively compelling message or symbol.

For the Grateful Dead, that message was embodied in their music and in the lifestyle and community that developed around the band's ceaseless desire to play that music live and improvisationally. In so doing, the band members, as collective CEOs of the business, owned the marketing function themselves. They never handed it off to a publicity firm or pushed it down into layers of a bureaucratic organization. By getting out with the customers more than any other rock band, the Dead created a visceral connection with their customer base and turned that connection into huge profits.

Like other great radical marketers, the Grateful Dead were their own customers. "The relationship between the band and the Deadheads needs to be nurtured because they are us and we are them," said Phil Lesh, the band's bass player and business leader, in a 1998 *New York Times* interview.

Like other radical marketers, the Dead started out with few resources and a modest plan. What they had was a product they believed in completely and a passion to share that product, the music, with an audience. In many ways, the equation was simple and failure was not an option. The idea that thousands of rock bands come and go and few reach star status was never a concern for the Dead. They just wanted to play. And in so doing, they followed a set of key radical marketing rules that fueled their success:

- They demonstrated love and respect for the customer.
- They spent most of their time face-to-face with the people who mattered—the customers.
- They celebrated rather than disdained uncommon sense.
- They created a community of users.
- They were true to the brand and managed to extend it with integrity.

Love and Respect the Customer

Spontaneity and rebellion are often hallmarks of great brands that appeal to the crucial demographic of eighteen- to twenty-four-year-olds, particularly males. Companies from Nike to Calvin Klein have built hugely successful franchises by pushing the marketing envelope to the farthest fringe. But unlike the contrived (and costly) "spontane-ity" of an athletic shoe or hip fashion, the Grateful Dead created a pow-erful and real emotional experience characterized by the longevity of its grip on the participants. Even after decades, Dead fans, having traded tie-dyed T-shirts for ties and crisp white shirts, cherish the product as a milestone experience in their lives. This devotion was a direct out-growth of the powerful and respectful connection between the band and its customer base.

Jerry Garcia, whose musical genius defined the band and its sound, set the parameters for the band's relationship with its audience. In an interview in *Dark Star,* Ken Kesey, author of *One Flew Over the Cuckoo's Nest* and an early Deadhead, explained Garcia's rapport with the audience. "He understood that he was in a relationship with his audience," Kesey said. "He was not playing at them, he was playing *with* them."

This two-way energy flow can flare up in bursts for successful prod-ucts like the new Volkswagen Beetle or Nantucket Nectars. But sustain-ing such a relationship for more than thirty years requires an unceasing commitment to improving the product and serving the audience. Respect and love of the customer must be demonstrated consistently as a brand attribute through actions, not lip service.

For example, when other rock 'n' roll legends like the Rolling Stones began to accept corporate sponsorship of their tours and raised ticket prices to astronomical levels—$100 or more—the Dead held the line, refused to cede control of its product in any way, and kept ticket prices at a ceiling of $30.

In 1983, to curtail ticket-scalping opportunities and to make sure all of its fans had equal access to tickets, the Dead set up its own mail-order ticket service. Thus, students willing to sleep out on sidewalks would not be the only ones able to get tickets to concerts.

The focus extended to employees as well. At its zenith, Grateful Dead Productions had more than eighty full-time employees, includ-ing a vast road crew that stayed on the payroll even when a tour ended. When the financial rewards began to grow astronomically, the wealth was shared. Like other great radical marketers, the Dead understood the value of employees who shared the enthusiasm for the product and would in effect represent the company to the customers.

The crew earned six-figure salaries, according to McNally, and the Dead was the first rock band to offer generous profit-sharing, retirement, and health benefits plans. Well before day care was a corporate issue, the Dead always had a secure children's play area backstage for the children of crew members and guests.

"There was simply no turnover," McNally said, "and no absenteeism." Indeed, Ram Rod, the crew chief, has held his job for thirty years. Such long-term loyalty, reminiscent of pre-downsizing days at IBM or AT&T, has long been a characteristic of successful companies. And such devotion to the crew was foreign to the rock 'n' roll business; most bands hired crews for the duration of a tour and then let them go. For a band that spent so much time on the road, such consistency kept the intricate machinations of touring at high levels for most of the band's lifetime. Ultimately, it benefited the fans most of all.

In order to put on the highest-quality shows, the Dead also invested millions of dollars in its vaunted "Wall of Sound" sound system, building perhaps the most sophisticated large-scale public address system in the industry. The band invested millions more to transport and set up the system at each venue on its endless tours.

Get Face-to-Face with Customers

The Dead played countless live shows and turned the accepted record industry formula on its ear. Rather than record an album and mount a tour to promote the album while visiting radio stations and schmoozing with disc jockeys, the Dead took the opposite view. They simply played as long and as often as possible in front of live audiences. The Dead annually mounted four regional tours that had, for their fans, the lure of a spiritual crusade. Each year they sold nearly two million tickets and played more than eighty concerts around the world, a workload that far surpassed that of any other popular rock band.

And when they played, they really played. While most rock concerts lasted a maximum of two hours, with artists' contracts limiting the required performance time, the Dead pioneered the four-hour concert and had it written into their contracts with promoters that they had a minimum of four hours' stage time so that arena operators were prepared for the lengthy shows. CEOs willing to spend four or more hours, day after day, with their customers are likely to spawn tremendous customer loyalty and devotion.

Indeed, though collectively the Dead sold millions of albums and reaped impressive profits, record sales have never been their trademark. The Dead believed their studio recordings lacked the spontaneity and energy of their live performances, and they never linked a tour to an album release. As a result, they have been all but ignored by the MTV generation, which only adds to the band's outcast allure. Though they wrote and recorded a string of memorable songs like "Truckin'," "Friend of the Devil," "Dark Star," and "Uncle John's Band," their studio recordings are merely an afterthought for Deadheads. The band had only one certified megahit, late in its career, the 1987 *In the Dark* album and its hit single "Touch of Grey." Neither came close, however, to the coveted number-one spot.

Celebrate Uncommon Sense

What characterized Garcia and his bandmates Bob Weir, Phil Lesh, Mickey Hart, and Bill Kreutzmann was the uniqueness of their product and their willingness to stick with the product against all conventional industry wisdom. They were first into this musical space and claimed it for their own. Like other radical marketers in this book—Iams pet foods, Snap-on Tools, and Sam Adams beer—the Dead turned the uniqueness into an advantage and built a lucrative market upon it.

And though they embraced different musical styles that encompassed rock, jazz, R&B, jug band music, country, and folk, the Dead in essence created its own genre, instantly recognizable, difficult to copy. There was a consistency to their sound, a consistency that lasted thirty years. Bill Graham, an early promoter of the band, said, "They are not the best at what they do, they are the *only* ones who do what they do."

The band embraced an improvisational style notable in modern jazz. Most of the show was unrehearsed and unplanned. Each song wandered off into a long, sometimes rambling tangent and then wound its way back. The band might plan two or three songs but then just play whatever they felt like doing at the moment. "That was the joy," McNally says. "They might start a song and then stop and say, 'Nah, not that one.' It was like being present at a conversation of musical friends."

"It was musically fascinating," adds David Gans, an author of three books about the band and host of the nationally syndicated radio show *The Grateful Dead Hour.* "That was what hooked me at first, the real-time, improvisational experience. The material and structures they'd bring onstage were fascinating, and they would take off from those structured places into unstructured places. We'd all wander along with it."

Gans compares the allure to baseball: improvisation within a structure. In baseball, you know the players, the rules of the game, the basic form of the event, but within that fixed structure everything is different every time. "The same was true for Dead music at its best, and the reward was to be there," Gans says.

In essence, the Dead weren't selling music, they were selling a unique, spontaneous experience, a version of lifestyle marketing embodied by Nike and Harley-Davidson. Because the music was essentially extemporaneous, songs could take off in many directions during live performances. Literally, no two concerts were the same. Each concert was a unique event, with the same songs rarely repeated for weeks or even years. While common sense and music industry history dictated otherwise, the Dead never wavered in their commitment to their own long, strange trip.

Paul Santinelli, a confirmed Deadhead and high-tech product manager who lives in Sunnyvale, California, says the Dead pioneered what he calls "the clayball" marketing method. "You take a piece of clay, throw it against a wall, and if it sticks, you take that and shape it from there," Santinelli says. "The Dead were constantly revisiting ideas. They were never afraid to go back to the drawing board or to make a mistake." Indeed, this willingness to allow its customer base to share this impossible quest toward perfection was a powerful marketing message.

Procter & Gamble's Elizabeth Moore calls this ability to continuously revisit and positively reshape a product "discontinuous change."

"The Dead didn't worry about following musical trends, but in doing that they created their own trends, which is what discontinuous change is all about," Moore says. These kinds of transcendent products, whether Tide detergent or the Dead's music, inspire tremendous long-term loyalty, she adds.

Loyalty is also inspired by strategic decisions that may fly in the face of accepted industry business practices but demonstrate respect for the customer. For example, in the 1980s the Dead decided to buck conventional wisdom and allow fans to tape its live performances. In an industry where bootleg records cost artists and record companies profits, such a decision was tantamount to heresy. But like other radical marketers, the Grateful Dead truly respected its customers. Jerry Garcia said, "If we're done with the music, you can have it." The band prevailed upon its fans to follow an honor system. They could keep or trade the tapes with fellow Deadheads, but they could not sell copyrighted material for profit. Hal Kant, the band's lawyer, says they spent a great deal of money tracking down and suing those who wouldn't honor the agreement. But the vast majority of Deadheads stood behind the band.

In fact, with the advent of the Internet, a vast virtual community of tapers has emerged, with Deadheads reaching out electronically via hundreds of homespun Websites to share the experience yet again.

The Dead didn't believe such taping would hurt record sales; in fact, they didn't produce a studio album from 1981 to 1987. The open policy, tantamount to Gillette offering low-priced razors in order to sell blades, fueled the creation of a Grateful Dead subculture and extended the brand. Those with the most extensive tape collections became masters of their universe, and thus the open-taping decision fueled ticket sales.

Every great brand can count on a deeply committed core customer base, and the tapers were that core audience for the Dead. The band even set up a special section for tapers behind the soundboard so they wouldn't interfere with other concert-goers. All this, along with the increasing global marketplace created by the Internet, has spawned a giant network of tape traders who share an adoration for the band. Santinelli says that he and a friend have amassed 1,600 hours worth of Dead tapes and estimates that he has purchased $20,000 worth of computer equipment and spent another $5,000 on digital audio equipment to pursue his habit.

But the tapes were just the beginning. The Dead, with the idiosyncratic nature of their shows, built a layer of mystery into their image. Serious Deadheads kept logs of each show, scribbling, on notepads during the concert, which songs were performed, in what order, and the quality of the performance. Each nuance, each note that Garcia missed or lyric he forgot, was logged in. Deadheads like Santinelli would sit for weeks poring over playlists, trying to predict what songs would be played at a show, comparing sets that were played at the same venue a year earlier or twenty years earlier. Would they play "Saint Stephen," an old hit that they hadn't performed since 1979? "I got caught up in the anxiety," Santinelli says. "The dynamic changed from show to show, set to set." Great brands inspire passion that may seem ludicrous to those on the outside. But fanatics, be they motorcycle enthusiasts, pet lovers, or rock fans, become important evangelists for the brand. This can be manifested by a tattoo of a corporate logo, a stock investment, or a prized tape collection.

The band's uncommon sense also led to sound strategic business decisions. Unlike most rock 'n' roll groups, the Dead never asked for big advances from concert promoters. Instead, they took on the upfront risk themselves and received royalties that were double the industry average. This practice proved to be incredibly lucrative for the band in the long run.

And the Dead never left a promoter in the lurch. If a concert was canceled because of bad weather or a competing event kept the crowds down, the Dead would make it up to that promoter with another concert date.

Create a Community

Great brands create a sense of community and belonging, and few did that better than the Dead. A virtual nation of Dead fans incorporated the band into their lives in a way that corporate marketers can only dream about. And the Dead were savvy enough, even in their early days, to tap into this community. They became database marketing pioneers well before the concept grew in more traditional business settings.

Steve Brown, an enthusiastic Deadhead and one of the founders of Grateful Dead Records, recalled the creation of the first Deadhead database in the early 1970s. In *Goin' Down the Road*, Blair Jackson's 1992 book about the band, Brown recounted:

> Around this time, we decided to plug in more idrectly to all the Deadheads. The "Dead Freaks Unite" campaign, introduced inside the *Skull and Roses* LP in 1971, had been a tremendous success—we'd built up a mailing list of 30,000 names—and we knew a direct mailing list and newsletter served as an effective communication link with the Deadheads. To reach even more people, we decided after the *Wake of the Flood* album to send a Grateful Dead Records promotion booth on our tour with the band. Our gambit worked: we signed up another 50,000 on the 1974 tours.

The tours themselves became the focal point of the emerging community. Every concert spawned a virtual city around the concert site, the show itself representing only part of the experience for the Deadheads.

Jay Novack is a thirty-six-year-old sales director in Framingham, Massachusetts, and a devoted Deadhead. "There's a sense of community, a feeling we're all in this together," Novack says. "You don't get that at other concerts where there may be thirty thousand individuals. With the Dead, you went to six shows in seven nights at the Boston Garden and saw the same people wearing the same clothes talking about the same things. That was the big draw for me, the sense of community."

"Dead concerts were designed to be transformational, spiritual experiences," adds Rebecca Adams, a sociologist at the University of North Carolina at Greensboro who is writing a book entitled *Deadheads: Community, Spirituality, and Friendship*. "The concerts took on more than entertainment value for the fans; they created a bond amongst the fans and between the band and the audience. This was a place they could count on these experiences happening with many of the same people, and that created a tremendous sense of community and solidarity."

Within this community, tens of thousands of otherwise rational adults have, over three decades, poured their souls and their wallets into the worship of the band with a level of adulation that borders on religious zeal or even cultism. Lifelong friendships were formed and a global network established that would be the envy of any successful marketer. Well-coifed baby boomer stockbrokers, lawyers, doctors, and academics now wear Jerry Garcia ties or carry Grateful Dead coffee mugs to board meetings and love to trade their acid-laced memories of Dead shows in the 1960s, 1970s, and 1980s. Second- and even third-generation Deadheads continue to worship the band.

Because of the eclectic—some say sophisticated—style of the Grateful Dead's music, it attracted an intelligent, educated crowd. As these early Deadheads aged, they entered high-profile and lucrative professions—Vice President Al Gore, Vermont Senator Patrick Leahy, and William Weld, the former Republican governor of Massachusetts, for example, are self-proclaimed Deadheads—and over the years these politicians, lawyers, doctors, academics, and entrepreneurs had more and more disposable income, which they happily spent on Grateful Dead tickets and merchandise.

The most fervent Deadheads attended literally hundreds of Grateful Dead concerts over the years, following the band from venue to venue, sleeping out on cold sidewalks, buying tickets for dozens of shows on a given tour, gobbling up Dead merchandise, and spending countless hours comparing set lists and finding endless nuances in the songs that were chosen and the order in which they were played.

This love and devotion translated into lucrative financial rewards for the band and the small universe of satellite businesses that revolved around it. The Dead became one of the top-grossing bands in the world, averaging $50 million to $75 million in ticket sales each year as they toured major arenas around the country.

In the parking lots around these concert halls and stadiums, a mobile village of merchandisers set up shop, selling tie-dyed T-shirts and veggie burritos, and generated many millions of dollars in additional revenues. In the early 1990s, after decades of ineffective outside management of its licensing and merchandising opportunities, the band hired Peter McQuaid, an experienced business manager, to bring these activities in-house under the banner of Grateful Dead

Merchandising. Grateful Dead–related merchandise now generates more than $60 million annually, with the band reaping 30 percent of those sales, far more than it ever received in the past.

Benson P. Shapiro, a consultant and former marketing professor at Harvard Business School, says the key to creating a brand is the pleasure a buyer gets in both acquiring and owning a product. Much of that is tied to joining and belonging to a group. "There is deep ego satisfaction and pleasure in belonging to some group," Shapiro says. "When you look at who the Deadheads are, they are people who were demonstrating in the 1960s and are now Wall Street lawyers. They occasionally take a pro bono civil rights case to feel good about themselves. But being a Deadhead is even more important to them. It helps bring meaning to a life that got co-opted along the line."

Rebecca Adams believes the Dead's improvisational music and penchant for playing a different show every night was the cornerstone to creating the Deadhead community. Most concert tours are built on the premise that an artist performs the music as close to the recorded version as possible. And each night, the song list is nearly identical to that of the night before. There is therefore no incentive for a fan to see more than one or two shows on a tour. The Dead, by eschewing this formula and essentially never repeating a concert twice, gave its fans a reason to come back again and again and thus see the same people repeatedly. In this fashion, the band, she said, made a lot of decisions that gave Deadheads a reason to know one another.

The band saw another marketing opportunity in this devotion and went so far as to create a vast database of shows and playlists they call the Deadbase, which became available in print and on diskettes.

All this created an urgency that translated into massive ticket sales. Even as the band grew older and Garcia, racked by illness and drug addiction, would play poorly, forget lyrics, and appear lost, the band retained its lure. "Even when Jerry was screwing up all the time, and he'd be horrible at Monday night's show, on Tuesday, he would sing something so beautifully it would bring tears to people's eyes," Novack says. "The feeling was they could be bad one or two nights in a row, but the next show could be *the* show, and you didn't want to miss that."

Shapiro says the ability to retain the cachet of a brand is crucial and requires careful nurturing. "If you make it too ubiquitous, it loses cachet," he explains. "What the Dead did is make sure they didn't let records or CDs cheapen their image or make it pedestrian. That's an important thing; there has to be a sense of 'I'm in, you're out.'"

The merchandising of the band, the catalog and all the Grateful Dead paraphernalia sold through retail channels, which might strike some as crass commercialism, has not turned off the band's followers because for them "it is more about affiliation, more of a sense of belonging, than crass merchandising," according to Shapiro.

Brand Extension with Integrity

Like other great radical marketers, the Grateful Dead inspired clever and innovative ways to extend their brand without damaging its integrity. From the current ambitious plans for Terrapin Station back to the earliest days of the band's popularity, they had an uncanny knack for extending the brand without diluting it. In 1972, for example, the Grateful Dead became one of the first bands to create its own record label, a radical concept at the time, but a way to control quality and retain the spirit of the music they played.

The Dead were also among the first bands to inspire vast merchandise sales, specifically T-shirts, posters, and stickers of the band's varied logos. Starting in the early 1970s, the drummer Bill Kreutzmann's wife Sussila started making Grateful Dead T-shirts for sale. She sold that business to the rock promoter Bill Graham, who incorporated it into his Winterland Productions merchandise operations, eventually a hugely profitable business. Graham's organization held exclusive rights to Grateful Dead merchandise for eighteen years, with the band getting royalties on sales. In 1992 the group decided it was time to bring the entire operation back inside, gain control of brand integrity, and increase the profits for itself.

The band members had always been loath to police their concert sites. For many years they were content to let entrepreneurial fans reap the rewards, as long as copyrighted material was not being co-opted, and allow this marketplace to exist in the parking lots of its concert venues. But they were eventually convinced that they were giving away more than $250,000 worth of potential revenues with each concert. Rather than force everyone out of business, however, the group made a radical decision: bring in the best and make them legitimate business partners.

"These people had a real respect for the band and the music," Peter McQuaid said. "It was far more satisfying to have a relationship with someone with high regard for the group than to create a stable of artists inside our company."

Greg Burbank, for example, was a twenty-one-year-old college dropout selling stickers and tie-dyed T-shirts in the parking lot of Grateful Dead concerts in the mid-1980s. One night he and his partner got a tap on the shoulder from a Dead crew member, who asked them to come in and talk to representatives for the band. "Rather than suing us for trademark infringement, they brought us on board," Burbank remembers.

Today Liquid Blue, Burbank's company in Lincoln, Rhode Island, is one of the largest licensees of Grateful Dead merchandise in the country. The company sells around $4 million worth of Grateful Dead paraphernalia to retail outlets each year. "The Grateful Dead always put out a quality product," says Burbank. "Their emphasis was always on putting on the best show and the best products. The band was uncompromising that the quality of the merchandise match the quality of the music."

Under McQuaid's direction, Grateful Dead Merchandising has soared. Its quarterly catalog and fan newsletter not only bring the Dead's brand to hundreds of thousands of Deadheads but provide a regular, uninterrupted connection between the band and its customers. Though a few aging hippies have complained, most Deadheads see no conflict between the band's counterculture roots and the commercialism of its merchandising. The Dead found a way to sell without appearing to sell out.

When Garcia died, for example, the company's toll-free telephone line rang off the hook and merchandise sales soared 25 percent for the next six months. The company logged fifteen thousand calls a day for several weeks. In a note to readers in the catalog, the band expressed sorrow over Garcia's death and then noted: "Deadheads have expressed an overwhelming desire to have something . . . anything . . . some music, a memento, an amulet, a power object . . . to console them, to inspire them, to remind them of the good times. And it's our privilege to be able to provide these things."

Like other great radical marketers, the band also found ways to extend the brand without spending its own money. In an unexpected but impressive crossover into mainstream markets, the Grateful Dead has achieved an accepted ubiquity that would have seemed inconceivable in 1967. Hundreds of licensees sell Grateful Dead merchandise at retail outlets—from head shops to Neiman Marcus to Disneyland—around the country. In the late 1980s, for example, Ben & Jerry's Ice Cream unveiled a new flavor called "Cherry Garcia," a tribute to the Dead's lead guitarist, which quickly became one of the company's most popular offerings. (Unfortunately, Ben & Jerry's hadn't asked for permission to use Garcia's name, but after a bit of legal wrangling, they agreed to pay him a royalty and everyone was satisfied, especially Deadheads. A severe diabetic, Garcia couldn't taste his namesake ice cream but expressed pleasure at the concept. "At least it wasn't motor oil," he said.)

The band's many logos, like the Skull and Roses, Dancing Bears, and Steal Your Face, can be seen on an endless stream of goods, from alcohol-free wine to baby clothes. Some of the symbols were inspired by drug-related paraphernalia, like paper for blotter acid (Dancing Bear), but have ironically become mainstream, their origins long forgotten. Indeed, Grateful Dead T-shirts have become so ubiquitous that they are now being worn by people who have never even heard of the band, says Rebecca Adams. "I see the Dancing Bear T-shirt all over the place," Adams says. "A lot of people don't have a clue what they are wearing. They like the bear because it is cute. In fact, real Deadheads don't wear those T-shirts anymore."

Because of the integrity of the brand, carefully nurtured by Grateful Dead Productions, this spillover effect has not turned off the core customers; in fact, they find the popularity of the merchandise both amusing and satisfying, a tacit stamp of approval for their obsession without minimizing the aura and mystique.

Meanwhile, the Deadheads do have disposable income and they are buying. McQuaid says business has grown 25 percent per year since the unit was created in 1992, and mail-order sales surpassed $8 million in 1998. He acknowledges that Garcia's death and the breakup of the band changed the dynamics of the business. Replacing the income generated by touring will be difficult. But he says that sales are stronger than ever, and he has plans to extend the brand into new retail channels like Nordstrom and other baby-boom buying bastions.

—— "I Will Survive" ——

So what happens now that the band is gone? For a band whose existence was based on live performances, the Dead may in fact be dead. But McQuaid believes the brand can live on indefinitely and has tremendous growth potential. He points out that the money Deadheads spent on concert tickets may now be aimed at merchandise and music sales.

Understanding how crucial the music is to the equation, the band had the foresight to tape countless concerts and studio sessions over its thirty-year run, resulting in an archive with more than twenty-five hundred tapes. The tapes are stored in a new state-of-the-art fireproof vault, and band members and technicians have been poring over the material to determine what is usable. The plans call for a steady release of recordings as long as good material is available. The band refuses to release inferior product and is well versed in the subtleties of retaining its customer base and remaining true to the brand. The plans for the Terrapin Station project are based on that very devotion to the core value proposition.

"We didn't want to just put out old live concerts until the material and interest dwindled away," Phil Lesh, the Dead's bass player and business leader, told the *New York Times* in an interview about Terrapin Station. "As big a draw as the music at our shows was the fellowship and community people had there with one another. We wanted to create a place that would be a representation of what we did musically and culturally and a place where people could gather and new music could be showcased."

And because of the archives of tapes, the band can be presented in many ways without actually being there. Indeed, the music has filtered down into new generations: the children and even grandchildren of Deadheads are already spending their disposable income on the brand. A Grateful Dead Bean Bear is a huge seller, Greg Burbank says, and second only to Beanie Babies as the most popular beanbag toy. Not to be outdone, the Beanie Babies have their own tie-dyed T-shirt–clad bear named "Garcia."

The remaining band members have all embarked on solo projects with new groups, and their presence on the road touring is likely to fuel sales of Dead merchandise and music as well. Add to that the mystique of rock stars who died young, like John Lennon, Elvis Presley, Buddy Holly, and Jimi Hendrix, and there is little doubt that Jerry Garcia's name will be added to that pantheon, with attendant sales of music and merchandise.

Ben Shapiro says the Dead built an institution, not just a rock band, and that they had the foresight not to stretch the institution too far. "It's amazing how brands have a hold," he says. "People get very attached."

Like other great radical marketers, the Dead is simply reinventing itself. Grateful Dead Records is creating and distributing its own CDs, and in its constant efforts to stay close to its customers, the Dead can offer these CDs at better prices—a double CD for $15, for example—and realize higher profits. The goodwill generated by the Dead and its organization has brought other musicians to them seeking the very expertise in brand development that the band has acquired over thirty years of dedicated hard work.

While he was still alive, Garcia, a noted artist, began extending his own personal brand by selling expensive ties adorned with his artwork. His ties became the most popular neckwear in the United States; even the president was reportedly seen wearing one. A successful new line of Grateful Dead ties not associated with the Jerry Garcia ties, along with other silk loungewear, shoes, and boxer shorts, have hit the stores. "T-shirts will be important, but they won't be the backbone anymore," McQuaid says. "An older, more sophisticated market will emerge, and people in boardrooms will wear Grateful Dead ties that only other Deadheads will recognize. It will be subtle."

In this vein, Peter McQuaid is planning to build the brand into a *lifestyle* product line for the retail market. He is hoping to sell products like an upscale, tie-dyed set of towels through retail outlets like Nordstrom. Without any reference to the Grateful Dead, these items have great cachet among the band's fans.

He adds that he is already looking off shore for additional marketing opportunities. Though the Dead toured mostly in the United States, the band has tremendous appeal overseas. "There is huge interest in Japan in the Dead," McQuaid says, "and we expect to find a big market there."

Greg Burbank says that new products keep the Dead in a growth mode. He points out that long-defunct acts like Jimi Hendrix or the Doors continue to be among the most popular in merchandising circles. "Hendrix only toured for four or five years before he died," Burbank says. "The Grateful Dead have touched millions of people, and there are fourteen-year-old kids who now think the Dead are a cool thing. That train was rolling for thirty years. It's not coming to an abrupt halt."

"This brand is very much alive," adds McQuaid. "And all signs point to wonderful, healthy growth before us."

4

Providian Financial

Mining Data for Gold

*"By analyzing the data, you can figure out
what they really buy rather than what
they say they will buy."*
—*Shailesh Mehta*

One common characteristic of radical marketers is that few carry the baggage of marketing training and expertise. Indeed, their success at marketing their brands is undoubtedly aided by their lack of theoretical know-how and preconceived notions of how things are supposed to be done. By bringing fresh and often radical ideas to the table, they are quietly reinventing the discipline of marketing.

No one embodies this freedom of thought and deed more than Shailesh J. Mehta, the chairman and chief executive of Providian Financial, the San Francisco–based financial services company.

Mehta's path into banking and financial services was only slightly less circuitous than his path to radical marketing. An engineer by training and an academic at heart, Mehta loves quantitative analysis and his haven is the back office—the computer systems and operations that hold a treasure trove of data about customers that most companies don't bother to mine.

Mehta is a data Midas, turning statistics and consumer credit histories into gold. Like other radical marketers, he has ignored traditional advertising and brand management. Instead, he has built a powerful direct-marketing organization on the back of sophisticated analysis of customer behavior—the "engineering approach to direct marketing," as Mehta calls it. What Providian does is not a secret; it simply requires a lot of sweat equity, which most competitors seem unwilling to invest.

For Mehta, the basic formula is simple: find the right prospects, make them customers by knowing them better than the competition, make sure they pay back the loans, and then retain them with a continuing flow of added value.

At first glance, Providian may not appear to be a radical marketer. Because of the focus on analytics, the passion may not initially be obvious. But once you realize how Providian uses these tools to create a visceral understanding of the customer and see how it employs that understanding, it becomes clear just how radical the company is.

What makes Providian radical is that its marketing is driven by operations and built upon engineering principles such as data modeling and feedback loops. From this, all product and marketing decisions flow. Senior managers constantly review the data and work in lockstep with marketing and operations to identify profitable price points and avoid poor credit risks. Thus, Providian's marketing people know they can make better promises to customers because the systems people can support those promises.

Within this framework, Providian is a prototype for the radical marketer we described in Chapter 2. Mehta leads the marketing effort himself. He eschews focus groups and traditional market research in favor of one-to-one customer contact. He embraces unconventional wisdom, spends nothing on traditional advertising, and has eliminated traditional marketing budgets within Providian. His employees are his passionate missionaries, as enamored of the quantitative approach as Mehta is. And by choosing to do business in a market that others have shunned, he views the impossible as simply another business opportunity.

—— Pushing the Limits of Risk ——

Providian sends out hundreds of millions of pieces of direct mail each year to a targeted, prescreened audience, offering its credit card. When a prospective customer responds, Providian initiates a detailed credit check of the applicant and then has one of its 725 customer representatives call the applicant personally. Providian's quantitative analysts use complex computer models to predict losses and assess how a person's financial profile will be affected by shifting economic conditions. The computers calculate the maximum credit line the company will offer and the minimum interest rate Providian will accept. All this up-front data allow Providian to push the upper limits of risk and still turn a handsome profit.

On the representative's computer screen is the customer's complete credit history, gleaned from three different credit bureaus, and with this data the marketing process gets under way. Providian's goal is to garner as much "share of wallet" as possible. If that customer has credit card accounts with a dozen other banks, Providian wants to consolidate all of it into one Providian account.

Armed with the essential data, Providian is able to tailor its credit card offering right at the point of contact. In so doing, Providian, like other great radical marketers, manages to establish a visceral connection to its customer base, essentially offering a custom-fit credit card to each customer, designed to accommodate the individual's particular financial needs. One customer might prefer airline miles with no annual fee, another a higher credit line. Most love simplicity and welcome the chance to untangle their financial lives.

Providian knows its customer base well. The company targets customers who are willing to carry larger balances at higher rates and shuns those who use credit cards for convenience, paying off entire balances each month. The ideal Providian customer is a middle-class homeowner with an income of between $30,000 and $75,000; someone who is budget-conscious and cash flow–oriented. Most don't have large savings accounts, and they use credit cards as a convenient tool for borrowing money. They fully intend to pay it back.

Mehta understands the importance of credit for people, especially for those who fall outside the accepted risk boundaries and have trouble finding banks willing to extend them credit. So Providian grants the maximum credit line it can justify and gets compensated with higher pricing on interest rates and fees for taking the risk. Mehta also knows that money is an emotional issue. Though these customers are not high-rollers, they don't want to be treated like second-class citizens either, so Providian provides them the opportunity to have gold and platinum cards. For the benefits and status that come with these high-end credit cards, some customers are willing to pay a higher price.

"People have emotional needs and can be very status-conscious," Mehta says. "They like to flash a gold card in a restaurant, and they want to be treated as no less than a millionaire." Mehta gleans this wisdom, not from psychology texts, but from the Rorschach tests of his data-driven operations. If you quantify everything and carefully study the results, patterns emerge, even behavioral patterns. And few in finance have been as adept at understanding these patterns as Mehta.

—— Eliminating the Marketing Boundaries ——

Working in virtual obscurity because Providian began as a business unit within a large insurance company, Mehta steadily honed his ability to recognize obscure patterns, devised algorithms, and built a state-of-the-art operations facility in nearby Pleasanton, California, as the engine of his emerging juggernaut. Like other radical marketers, he carefully hired the best and brightest risk managers, quantitative analysts, and operations engineers he could lure to Providian, and around them he built a prototypical boundary-less organization in which marketing was not segregated as a separate function but integrated into every discipline.

In most financial institutions, the marketers are constantly at odds with the credit managers. Marketing wants to issue more credit, and credit wants more control. At Providian the skill set for marketing is the same skill set as for credit. Everything is based on operations, and without a deep knowledge and understanding of math and statistical and quantitative analysis, a marketer couldn't survive at Providian. The functional boundaries simply don't exist because everyone is focused on the same target: selling credit.

The company, Mehta says, sells customer service, not brands or products. A traditional brand manager would be lost in Providian's linear marketing structure. Providian marketers don't spend their time developing brand plans or meeting with advertising agencies. They are analytically competent and adept at using the company's systems to conduct extensive analysis of customer behavior and thus have no need for an interpreter between them and the customer base.

Employees are encouraged to be entrepreneurs, and good ideas are the currency for corporate recognition and advancement. From such encouragement comes a raft of profitable employee-generated ideas that traditional marketers would admire: using a special gold-leaf paint so that Providian can give customers a "real" gold card; adding a blank check for cash advances to every credit card bill so that customers can borrow more money even while paying current bills; and providing a "personal banker," a special representative who works with Providian's biggest borrowers to find ways to consolidate loans and credit cards into a single manageable account.

—— Analysis into Profit ——

Mehta's senior executives insist there is no magic to the formula; from the outset, Providian built a quantitative model for doing business that favored computer-based analytical tools and software that tracked the usage patterns and profitability of each customer, setting pricing and service levels accordingly. Added to that are stringent cost controls and demanding collection measures, crucial requirements if the formula is to succeed.

If it sounds hard, it was. And it has worked.

In just over a decade at the helm of Providian, Mehta has transformed a small, unknown credit card provider with $100 million in assets and less than $1 million in profits into a powerhouse player in the financial services industry, managing more than $12 billion in assets with more than six million customers and $300 million in profits. Though it is dwarfed by giants like the newly merged Citigroup and BankAmerica in the $800 billion domestic credit card business, Providian has staked out an enviable niche. By eschewing massive advertising and brand building, Providian is able to channel its assets into creating customer value, offering not only access to credit but customized credit that its customers are unable to obtain elsewhere.

For its size, Providian is consistently among the most profitable credit card companies in the industry. Having spun out from the insurance company, Providian went public in 1997, and within a year its stock value had more than doubled and was selling at more than 1,000 percent of book value, making it a darling of Wall Street analysts and a potential takeover target in a merger-hungry financial services industry.

A truly radical marketer, Providian achieved all this without a formal marketing department, without spending anything on traditional brand-based advertising, and, in a marketplace characterized by recognizable and heavily promoted brands, without bothering to build a brand of its own. Mehta, for example, believes there is no brand loyalty for credit cards. A customer doesn't care if it's a Citicorp Visa or a Wells Fargo Visa. Visa itself spends hundreds of millions of dollars promoting the product, so why should Providian? Providian can ride those coattails quite nicely.

And most important and most radical, the marketing charge is led by Mehta himself, not handed down through layers of marketing bureaucracy. To traditional marketers, most of Mehta's ideas are anathema, and that is fine with him. He rarely speaks with the media or at conferences because he is quite content to stay off the competition's radar screen and not direct them to the gold mine he has unearthed.

—— Banking the Unbanked ——

In a business where the product is credit and the goal is to turn managed risk into profits, Mehta has ventured into new markets that the traditional lenders like Citicorp, Chase Manhattan, and MBNA have largely ignored. Like other radical marketers, Providian finds new markets by paying close attention to its existing markets. While conducting tests to try to increase the approval rate of its existing credit card business, for example, Providian's marketers uncovered a rich new revenue stream.

Mehta is a highly practical businessman and has no interest in bad debt, charge-offs, and delinquencies. But over time, while dissecting why some customers declined Providian's solicitations, he and his senior managers kept noticing that the lower end of the market was being cut off arbitrarily. Traditional credit formulas dictated that a line be drawn; you must market only to people above that line, conventional banking wisdom decreed. But in Providian's radical culture, researchers and marketers kept asking, "Why?" Eventually, Mehta decided it was folly to rule out these potential customers.

Mehta and his staff created a new algorithm for finding, acquiring, and retaining customers who fell between the cracks of traditional lending requirements and regulations and built models that would allow Providian to safely and profitably market to those customers. Part of the requirement, for example, was that the customer "secure" the account by opening a savings account for up to $1,000 as collateral against the credit card.

Providian now targets these higher-risk customers, the "unbanked," in industry vernacular, those traditionally called "bad credit risks," such as new immigrants trying to build credit for the first time or bankrupt professionals trying to rebuild tarnished credit histories. Providian has developed a highly profitable business around these twenty-five million families who don't qualify for regular credit. In the process, Providian has taken control of this business and annually achieves record growth. It is, in fact, the fastest-growing part of Providian's business. In the market for "secured" credit cards—those that require a savings account as collateral—Providian is the top player, with more than one million customers in that segment alone.

Providian has now established a huge and loyal customer base, no mean feat in a competitive, mainstream money-lending market that is happy to compete aggressively for these once-outcast customers after

Providian transforms them into creditworthy customers. By keeping its customers loyal, Providian, like other radical marketers, has created an invaluable community of users.

It has also made the publicity-shy Mehta one of the highest-paid executives in the United States and placed him in the legion of radical marketers. He has earned high praise from industry analysts, who call him a "genius" and mention his breakthrough thinking in the same breath as Thomas Edison and Henry Ford. That he has earned kudos as a marketing genius at all is remarkable considering his unusual path into banking.

—— Seeing Things Differently ——

Born into a family of diamond merchants in Bombay, the forty-nine-year-old Mehta earned a degree in mechanical engineering at the Indian Institute of Technology in Bombay and came to the United States to do graduate studies at Case Western Reserve University in Cleveland. A straight-A student, Mehta quickly earned both a master's degree and a doctorate in operations research and computer science. He was heavily recruited by Bell Labs and other prestigious companies for his math and engineering skills, but he'd already committed to what many viewed as a highly unconventional career path for an engineer.

While at Case Western, Mehta got an opportunity to do a research project for Cleveland Trust, at the time the largest bank in Ohio. The bank needed a graduate student to study what they believed was a transportation problem. It was 1973, the Arab oil embargo was in full force, and the bank wanted its cumbersome delivery system analyzed. The bank had eighty-three branches in Cuyahoga County, and each day a squadron of thirteen drivers drove back and forth to the branches picking up the mail that brought in thousands of customer checks. The bankers wanted to know, in the face of escalating gasoline prices, whether the drivers were making optimal use of their time and resources. Was there a cost savings available by cutting routes and scrimping on pricey gasoline?

For $7 an hour, Mehta took on the challenge—a perfect one, he figured, for an operations research major. Mehta had an uncanny knack for seeing solutions that were often invisible to others. In a math class at Case Western, for example, he'd solved a century-old problem in graph theory that his professor had believed to be unsolvable. The awed professor allowed Mehta to use the solution as the dissertation for his doctorate if Mehta completed the required course work.

At Cleveland Trust, as he studied the bank's problem, Mehta realized that the real issue was about float—the time between processing a check and having it credited to an account—not about saving gasoline. The branches received thousands of checks in the mail every day. The goal was to get these checks processed as fast as possible and shorten the float. Checks that arrived early at the local Federal Reserve bank were credited with an extra day of interest. The bank processed $100 million worth of out-of-town checks every day, and Mehta concluded that the bank was losing $200 per $1 million, owing to the delay in getting the checks processed.

For Mehta, the situation was clear: as he analyzed the data, he saw that some suburban branches received less mail and fewer checks than the larger branches closer to the city.

He suggested a new pickup and delivery schedule based on the number of checks at each branch, a route that maximized the number of checks that could be delivered to the Federal Reserve each day. If the bank could get the bulk of the checks in more quickly, it would earn substantial profits from reducing the float.

His supervisors, being bankers, were both shocked and pleased by his recommendations. Mehta was amused at the excitement about his revelations. It had seemed pretty obvious if one just took the time to use the available data. But banks, in the 1970s, were woefully inept in the back office, far behind other industries in using computers and quantitative information for strategic advantage. The bank immediately offered him a job, and Mehta accepted. "This is easy," Mehta thought. What he'd learned about operations in manufacturing companies put him well ahead of his banking colleagues. "Here I can be a genius," he figured and took the job.

Mehta ran the bank's back office systems for the next thirteen years,

amassing a storehouse of knowledge about banking industry operations that would lay the groundwork for his success at Providian. In
1986 he joined Providian, then known as First Deposit Corporation,
as chief operating officer with the promise that he'd be CEO in two or
three years.

Part of an insurance company known back then as Capital Holding,
Providian was a credit card business created by another eccentric financial genius, Andrew Kahr. Kahr had designed Merrill Lynch's innovative
Cash Management Account, an integrated brokerage account that provided customers with checking and savings accounts and Visa cards, all
on a single monthly statement. It was a breakthrough in the use of technology in the consumer lending arena and became widely copied
throughout the industry.

At Providian, Kahr continued to innovate, creating the first Visa card
with no annual fee and a 1 percent cash rebate on purchases. The card
had a steep 21.9 percent interest rate and also required the customer to
borrow at least $1,000 in a cash advance or savings account. But it
proved alluring to customers who needed access to credit; their immediate need for cash outweighed any concern about interest rates and terms.
It also introduced another first, one that has since become common
throughout the credit card industry: a minimum payment of only 2 percent of the balance. If credit cards were among the most profitable of
banking products, these credit cards were even more profitable.

But despite these innovations, Providian was growing at a snail's
pace until Mehta arrived. The tiny business had eighty employees,
had under $100 million in assets, and was barely turning a profit.
Still, Mehta saw vast potential. The consumer lending business was in
the midst of dramatic change—shifting away from the old bricks-and-
mortar model and into a new high technology–driven paradigm—
and this gave a small upstart like Providian an opening. Most of all,
Mehta was surprised by the concentration of intellectual talent he discovered at Providian. He believed that the profits in banking would be
leveraged more and more by the intellectual capital of the lending
institution. Smart people might cost more to hire and retain, but they
would pay off in spades in generating new ideas, running the back
office more efficiently, and mining the data for quantifiable benefits.

But the assets were without value if Mehta couldn't create a marketing plan and find a way to implement it. Like other radical marketers, he viewed the competitive landscape with the innovative eye of someone with great ideas, grand plans, and limited resources. The best brands, like American Express and Citicorp, had been built up over many years. Mehta didn't believe he had the time to build a mega-brand. Giant regional banks like BankAmerica and BancOne had established vast branch networks that Providian couldn't hope to match.

"When you don't have those kinds of advantages, how do you compete?" Mehta asked himself. "Just being a product innovator doesn't solve the problem. Product innovation gives you some edge, but it's not sustainable. A great product will be copied. American Express created the Platinum Card, and now sixty other companies are using platinum. So where is the advantage?"

—— Cookies and Milk in the Back Office ——

To find the answer, Mehta turned back to his roots in the back office. Even a decade or more after he had left graduate school, banks had done little to improve the back office. Banking operations were buried under mountains of paper, the back office was populated by high school graduates, and the MBAs were out front in the credit and financial services areas. The back office was, in fact, the domain of computer vendors, who pushed their proprietary hardware and software products into the data centers and left dazed information technology executives at the bank to piece together coherent systems.

What most bankers viewed as dirty detail work, Mehta saw as a mother lode of untapped data. He believed he could create his advantage right there among the computers and disk drives. "The risk is in the execution," he says, "but if you do it right, it's a lot harder to duplicate than a product."

Like other radical marketers, Mehta knew that quality would beget results. He decided he would build the best back office in the industry, a state-of-the-art facility populated with the best and the brightest. He immediately hired David B. Smith, a twelve-year BankAmerica systems and risk management veteran who built Providian's back office in Pleasanton. Starting from scratch gave Providian a huge advantage.

While competitors, saddled with outdated infrastructures, focused on controlling and even decreasing back-office costs, Mehta viewed the back office as his key investment and poured resources into its creation. He himself spends two days a week away from San Francisco headquarters and in his Pleasanton office, working with senior managers and analyzing the ceaseless stream of data generated by Providian's quantitative analysts. "That is where I maintain my sustainable advantage," Mehta says.

Visitors to Pleasanton walk away impressed, not only with the operations but with Mehta's enthusiasm. "There's nothing he prefers more than spending an afternoon there, arriving with boxes of cookies and milk, and sitting around looking over the last thirty bankruptcies to determine how they could see that coming," says Charlotte Chamberlain, a financial analyst with Jefferies & Company in Los Angeles. "Nothing in the data world goes to waste. It is mined and refined to increase profits going forward."

The core of the Pleasanton operation is behavioral testing, according to Smith. Providian representatives speak to anywhere from twenty thousand to seventy thousand customers a week. If the company is planning a mailing of five million pieces, it might send out fifty thousand pieces with a slightly different offer or feature as a test cell and have those responses come back to the test center, where they are carefully scrutinized. In this way, Providian can determine price points, credit lines, and packaging that attracts a higher response. In fact, Smith says, all of Providian's products have emerged from this "rapid evolution," including its fast-growing secured credit card business.

By focusing on markets, such as the high-risk segment, rather than products, Providian tests and retests its assumptions about customers and hones them to a fine edge. When soliciting new customers by phone, for example, Providian tracks the script in precise detail to test what works. If a call is unsuccessful, Providian even monitors which word the representative was saying when the customer hung up.

Such obsession with the details of customer interaction is an earmark of radical marketing. Rather than depend on focus groups or contracted market research from an outside consultant, Providian uses this kind of analysis to get out of the office and next to its customers. In essence, this is how Mehta echoes the sentiments of Iams' Clay Mathile, Harley's Rich Teerlink, and Boston Beer's Jim Koch: marketing and advertising are no substitute for staying close to the customer. Seventy thousand phone calls may result in a lot of hang-ups, but it also provides a remarkable wellspring of customer intimacy.

It has a similar effect inside the company. "When you have an infrastructure and people dedicated to testing and reporting on the results in a credible way, it creates a culture of implementation," Smith says. "In other, bigger organizations, without the same level of testing, if a marketing person has a brilliant idea the credit people will find a reason why it isn't a good idea. But when you've tested something and can say, 'Here is the credit quality, here is the profitability,' it becomes less about whether or not it's a good idea and more about how fast can we implement it."

From this command center, Providian is able to achieve what most corporate leaders can only aspire to: a personal connection to a vast customer base. All of Providian's senior managers are deeply involved in hands-on analysis of data and customer interaction. They even write the scripts used by the company's telephone representatives.

Debunking Conventional
—— Marketing Wisdom ——

Seth Barad, an executive vice president in charge of Providian's secured credit card business, spent eight years with American Express and another eight with Bain & Company, an international consulting firm, and says he has heard all the buzzwords about the value of listening to customers and delayering organizations. Few organizations actually embrace those ideas, he says, but at Providian the culture and business model are based on those very tenets.

There is minimal hierarchy and widespread collaboration. "We manage hearing from the customer at a very senior level here," Barad says. At Friday morning meetings, for example, the top executives review complaints from customers. The goal, Barad says, is not to respond—others at Providian handle that—but to learn, from what is being done wrong, how the product is flawed. Senior managers regularly pull and review hundreds of bankruptcy files to analyze the data and find cues, such as in cases of divorce, that might tip off bankruptcy risks that can be avoided in the future. In such cases, a Providian customer service representative will watch the account more closely, contact the customer, and seek ways to limit the risk.

Such insights, Barad says, can come only from senior people "eyeballing hundreds of files," seeing trends, and understanding the details. The alternative, as practiced by most competitors, is to hire an outside consulting firm to conduct a market research survey, followed by focus groups. Such research inevitably leads to mass media campaigns designed to launch new products, retain current customers, build a brand, and grow market share. This share-building process is to marketing what drift-netting is to fishing. It is inefficient, highly expensive, and not part of the Providian marketing culture.

Not surprisingly, Mehta has long believed that traditional marketing vehicles are flawed. Demographics, he insists, is not a good indicator and predictor of buying behavior. It's possible, even probable, he states, to have two demographically identical people—same sex, age, income, and zip code—with totally different needs and behaviors. Focus groups are also intrinsically inept at culling out behavior.

In his early days at Providian, for example, Mehta hired a traditional marketing manager whose experience had included stints at Citibank, Philip Morris, and Bank of America. The marketing manager suggested using a focus group as a way of gaining insight into what consumers wanted from a money market account. The people in the room—typical consumers spanning various demographics—gave thoughtful answers about wanting the best rates and lowest requirements. But Mehta, ever the radical marketer, was not satisfied that the data were authentic. He tossed in his own bonus question: What money market account did they currently have? Most, he recalls, had nowhere near the interest rates they claimed they had to have to consider such a product, and there were other accounts in the marketplace with higher rates. Why hadn't they switched?

"People tend to do and say things differently in focus groups,"

Mehta explains. "They tend to be rational in focus groups because of peer pressure, but they buy in a totally irrational fashion. By analyzing real data, you can figure out what they really buy rather than what they say they will buy."

Mehta also believed that the traditional models used to identify markets and product development in consumer lending were flawed. Most competitors identify a product and then conduct focus groups and market research to justify that product's development. Distrusting focus groups, Mehta decided to find the market first and then deliver the product based on what consumers actually wanted.

"We're in the business of selling service," Mehta says. "Our focus is on asking what is the most efficient and profitable way to deliver money to customers? Not everyone is looking for the lowest price or all the features you are peddling. Some customers would rather settle for cash rebates rather than airline miles. Others say, 'Give me the miles.'" Mehta has made a profitable business and created a niche opportunity by understanding these factors. He understands, for example, that the definition of low price varies from person to person. One person might think a 9 percent interest rate is low, while to another, 12 percent is low enough. So how do you price the product?

Though competitors are focusing more than ever on price, the truth is that customers care far less about that than the bankers. "The difference between 9 percent and 12 percent interest on a $2,000 loan is about $1.50 a week—less than a cup of Starbuck's coffee," Mehta says. "To a banker, that is huge. But to a customer, it's a nuisance. They say, 'I'd rather have your card and these features than shop around to save $1.50.'" In a focus group, however, that same customer, trying to sound rational among his peers, would most likely say he'd take the card only at a 9 percent APR.

What Providian has discovered, in fact, is that the consumer tends to value simplicity above all else. "We are all pressed for time," Mehta says. "Time is becoming a precious commodity to all income bracket groups. Those with lots of money need time to spend it, others need time to make it. Customers say, 'I am willing to pay extra if my life can be simplified and my time can be freed up.'"

To Mehta, Providian's ability to not only consolidate its customers' debt into one credit vehicle but to customize that vehicle with all the specific features a customer desires is the foundation for a powerful competitive advantage.

And while Providian has been taken to task by some industry analysts for targeting such a high-risk market, Mehta insists, in true radical marketer fashion, that Providian is simply broadening its opportunities.

Mehta says Providian's loss rate is about the same as that of the large banks. But more important, Providian manages risk-adjusted revenues rather than just pure loss rates. By avoiding the convenience users—those who pay off their monthly balances—Providian has one of the highest margins of any credit card company, allowing it to operate comfortably in markets that others fear. "You can't make money lending money if you don't take risk," Mehta says.

—— Banning the Budgets ——

Traditional marketers would also be perplexed by Providian's strong cultural bias against marketing budgets and quotas dictated by spreadsheets. Radical marketers are unhindered by conventional wisdom about marketing budgets. Seth Barad says that such requirements, de rigueur in the banks and big financial services companies, simply become entitlements and shift the focus away from the creativity and entrepreneurship that drive a radical marketer like Providian.

"If you were in charge of the Gold Card Rewards program at American Express, you might have a $20 million budget at the beginning of the year to market that card and get new customers," Barad says. "In most traditional marketing companies, that $20 million is an entitlement: it defines you as an individual and gives you a mandate to spend that amount."

The mandate, he continues, is based on targeted results set at the beginning of the fiscal year or quarter. In the credit card industry, for example, an accepted industry measure of success is the number of cards in force or out in the wallets of consumers. Analysts who track companies use that as a barometer for gauging financial success, regardless of how much profit is being made. So American Express might set a target for Gold Cards shipped in the fourth quarter and its marketing people would then focus solely on that number, even if it meant giving out free cards for spouses or using other promotional gimmicks that don't generate earnings.

At Providian, Barad says, the engineering mentality, supported by the company's computer models, changes the focus. Decisions are made daily, weekly, and monthly on how many pieces of mail to send and what to offer in each mailing. If Barad spends more money than anticipated, he is never criticized for it. "If I'm making a decision that produces smart economic value, it is not questioned," he says. "In a big company, I'm a hero if I spend only $19 million of the $20 million budget. Here I'd more likely be asked, 'How much could you have done if you had another $19 million?'"

Thus, Providian does not set out to establish a target number for pieces of direct mail at the beginning of the year. Instead, at regular meetings, Barad and his team study the current data, examine response rates, fulfillment rates, and return on capital, come up with an educated estimate of return and net present value of the cards, and then decide how big the mailing will be that week.

In such an environment, with well-honed and -vetted models, marketers can get away with a much less scripted and budgeted marketing approach. And unlike the shotgun approach of most traditional marketers, Providian spends as much time reexamining its decisions on the back end, testing to learn from what worked and what didn't.

The engineers call it a feedback loop. "Let's go back to a decision from last April, even if it was a terrible decision, and learn from it," Barad says. "The only bad test is a test you don't learn something from. Most tests are not going to turn into brilliant products, but you can learn a lot about what not to do and save yourself a lot of headaches in the future."

In addition, Providian understands better than most of its competitors what its cost structures are and how they can be leveraged. The company's marketers understand that they are engineering a purely financial product; there is no toothpaste to sell. They also acknowledge that Citicorp can service and process a credit card account more cheaply, owing to its sheer size and economies of scale.

But, as Barad points out, Providian, by focusing on its niche markets and using its culture and computers, has advantages of its own. "The big guys have massive cultural barriers to making decisions," he says. Big corporations like American Express or Citicorp often create vast marketing departments around individual brands and products, entrusting valuable corporate assets to groups of young marketers who might be six or seven layers removed from the core customer base.

And perhaps more important, the big players simply don't view the world radically enough to tread into Providian's markets. Some simply don't want to enter these markets for image reasons; others find the barriers to entry—Providian's complex technology and data collection infrastructure—much higher than anticipated.

By focusing so deeply on its core market, Providian has gained a substantial advantage over competitors whose focus is diluted by involvement in too many businesses at once. More important, Providian has honed its model over a decade and found ways to measure and assess risk that can't be purchased from credit bureaus. Thus, most competitors just don't have the will to devote the time and resources necessary to learn how to turn a profit in this higher-risk segment. "You have to learn this by trial and error," says Barad.

Whether Providian can sustain its remarkable growth as an independent entity in a financial services industry rife with mergers and acquisitions may well be Mehta's sternest test. Mehta purposely maintains a low profile. "I like to keep my ideas fresh and not easily available," he says.

In a business where the best ideas are quickly appropriated and copied, Providian has managed to stay ahead of the pack by adhering to its radical roots and maintaining a corporate culture that keeps its talented young staff motivated and loyal. "I put a high price on intellectual capital," Mehta says. "If you have smart people, smarter than the person the competition has in that same position, you have a much better chance to succeed."

Especially if that person is the CEO.

5

Harley-Davidson

The Deafening Roar of a Lifestyle Brand

"Let's turn left when the competition turns right."
—Clyde Fessler

If radical marketing is about creating a community around your brand, there have been few better displays of radical marketing than this. On June 13, 1998, amid a deafening roar and a river of black leather and blinding chrome, more than fifty thousand Harley-Davidson motorcycles thundered east along Interstate 94 into downtown Milwaukee as part of the company's ninety-fifth birthday celebration. It was a stunning sight, awesome in its scope and emotionally powerful in its message: owning a Harley makes you a member of a very unique community.

Harley-Davidson holds a birthday party for itself every five years, each successive gathering outdoing the one before. For the ninety-fifth, Harley owners were invited to join a cross-country pilgrimage, originating from five different cities and converging in Milwaukee, Harley's home city. "Come Home" was the company's message, and the word spread—through the dealer network and the company-sponsored Harley Owners Group—that Harley enthusiasts should come and participate in what was conceived as a "family" celebration. Hotels as far as one hundred miles away had been booked solid for a year or more,

125,000 Harley owners showed up on their bikes (only fifty thousand were permitted on the parade route), and the city orchestrated a weekend-long celebration to honor its favorite corporate citizen.

Because they are radical marketers, Harley executives were not simply waiting in suits and ties on some downtown viewing stand. All the senior executives, from Chairman Rich Teerlink to CEO Jeffrey Bleustein, and hundreds of other employees had ridden into Milwaukee on their own Harleys from one of the five originating cities. Harley's executives and managers, along with a good percentage of its fifty-five hundred employees, have a visceral connection to the brand because not only do they make and sell the motorcycles, they are customers. They understand that a Harley is more than just a motorcycle, it is a lifestyle, a work of art, an emotional connection to a widespread and unique community.

Indeed, what Harley-Davidson has created is a prototypical example of radical marketing. Much has been written about the company's remarkable rise from the ashes in the mid-1980s to become a darling of Wall Street and a symbol of rugged American determination. But Harley-Davidson, at its core, is a story of a deep-seated understanding of and belief in an enduring brand and the brilliant management of that brand in the face of daunting odds.

Harley made very clear and decisive moves based on a simple value proposition, one common to the top brands, from Rolex watches to Ferrari sports cars: there is no substitute for the best. Trends shift, status symbols fade, market leaders stumble. But radical marketers thrive because they refuse to act like the competition. Like Thoreau's different drummer, they insist on stepping to the music they hear, however measured or far away.

When foreign motorcycle makers found profits over the past decade in sleek, fast, futuristic-looking sport bikes, Harley focused even harder on its traditional design heritage. The styling cues, direct from the 1940s and 1950s, were designed by Willie G. Davidson, grandson of one of the company's founders, head of the company's design department, and a legend of rock star proportions among the Harley cognoscenti. Davidson's connection to the company's past has become a signpost to the future. He is constantly on the road, listening to customers, riding with Harley owners, incorporating their suggestions.

Though many have conjectured as to the lure and mystique of the Harley-Davidson motorcycle—its unique styling, its distinctive rumble, the sense it brings of freedom and rebellion and rugged American individualism—there is, in fact, no simple explanation for its appeal. Harley executives claim that they have never tried to define the mystique. "If you could really define the mystique, it wouldn't be a mystique anymore," says Harley CEO Jeff Bleustein. He believes the appeal lies deep within the human spirit, a desire for freedom and adventure that has always been a part of human nature. "It's not something that can be artificially created on Madison Avenue," Bleustein says.

But it can be embraced and exploited, not only by the company itself but by others. Madison Avenue thinks Harleys are so cool, for example, that the company reaps millions of dollars worth of free advertising by appearing in ads for countless other products such as cars, clothes, and even the New York Stock Exchange. Harley's marketing department logs at least five requests each month for the use of its products in other companies' advertisements. While companies paid $1 million for thirty seconds worth of advertising during the 1997 Super Bowl, for example, there were one hundred Harleys on the field as part of the halftime show, at no cost to Harley-Davidson. And Harley's marketing vice president, Joanne Bischmann, reports that she is constantly barraged by requests from celebrities to serve as Harley's official pitchman. With no national television advertising and a small print campaign, she politely declines all requests.

What is at the heart of all this fuss about a motorcycle? Company executives have carefully studied the emotional bond between Harley riders and the product and have followed strict parameters in all aspects of the design, manufacture, and marketing of the motorcycles to enhance the mystique and further cement the bond. Harley-Davidson, for example, has filed with the U.S. Patent and Trademark Office a trademark on the very noise the bikes make, the distinctive *"potato, potato, potato"* lumpy rumble that comes from its patented V-Twin engine. The company feels that competitors, already copying Harley's styling, are also trying to re-create its sound, which Harley executives say is as much a unique product attribute as the engine or body design. If NBC can copyright its three-tone signature and MGM its lion's roar, why not the Harley rumble?

For many, the Harley roar is classic noise pollution. But for Harley lovers, it is a mating call. And it is also a perfect example of what great radical marketers do to build their brands. Like other radical marketers, Harley did nothing less than reinvent the company while transforming many negative images into positive ones. Out of the stereotypical menacing image of biker gangs, for example, Harley created a worldwide club, became affiliated with a reputable charitable foundation, and celebrated the bonding experience of road rallies and annual biker gatherings in places like Daytona Beach and Sturgis, North Dakota.

To fend off an aggressive onslaught from foreign competitors, Harley decided to adhere strictly to its quality standards, even in the face of massive unmet demand; to build a broad sense of community around the product; and to solidify the core constituencies—the employees, dealers, and customers.

In this way, Harley-Davidson emerged as a brand that crosses a raft of formidable boundaries: age, gender, income, education, ethnic background, and political outlook. What other product could claim the fierce loyalty of both the Hell's Angels and business tycoons like the late Malcolm Forbes, who liked to ride around Wall Street on his Harley during lunch hour?

——— Big Name, Little Advertising ———

How powerful is the Harley brand? The numbers tell an impressive story, but hardly the whole story. In 1997 Harley-Davidson Inc., a company that was nearly bankrupt in 1985, reported its twelfth straight year of record sales and earnings with revenues of $1.8 billion, up 21 percent from the previous year. The company sold 132,000 motorcycles, up 11.4 percent from the year before, and dealers said they could easily have sold twice that number if the company had had the capacity to build them.

Like other radical marketers, Harley-Davidson's marketing prowess is not dependent on massive advertising expenditures. In 1997 Harley spent just $1 million on advertising, which was $1 million more than it spent the year before. Compare that to the nearly $100 million

Toyota spent on advertising for a single car model, the Camry.

Harley doesn't rely on huge advertising expenditures to generate interest because it simply doesn't have to. Harley-Davidson motorcycles are in such demand today that dealers consistently report waiting lists of a year or longer. Even the wife of Harley's chairman had to order a new bike nearly a year in advance to get it in time for his birthday.

All this has fueled enviable shareholder value: $10,000 invested in Harley-Davidson stock in 1986, when the then-beleaguered company went public, was worth $312,500 at the end of 1997. Most employees and many customers are shareholders.

Harley's true radicalness, however, lies in its adherence to the rules we presented in Chapter 2, from the CEO owning the marketing function to creating a community of users while remaining true to the brand.

—— The Lure of the Community ——

Despite its long, colorful history, the company's true golden era has blossomed in just the past fifteen years as the brand caught hold with a baby-boom generation that had long harbored Harley dreams and had now acquired the disposable income to indulge those dreams. Suddenly, Harleys weren't just for the stereotypical blue-collar biker crowd, the company's primary customer base for most of its history. As the company experienced its resurgence and prices rose, the demographics started to change.

The average age and income of Harley owners shot up, and Harley rallies around the country were suddenly populated with lawyers, investment bankers, and chief executives rubbing elbows and comparing notes with ponytailed motorheads. Celebrity Harley owners like Jay Leno, Arnold Schwarzenegger, and Billy Joel provided added cachet. Like other great radical marketers, Harley-Davidson not only created an expansive community but instilled it with a crucial ingredient: common ground.

When the usual crowd of bikers gather on Sunday mornings at the Marcus Dairy in Danbury, Connecticut, there is no way to tell the corporate executives from the plumbing contractors, and everyone is far more focused on admiring the other motorcycles and retelling old rally stories than comparing résumés and social status. Corporate leaders, in fact, agree that riding is an effective stress reducer, a transcendent experience that requires total concentration and provides a much-needed respite from the pressures of daily business life.

Regina Burston, a consultant, Harvard graduate, and Harley rider in San Anselmo, California, says that Harleys attract passionate entrepreneurial types because riding is an outlet for their propensity to take risks. "This is about danger, about being out in the sun and the wind," she says. "It's raw and sensual."

A few hard-core Harley traditionalists scoff at these "Rubbies" (rich, urban bikers) and wonder if Harley is selling its soul to a new moneyed crowd. But Harley executives saw the obvious value in embracing new customer sets and understood immediately that the best way to bring in a wider audience was to stay true to the message. "We market fun," Teerlink says. "We don't market to any specific group. The Harley family is a very diverse group who do all things imaginable for a living. If the world could get along like Harley owners, it would be fantastic."

—— Hiring Passionate Missionaries ——

Like other radical marketers, Harley has kept its marketing organization small and flat. Bischmann says she hasn't had a new hire in her twelve-person department in more than four years. "We're a lonely group," she says, laughing. And Harley puts on mega-events like the ninety-fifth birthday entirely from within. Most large corporations hire out such galas to professional event consultants, but Harley forms, from its employee population, more than eighty volunteer committees that spend three years on the project.

Radical marketers hire carefully and well, summoning the same visceral connection to the employees as they do to the customer base. What they end up with are passionate missionaries who evangelize the brand. Harley employees take personal responsibility for maintaining the luster of the brand—so much so that the company was able to shut down its branding department in 1995. Harley employees not only model motorclothes in the catalog but lead tours of the company's factories, ride to HOG rallies, and wear Harley T-shirts on the assembly line. "We didn't need the branding department," says Bischmann. "We're all brand managers."

In a manufacturing-intensive environment like Harley-Davidson, which is a union shop to boot, the management-employee cohesion is striking. Though owning a Harley is not a requirement for employment, most new hires come in with a passion for the company and its products. If not, that passion is generally ignited pretty quickly.

Nearly every résumé is accompanied by a cover letter that tells a story about a relative who worked there or a Harley experience that conveys the depth of the bond between the company and the community. Part of the work requirement is to attend rallies and company-sponsored events, and rather than complain, employees wrangle to get these assignments. Customers are thrilled to meet a genuine Harley factory worker. Indeed, sixty thousand people tour the assembly plant in York, Pennsylvania, and another twenty-five thousand visit the Milwaukee engine plant each year. Employees proudly take turns as tour guides.

"If that feeling ever faded, so would the authenticity of the brand," Bischmann says. "If the customers didn't feel it from us, they wouldn't feel it either."

—— Out of the Head Office ——

Harley executives eschew focus groups and market research and data for a more visceral approach to their customers: they ride with them. Bleustein, a twenty-three-year Harley veteran who succeeded Teerlink as CEO in 1997, led the riders from York, Pennsylvania, to Milwaukee for the ninety-fifth anniversary celebration. But the executives don't just ride in Harley-sponsored events. Finding the leather-clad Teerlink, an accountant by training, at Daytona Bike Week in Florida in March or at the mammoth motorcycle rally in Sturgis, North Dakota, in August is nearly impossible, like finding Waldo in *Where's Waldo?* He looks just like his customers because he is one.

Indeed, like other radical marketers—EMC's Dick Egan, Boston

Beer's Jim Koch, Iams' Clay Mathile, or the NBA's David Stern—Teerlink shares the emotional connection to his product that his customers have. He is as likely to ride seventy miles to a morning meeting in Madison aboard his own Heritage Springer as any employee or customer. And he is happiest when meeting true Harley enthusiasts—those who own two or more Harleys—to talk about the bikes.

George Conrades, a former senior marketing executive with IBM and now chief executive of BBN Corporation in Cambridge, Massachusetts, is a longtime enthusiast who owns three Harleys. When he worked at IBM, he got to know the Harley management team because Harley-Davidson was an IBM customer. As a rider, Conrades was a lifelong Harley fanatic, but he bought the company's stock after meeting and riding with Teerlink and his executive team. "The Harley management team has the best understanding of its customers and works as hard on those customer relationships as anyone I know," Conrades says.

In the late 1980s, Conrades introduced a fellow IBM executive, Michael Armstrong, to Harleys, and Armstrong quickly got hooked. In 1990, at Teerlink's invitation, Conrades and Armstrong flew to Milwaukee, toured the Harley plants, and then were joined by a group of Harley executives and provided with Harleys to ride. The group took off on a three-hundred-mile journey to tour IBM's manu-facturing plant in Rochester, Minnesota. Not your typical customer-supplier meeting, but it made an impression.

For Armstrong, now chief executive of AT&T, the ride was cathartic. "When you come into a small town with a big group of riders, the Harleys tell everybody they are around with that wonderful distinctive sound," Armstrong recalls. "All the men and boys turn and look at you, and that smile comes across their face; you can hear them thinking, 'I wish I was on that bike.'"

—— How They Got Here ——

Like other great radical marketers, Harley-Davidson has been able to reinvent itself many times over in its long history. Harley, in fact, has managed to do what few old-line manufacturing companies have accomplished: retain a few critical positive elements from its long heritage and make the world forget the rest of what eventually became a dismal business story. Harley is essentially a new company, having remade itself yet again in the early 1980s, this time in a most dramatic fashion. Yet Harley manages to retain the mystique of its own early history, which management wears like a badge of honor, brandishing the Harley tradition as a key marketing tool.

Harley didn't truly become a radical marketer, however, until the new management team took over in 1981 and turned the company into a case study for success. If there is evidence that more mature and traditional companies can become radical marketers, Harley-Davidson is it.

Throughout its early history, the Harley-Davidson earned a reputation as a sturdy and reliable motorcycle and became popular with both the hobbyist and racing crowds. During World War II, Harleys were enlisted as military vehicles, and a spillover effect during the postwar period made Harley a popular brand among returning veterans.

Ironically, both police forces and a spate of new outlaw motorcycle gangs embraced Harleys, creating a marketing juxtaposition that the company wrestled with for years. Harley-Davidson designers set the standard of the day with distinct styling, heavy chrome, and a wide assortment of accessories that adorned the bikes. During this period, a cottage industry of "chop shops" began to blossom. A small but enthusiastic group of riders liked to strip down the bikes to their bare minimum for speed and create a certain aesthetic look that not everyone appreciated. These choppers, or "hogs," as they became called in the press, added to an unwanted disreputable image.

Clearly, for Americans, motorcycles were no longer mere modes of transportation, as they had been in pre-war years. They stirred a sense of freedom, rebellion, and individuality, in some ways replacing the cowboy's horse from the Wild West. And Harley-Davidsons, big, powerful, and loud, epitomized the classic motorcycle to a growing legion of enthusiasts.

In 1947 a single incident—at a July 4 rally of the American Motorcycle Association in Hollister, California—galvanized the country and set the tone for Harley for the next several decades. A group of about five hundred drunken riders rode into the tiny northern California town and broke windows, trashed restaurants and bars, and terrorized the local population. It took forty police officers and state troopers to get the situation under control. Several people were injured, and many arrested. A *Life* magazine photographer snapped a picture of one of the "outlaw" riders, clearly inebriated, with his stripped-down Harley atop a mountain of empty beer bottles. He held a beer bottle aloft in each hand and leered drunkenly at the camera. The picture ran on the cover of the popular magazine, much to Harley-Davidson's chagrin.

The incident became a national sensation, spawning great media interest, and in 1954 the film *The Wild Ones,* based loosely on the Hollister incident and starring a youthful and swaggering Marlon Brando, became a hit. Outlaw motorcycle gangs, most notably the Hell's Angels, began to proliferate around the country. The motorcycle of choice was a Harley. Though most motorcycle enthusiasts were distinctly blue-collar types who smoked cigarettes and drank beer, they were neither gang members nor troublemakers. But in a short time, the sight of any large group of leather-clad motorcyclists entering a town set off alarm bells and helped solidify a growing notoriety. In 1969 the hit film *Easy Rider* portrayed two drug-dealing Harley riders on a journey across America, further enhancing Harley's "bad boy" image.

Harley, despite the negative stereotypes, never strayed far from its original value proposition: to build its sturdy, powerful motorcycles for enthusiasts. Moreover, Harley executives couldn't help but notice that the outlaw image had its merits in enhancing Harley's lure. The "bad boy" image gave the brand a sharp edge and tapped into the rebel inside its mostly male customers. "Harley reflects many things Americans dream about," says Benson P. Shapiro, a consultant and former Harvard Business School professor. "They're a little bit naughty, a little bit nice, which is a very attractive brand image to have." And a perfect profile for a radical marketer.

By the late 1950s, Harley had captured much of the market share for big touring bikes and for police forces. But in the golden era of the automobile, American motorcycle sales in general were slowing dramatically. In fact, by the mid-1960s, Harley-Davidson was the last of 214

American motorcycle makers to survive. Poor family management and the sudden flood of cheaper, higher-quality Japanese motorcycles from Honda, Kawasaki, Suzuki, and Yamaha into the U.S. market pushed Harley to the brink of bankruptcy. The company was rescued when it was purchased by American Machine and Foundry Company (AMF) for $21 million in 1969.

—— **Saving the Brand** ——

AMF saved Harley only to run it back into the ground. AMF, to its credit, poured millions of dollars into facilities and manufacturing. By 1973 Harley was turning out thirty-seven thousand motorcycles a year and pulling in $122 million in sales. But AMF forced the company into overproduction, simultaneously driving quality down. The Harley, which already had a reputation for its leaky and sometimes temperamental engine, was losing appeal even with hard-core Harley loyalists who loved the look and feel of the bikes and were happy to spend weekends in their garages, up to their elbows in motor oil and grease.

In the late 1970s, however, AMF went too far and insisted on putting the name AMF rather than Harley-Davidson on the motorcycles. Sales dropped, and AMF began looking for a buyer. Such hubris and lack of understanding of the brand struck a decisive blow with Harley's executives. In 1981 Vaughn Beals, Harley's chief executive, pulled together a dozen company officers, including Jeff Bleustein, found outside financing, and bought Harley from AMF. It was a radical move considering the raging recession, staggering interest rates, and marketplace dynamics of the day. But like other radical marketers, Beals and his team believed so deeply in the product that they were willing to mortgage their homes to try to save the brand. Indeed, radical marketers view the impossible as just another opportunity, and that made rescuing Harley-Davidson a great opportunity, for the company was surely in an impossible situation.

Saddled with $70 million in debt from the buyout, amid a terrible recession and the onslaught of Japanese competitors, Harley-Davidson was a company on life support for the next several years. Harley lost more than $50 million in 1981 and 1982, and by 1983 it was facing bankruptcy yet again. The company publicly railed against the Japanese for "dumping" bikes into the U.S. market and pressed Congress and President Reagan to impose a stiff tariff on Japanese imports. Ironically, at the same time, Harley executives, like many American business leaders at the time, were touring Japan and bringing back vaunted Japanese production methods—such as just-in-time inventory control and quality circles—to the beleaguered company.

Beals later acknowledged to the *New York Times* that after years of blaming the Japanese, Harley-Davidson admitted that its troubles were internal. "We realized the problem was us, not them," he said.

Few brands tarnished for so long are able to bounce back. But Harley's cachet had endured, and in the nationalistic, anti-Japanese fervor of the 1980s, Harley-Davidson became a rallying symbol for American resilience and business moxie, an underdog to cheer back to the top. Taking advantage of the timing of this fortunate bit of economic nationalism, Harley-Davidson's management team employed a radical marketing effort to seize the opportunity.

After refocusing its manufacturing efforts with a heavy dose of quality control, Harley began to win back converts. Desperate for much-needed capital, Harley went public in 1986 and received strong support on Wall Street. Its stock became a favorite for investors, particularly those white-collar executives who'd harbored lifelong secret dreams of becoming Harley owners themselves.

Teerlink, who succeeded Beals as chief executive, understood, like other great radical marketers, that Harley had survived because it had a dedicated, hard-core customer base with hundreds of thousands of happy Harley stories spun over eight decades in the business. He also understood the value of a dedicated network of six hundred dealers, including some like A. D. Farrow in Columbus, Ohio, which sold its first Harley in 1912 and had stood by the company throughout its fiscal crises. And he understood that the Harley brand had survived even the darkest hours because Harley owners were dedicated to preserving the bikes they owned, even if they were uncomfortable buying new ones. Such brand loyalty is rare but powerful. And it can be highly contagious.

At Milwaukee headquarters and Harley's manufacturing plants, the employees, most of whom were veteran Harley workers, displayed an emotional commitment to the long-term viability of the company characterized by "a high level of intrinsic motivation," which stems from the legacy, Teerlink says. "We've been up and down," he says. "When we haven't been sensitive to that legacy, to the employees or customers, and made products that were not up to standards, our market share went to hell."

Harley carefully plotted the blueprint for its rebirth, a radical marketer's manifesto for recasting and refurbishing the brand. The blueprint included:

- a complete quality overhaul
- a recommitment to the design and styling that was the company's trademark
- the building and support of the Harley community
- a commitment to brand integrity
- positioning for success

—— Getting Back on Track ——

Clyde Fessler, who joined Harley-Davidson in 1977 as advertising and sales promotion manager, became part of the marketing strategy team in the early 1980s with the mandate to put a new face on Harley's tarnished image. Fessler recalls a four-day strategy meeting he held with Harley-Davidson's new ad agency, Carmichael Lynch in Minneapolis, in 1981. The focus was on Honda, Kawasaki, Yamaha, and Suzuki, the tough Japanese competitors.

"On a big piece of paper, we drew up a list of comparisons between the Japanese bikes and ourselves," he says. "We put down all the strengths and all the weaknesses. The Japanese were global, into long-term strategic planning, did a lot of advertising, and had great diversity in their global markets. They could take a concept from idea to product in eighteen to twenty-four months.

"Harley-Davidson had both a positive and negative image," he continues. "We had heritage, tradition, mystique, and we said, 'With that, how do we compete against these giants?' We looked at where they had been the previous five years and were able to project where they were going in the next five . . . new engines, new frames, new suspensions, very high-tech. So we decided to be the alternative. We said, '*Let's turn left when they turn right.* Let's be the alternative and do the things they can't do.' And that became our strategy in everything we did and still do."

—— Getting Good Again ——

Under AMF, the quality of Harley motorcycles sank so low that they inspired heavy sarcasm in the biker community. "Buy a Harley, buy the best—ride a mile and walk the rest!" went one popular ditty. By the mid-1970s, for example, the California Highway Patrol stopped riding Harleys because they were unstable and sprayed oil. Things got so bad that Harley-Davidson actually instituted a policy of putting final quality inspection responsibility on the shoulders of its dealers rather than on its own factories.

To resuscitate the brand, the company began to retool its entire manufacturing process. "Quality became our method of survival," says Ken Sutton, vice president and general manager of Harley's engine plant in Milwaukee. Indeed, quality has driven the dramatic Harley turnaround story more than any other single factor. By cutting head-quarters staff, reengineering production methods, redesigning and building high-quality engines, and instituting a raft of Japanese-style manufacturing and quality control methods, Harley coupled its sur-vivor's mentality with an aggressive revitalization of its brand. The result: demand so high that Harley cannot increase production fast enough.

In the mid-1990s, the company spent $200 million to increase production, and a new Kansas City plant began shipping motorcycles in early 1998. Harley's stated goal is to produce two hundred thou-sand motorcycles by 2003, the company's hundredth birthday. But to its credit, Harley refuses to sacrifice quality for speed. Having experienced several brushes with oblivion, management has taken on the classic, paranoid Depression-era mentality of the best radical marketers. Failure is impossible if you focus on the proper precepts for growth rather than sacrificing everything for quick profits.

"We think it's unfortunate that customers have to wait," says Teerlink. "But we are not purposely keeping our numbers down. We say to customers, 'Would you like us to go back to the quality of motorcycles you got in the seventies and early eighties?' When they hear that, they are not happy, but they understand."

Like other radical marketers, Harley had few resources after the 1981 buyout, so the company instituted nontraditional policies aimed at keeping quality high and costs low. Beginning in 1983 with the introduction of the new Evolution engine, the company has made extensive technical changes to its engines and parts, curing the ever-present oil leaks, cutting emissions, enhancing performance. "We've maintained the Harley look, not the Harley leak," said one executive.

Bikes are built strictly on advance orders from dealers rather than anticipated market demand. Every motorcycle has a dealer invoice number on it before it leaves the factory. Indeed, such is the demand that the corporation itself owns just twenty motorcycles, one of each model, to use for photography purposes. This policy allowed Harley to do away with vast stocks of parts awaiting assembly and adopt the Japanese just-in-time method. A continuous flow of quality parts into Harley's factories not only reduces the amount of money tied up in inventory but drives the quality process throughout manufacturing.

Harley's salaried staff receive bonuses not only for financial performance but for warranty performance. The fewer returns, the better the bonuses. Hourly union workers are given similar incentives: their quarterly bonuses are based on meeting quality targets that have been negotiated with the unions.

Much of Harley's quality edge comes from an intensely loyal employee population, half of whom are veterans of twenty years or more who have survived the company's brush with bankruptcy. A visit to the company's vast engine plant on Capitol Drive in Milwaukee provides a vivid visual display of employee commitment. A parking area in front of the plant is filled with hundreds of gleaming Harleys, all owned by employees. Sutton says that fully 40 percent of the eleven hundred employees in the plant ride Harleys. Woe to the employee who parks a Honda or Kawasaki anywhere nearby. Inside, most employees wear Harley T-shirts or some other form of company paraphernalia, even though it isn't required. It is a matter of pride. In Milwaukee a job at Harley is a "badge of honor," according to Joanne Bischmann.

And though no hard data exist, anecdotal evidence suggests that more Harley employees have the company logo tattooed somewhere on their bodies than do the employees of any other company. Customers are not far behind. Rather than distance themselves from this socially controversial practice, Harley executives openly brag about the phenomenon, even in the company's annual report.

And like the best radical marketers, the visceral connection to the customers pervades the entire employee population. When a decision on quality needs to be made, the employees have little trouble thinking like customers since so many *are* customers. "The catchphrase around here is 'I wouldn't put that on my bike, so I'm not going to put it on someone else's bike,'" Ken Sutton says.

The payoff has been dramatic. Harleys have become far easier to operate and maintain. By the mid-1980s, the California Highway Patrol returned to Harley-Davidson, and the motorcycle has once again become the vehicle of choice for most police departments in the United States.

Quality remains the key differentiator as Harley seeks to extend the brand with clothing, accessories, toys, games, and other licensed merchandise. "The biggest problem isn't extending the brand to a variety of merchandise, but to merchandise that is poorly made and expensive," says Christopher Hart, a management consultant in Boston. "That is a trust defect. Whether they own a Harley or not, if people consider themselves Harley people, they have created a trust bond with the company. And to get poor-quality, expensive junk foisted on them cheapens the image and weakens that bond."

To that end, Bischmann, Harley's marketing vice president, says the licensing department is extremely cautious about the products it endorses, selecting them based on quality and management. "We've been around almost one hundred years, and nobody wants to be the one to screw it up so that we're not here for the next one hundred years."

—— Creating Design Envy ——

One of the tenets of radical marketing is staying true to the brand. Few can claim such devotion to their brands as Harley-Davidson. Like the Grateful Dead with their music, Harley-Davidson has maintained a consistency in its product design that is the envy of designers in many other fields and the basis for a powerful brand. In an exhibit of global design at London's Victoria and Albert Museum, the object chosen to represent American design was a Harley-Davidson. Harleys were also on display in a highly popular exhibit at New York's Guggenheim Museum.

Building on its unique heritage, Harley makes bikes that look as if they were packed in crates in 1947 and unpacked in mint condition today. According to Fessler, the company experimented internally in the early 1990s with new, futuristic designs. But no one—customers, dealers, or employees—liked them. Instead, Harley's response to the trend toward sleek, speedy sport bikes, which the Japanese, Germans, and Italians began to export to the United States in the 1970s, was to acquire Buell, a small American sport bike maker, to grab market share in that growing category.

Harley-Davidson thus made a clear choice to stay with its traditional styling, a classic 1940s and 1950s design whose features epitomize what aficionados believe motorcycles were meant to look like: colorful teardrop gas tanks, the patented V-Twin engine, lots of sparkling chrome, and an open invitation to modify and accessorize every bike in the owner's personal style and taste. "They are Barbie dolls for grown-ups," the Harley enthusiast George Conrades says. "The fun is dressing them up to suit your taste."

Even the Harley model names—Electra Glide, Hydra Glide, Bad Boy, Road King, and Softail, among others—connote the styling and elegance that make Harley lovers weak in the knees, unable to decide whether to ride the bikes or park them in their living rooms as sculptures.

The Japanese, in their traditional marketing fashion, decided as far back as 1979 that they could copy the Harley styling and introduce Harley-like cruisers in the United States. Figuring they could carve out market share by offering higher-quality, lower-priced machines, the Japanese companies all entered the market with a vengeance. And they've been successful, grabbing 50 percent of the market over the past twenty years. That market share is spread, however, among four or five other manufacturers. Harley-Davidson's market-share growth has been stunted more by production limitations than by competitors.

Mark O'Neil, the marketing manager at Cycle-Craft, a forty-year-old Harley-Davidson dealership in Everett, Massachusetts, points out that first-time buyers may be lured by competitive offerings or the immediate availability of bikes, but customers who know the market scoff at the competition. "Good try, bad result," is what they say, according to O'Neil. He is adamant that even an untrained eye can quickly see the difference. "Harley's heritage evolved over a long time," he says. "You can't just come in and say, 'We have that, too.'"

Having a consistent design vision is crucial to sustaining the brand. In Willie G. Davidson, the company has a vital link to its design heritage. The sixty-six-year-old Davidson—"Willie G." to adoring customers and employees alike—has headed up the design department since 1963, and dressed in black leather and beret, he takes to the road throughout the year and meets with Harley customers. They throng around him, asking for autographs and posing for pictures. Radical marketers love and respect their customers, and Willie G. embodies that for Harley. He really does listen to his customers. For example, based on customer input, he designed new lines like the 1997 Softail to mimic the beauty and elegance of 1940s classics like the Hydra Glide.

According to *Financial World* magazine, when the company was in tough financial straits, unable to bankroll innovations in engineering, Willie G.'s deft touch with paint and decals kept new designs rolling out of the factory. When bikers were paying small fortunes to customizers to remake their bikes, Willie G. began to design new models to look custom-made straight from the factory. And like the other radical marketers at Harley, Willie G. believes the magic emanates from the closeness to customers and a vital link to the past. "It's no one thing," he told *Financial World*. "I feel we never really lost track of who we are. We've created an identity that is loved all over the world. It didn't happen overnight, it happened over ninety years. We keep that sacred in our thoughts." Willie G.'s three children are all involved in product design for the company, ensuring that yet another generation of Davidsons will keep the tradition intact.

── It Takes a Village ──

Radical marketers understand that a signature of great brands is the sense of community that they spawn. From its earliest days at the start of this century, Harley-Davidson recognized the primal urge that bikers have to gather and share their passion about their sport.

Clyde Fessler, who was then Harley's advertising and promotion manager, set out to formalize that need, at Vaughn Beals's suggestion. Ever the radical marketer, Fessler approached the task by looking for opportunities to turn negatives into positives.

For as long as anyone could remember, Harleys had been called "hogs," though no one could recall the exact origin of the name. The connotation was a negative one: Harleys were seen as big, loud, road-hogging bikes driven by outlaw bikers. Turning the stereotype on its ear, Fessler created the Harley Owners Group, or HOG, in 1983 and drew applause for the idea. HOG was an organization that would sponsor rallies, organize events, offer special promotions, and keep Harley owners in close contact with the company and each other.

Fessler had an additional purpose in mind for the Harley Owners Group. He knew that another age-old stereotype, left over from the Hollister, California, incident in 1947, was the image of *The Wild Ones* that Harley evoked for many Americans. The sight and sound of an entourage of Harleys roaring into town still meant a nasty motorcycle gang had arrived. So Fessler pushed hard to get HOG associated with the Muscular Dystrophy Foundation, an honorable and highly visible charity. Under the club's banner, groups now ride for charity and over the past fifteen years have raised more than $25 million for MD research. Today

HOG members constitute the fourth largest contributing group to the Jerry Lewis Telethon each September.

At the first HOG rally in 1984 in California, 28 people showed up. Today HOG has 365,000 members in 940 chapters all around the world. The organization sponsors hundreds of rallies around the country each year, including the September Posse Run from Portland, Oregon, to Portland, Maine.

For a company that markets emotion, the gatherings take on a familiar spiritual feeling, evoking a sense of family and devotion that surprises even hardened Harley veterans. Teerlink recalls a moment at the company's ninetieth birthday celebration in Milwaukee in 1993. After tens of thousands of Harley riders roared into downtown Milwaukee, three abreast amid thousands of cheering spectators, a burly man walked up to Teerlink, lifted him off the ground, looked him in the eye, and said, "Thank you." Teerlink asked, "What for?" The man replied, "For giving me the parade I never got when I returned from Vietnam."

Harley also recognized early on the unusual path that most Harley lovers took from wanna-bes to members of this elite club. Most neophyte riders buy smaller Japanese motorcycles to learn to ride. They quickly trade up to used Harleys and eventually make the plunge and invest in a brand new bike. Fessler saw an opportunity in this pattern. In the late 1980s, he met with Harley dealers and created the Ride Free campaign. The company promised that customers who bought new Harley Sportsters, the entry-level bike, which sold at the time for $3,395, could trade them in a year later for a bigger Harley and get credited for the full $3,395 toward the new bike.

Today Harleys are not cheap, selling for between $6,500 and $17,000. But the bikes are in such demand that they actually appreciate as they age, fetching more than full price in resale value. One dealer says that he sold a Harley to a customer, and before the customer even left the lot he had resold it to someone waiting outside, for a $2,000 profit!

Coupled with the fact that Harley owners often spend more to customize the bikes than they paid for the bike originally, there is a huge after-market industry in parts and accessories for customizing the motorcycles. Radical marketers constantly rethink the marketing mix, and Harley, which already has a successful parts and accessories business, is stepping up its efforts in that business.

—— Maintaining Brand Integrity ——

Radical marketers find ways to extend their brands without diluting them. Harley's internal licensing department struggles to determine which products deserve to carry the Harley brand. Over the past fifteen years, the company has licensed its popular shield-and-bars logo to hundreds of products, including train sets, Christmas ornaments, art kits, clocks, watches, and cigarette lighters. Harley's name and logo have such cachet that they adorn a popular Manhattan café, a L'Oréal cologne in Europe, and a limited-edition, leather-clad Harley Barbie doll. The company, through its Eaglemark Financial Services unit, introduced a Harley Visa card—not gold or platinum but chrome—with an option for the cardholder to have a photo of his or her Harley emblazoned on it.

The Harley Cafe, modeled after the Hard Rock Cafe, has become a highly popular destination in midtown Manhattan, and a new one opened in Las Vegas in 1997. Harley-Davidson shops have become familiar tenants in malls around the country. Clyde Fessler says that Harley insists that the merchandise be durable and high-quality to win over its riders. The logo was licensed to a Zippo lighter, for example, rather than a Bic disposable.

Harley executives know they walk a fine line between prostituting the brand and enhancing the customer's relationship with Harley, and they admit to mistakes along the way, like licensing the Harley name for a line of cigarettes. But the company sticks to a clear three-point strategy for licensing its hallowed name: (1) to provide practical products that customers require, such as leather jackets, boots, and other functional riding apparel; (2) to provide items that enhance the general public's view of the brand; and (3) to provide toys and other items for children as a way to build relationships with future customers.

Critics suggest that Harley-Davidson is "selling out" and diluting its brand by putting its logo on so many products. But proponents don't believe Harley has come close to burning out its brand, and as long as the company doesn't get distracted from its core business, the brand extension helps fuel the mystique. Radical marketers are acutely aware that brands must continually evolve or die. A company selling a high-ticket item like a Harley across a wide range of economic and social strata must find ways to make the brand accessible to those who can't own the product itself. Indeed, the aura of Harley as a shared community can be experienced by someone wearing a Harley T-shirt on a grocery store checkout line or a cabdriver wearing a Harley belt buckle. Conversations start, experiences are shared, and both the community and the brand are extended.

Bischmann adds that Harley toys, built by the likes of Mattel and Kenner, are an excellent way to extend the passion for Harleys to a younger audience; with an aging customer base, this is a key marketing challenge for the company. Pointing to a Harley Barbie, she asks, "What better way is there to get a three-year-old girl to feel the Harley motorcycle experience?"

Harley also recognizes that it is in the motorcycle business, not the toy or apparel business, so licensing deals are essential. Like many other radical marketers, Harley used models such as Walt Disney to piece together its own licensing program. Where can value be added to the brand without straying too far from the core attributes of the brand? Bischmann says that the motorcycle is the center of every discussion. Harley rarely initiates licensing deals but rather fields countless requests. The common thread in every decision is how well a proposed product or service leads customers back to the motorcycles. Rumors about a Harley theme park, for example, have circulated for several years, but Bischmann says that if such a park were to be built, it would have to provide something tangible, like the Harley experience of riding out on the open road, to be considered.

Fessler also realized that legions of Harley riders in black leather jackets and black T-shirts helped perpetuate the outlaw biker image. But a limited line of black Harley apparel was all that was available. Harley began licensing its logo for blue jeans, T-shirts, baseball caps, and footwear to be sold through outlets such as Sears and JC Penney.

"We licensed our name because it was valuable," Fessler says. "People paid to wear it."

In 1986 Fessler officially launched Harley-Davidson Motor-Clothes, a business unit that has become the Lands' End of biker apparel. Through its catalog and the dealerships, the company markets everything from black leather jackets to baby clothes to French-cut women's underwear. The riding clothes are rugged and durable, designed not only for motorcyclists but for pilots and car enthusiasts as well—"people who want their clothing to be a symbol of strength, freedom, individuality," Fessler says.

A $20 million business in 1988 grew to $100 million by 1996, when seven million Harley-related garments were sold around the world. "People love the logo, and this helped change our image," Fessler says about shifting negatives to positives.

But people felt uncomfortable shopping for clothes in motorcycle dealerships, where grease and fluorescent lighting combined to create a rather inhospitable atmosphere. Realizing that most dealers were ill equipped to sell fashion items, Bleustein suggested a redesign of the dealerships to accommodate merchandise sales. Harley paid for the interior designers and offered to help all of its dealers to remodel their stores (at the dealers' expense) to showcase the merchandise. Despite some anger and grumbling from a few of its six hundred U.S. dealers, the payback was almost immediate. Most dealers recouped their investments in two years and welcomed the change. Cycle-Craft's Mark O'Neil says the dealers really have no choice if they want to keep up with demand.

"Our business has increased every year," he says. "When I started ten years ago, all we had were some jackets, boots, and gloves. Now the catalog constantly grows. There are train sets, popcorn machines, coffeemakers. . . . If you can stamp Harley-Davidson on it, people want it."

—— Supporting the Evangelists ——

Harley-Davidson, even throughout its bleakest period, has maintained close ties to its dealers. Like other radical marketers, Harley understands the power of its retail channel and considers the dealers part of the family. Of the six hundred domestic dealers (there are one thousand worldwide), most have been Harley dealers for decades, with second and even third generations running the dealerships. Harley is looking to expand its international business, though it is hampered by the production shortfall. In the fall of 1997, the company opened its first dealership in Saudi Arabia, selling most of the allotted bikes in the first few days.

The company relies heavily on dealer input in all aspects of its business, from design to marketing. Harley holds quarterly meetings with an elected ten-member dealer advisory council, and an annual July dealer meeting, where new models are previewed and problems get aired, is attended by every senior Harley manager.

Harley sponsors basic training for service technicians, an especially crucial offering since engines and other mechanical devices have become increasingly high-tech. Six years ago the company began offering the Harley-Davidson University each year: dealers spend three days taking courses such as "How to Manage Your Business" and "How to Create a Succession Plan."

The company provides a steady flow of support material such as video productions, collateral brochures, and backup advertising for the dealers to use in local markets. Harley also publishes magazines, such as *The Enthusiast* and *Hog Tales,* that get funneled to customers through the dealers. In addition, the company sends its traveling Harley museum to dealerships around the country for special events.

The dealers, in turn, serve as local conduits to HOG and provide support for local rallies, rental programs, and national promotions. "We depend on the dealers, and we're in touch with them all the time," Bischmann says. "They're the ones who deal with the customers."

Harley-Davidson, says the consultant Chris Hart, is cognizant of the fact that it was the dealers who came to the rescue as the company went through its rebirth during the mid-1980s. During the management buyout, "the quality of the bikes was terrible, and Harley counted on the dealers to fix the bikes," Hart says. "They went through the war together, and the dealers didn't charge the company back for any of this."

The dealers have also stuck by Harley during the extended production shortfall, which still has not eased. The company cannot dictate what dealers charge the customers, it can only suggest a retail price. A few dealers, taking advantage of the eighteen-month-long waiting lists, have jacked up prices by $5,000 or more above the invoice. But most dealers, Bischmann says, have maintained prices in order to nurture crucial customer relationships. Bischmann explains that in the early 1990s the situation was far worse: there were two- to three-year waits for some models, and many dealerships didn't even have a demonstration model to show prospective customers. In 1996 the company channeled all available resources into increasing manufacturing capabilities, even cutting its advertising budget to zero in 1996. Harley has upped production 10–15 percent annually and opened two new production plants in 1998, but the demand grows stronger. Bischmann stresses that Harley is not happy about the shortfall, which gives customers a reason to look at competitive offerings.

"The mystique is not about being hard to get," she insists. "This is just an obstacle we want to get out of the way."

Of course, the dealers make more money from service and the sales of parts and accessories than from sales of the motorcycles, so few are complaining. The relationships are long, deep, and symbiotic. Harley understands that the dealer is the customer's conduit to the company. Indeed, for many Harley owners, the local dealership is a second home, a gathering place. "I can set my watch by certain people coming in every day," says O'Neil of Cycle-Craft.

—— Staying Radical ——

Like all great brands, Harley-Davidson has found that success makes it an attractive target for competitors. The foreign competitors have lined up to grab market share, seeing a lucrative revenue stream in the heavyweight cruiser market and sensing Harley's vulnerability due to its production delays.

Marketing professionals suggest that competitors have an opportunity to redefine the cruiser market, sidestep the hard-core Harley devotee, and find a way to make their own motorcycles cool enough to build momentum and outflank Harley. If they can find the riders who simply don't require a Harley, they can build a community of their own. Harley CEO Bleustein is undaunted. He says it is one thing to copy the products but quite another to create the lifestyle and total experience of a Harley—from the bike itself to the clothes and rallies and cachet. "We've found that providing the total experience is key, and that is not quite as easy to copy."

As with other radical marketers, courage may be Harley's greatest strength—the courage to stick with the formula that got them where they are and to not deviate from it and play the competition's game. "The worst thing Harley could do is to act like those other guys," says George Conrades, the Harley lover. Harley, he says, has driven its brand deep into the culture and built an intimacy with its customers that is unmatched in not only the motorcycle industry but the automotive industry as well.

"Harley has done an amazing job with customer intimacy," Conrades says. "They've got a lot to lose if they deviate too far from the customers they understand so well."

To broaden its reach, Harley has picked up its advertising efforts with print campaigns in motorcycle enthusiast magazines and such popular publications as *Rolling Stone, Sports Illustrated, Playboy,* and *Popular Science.* But with ads that are targeted and efficient, Harley keeps its advertising expenditures to a minuscule level compared with the advertising budgets of its giant competitors like Honda and Yamaha.

For Teerlink and Bleustein and the rest of Harley management, the crisis of success is ever-present. "Greed, arrogance, and complacency will get us faster than any competitor," Teerlink says. Like true radical marketers, the watchword at Harley headquarters is "We're not as good as everyone says we are."

But when it comes to radical marketing, Harley-Davidson is as good as they come.

6

The Iams Company

Marketing a Mission, Remaking an Industry

*"We think of ourselves as missionaries,
out there saving the world's dogs and cats."*
—Clay Mathile

Radical marketers believe in their product, whether it be rock music or ratchet wrenches, with a conviction bordering on religious fervor. Clay Mathile, the chairman and chief executive of the Iams Company, is no exception. Mathile sells his pet food with missionary zeal and a deep belief that Iams is "out there saving the world's dogs and cats."

Radical marketers find a way to project their enthusiasm for their product into the marketplace without the massive advertising budgets or strategic brand management that traditional marketers rely on. Iams, which as early as the 1950s pioneered premium-priced, high-quality dog and cat food, did nothing less than change the face of the $10 billion pet food industry.

Until the 1980s, most pet owners were content to buy a bag of *Dog Chow* or *9-Lives* off the supermarket shelf for their dogs and cats. Preaching the gospel of superior animal nutrition, Iams convinced a significant and increasing number of consumers to stop at a pet shop or feed supply store, pay two to three times more than for the supermarket brand, and take home a brightly colored bag of Iams or its exotically named sister brand, Eukanuba. The premium pet food segment now totals more than $2 billion of that $10 billion market, and much of the estimated 7 percent growth in the overall pet food market in 1997 was in premium brands, according to the Maxwell Report, an annual industry trends survey published by Davenport & Company in Richmond, Virginia.

Iams has evolved, through a true grassroots, word-of-mouth marketing strategy, into the seventh-largest pet food company in the United States. Until the mid-1980s, when it became a national brand, Iams' annual advertising budget was $12,000: it bought a single ad in the monthly magazine *Dog World.* The privately held Iams, based in Dayton, Ohio, has surged from a sleepy, $16 million regional brand in 1982 to more than $500 million in sales in 1997. Sold now in seventy countries, Iams is among the fastest-growing pet food companies in a worldwide market estimated at $25 billion.

From its gleaming headquarters building in Dayton to its campus-like research and development facility in rural Lewisburg, Ohio, Iams is a model of high-quality product development, production, distribution, and customer service. Iams has flourished for a wide variety of reasons, but its success can also be tracked to a simple yet radical notion conceived by the company founder, Paul Iams, and put in place by Mathile: people will pay a premium price for dog and cat food if they honestly believe it enhances the well-being of their beloved companion animals.

Like other great radical marketers, Iams also succeeded because its CEO clearly owns the marketing function; it has successfully created a community around its brand; it has stayed true to that brand; and perhaps more than anything else, it has displayed great love and respect for its customers, the dogs and cats of the world.

—— Stow Cute, Sell Nutrition ——

While Madison Avenue created an anthropomorphized world of talking cats and dogs who long for gravy on their dinners, Iams eschewed cuteness and made animal nutrition its yardstick. Let the breeders, pet store owners, and veterinarians see the shiny coats, the muscle tone, the clear eyes, the high energy, and word would spread to the owners. Those who cared enough would happily pay a premium to give their pet the best.

The lesson was clear to Mathile. "I learned early on," he says, "that the product is king. If you have a great product, you can make a lot of errors. . . . You don't want to, but if you've got a great product and don't let that slip, you can get the rest of the equation right."

As with some other radical marketers, Iams' success has translated into profits that allow it today to embrace such traditional marketing techniques as television advertising and market research. But Iams' spending in those areas is paltry compared to that of its competitors like Ralston-Purina. Iams, in fact, prides itself on staying close to its customers by maintaining well-established channels of marketing and distribution in the face of constant pressure to join the supermarket brands.

Tom MacLeod, Iams' president and chief operating officer, has the résumé of a classical marketer: a short stint at Procter & Gamble, nine years at Pepsico, and seven years as chief executive of Sara Lee Bakeries. He says that the opportunity to escape from a traditional marketing environment and return to "real selling"—targeting users one at a time—was the lure that convinced him to join Iams. Since doing so in 1990, MacLeod, like Mathile, has become a proponent of nontraditional marketing.

"It's much easier to go hire a couple of Harvard MBAs or Procter guys, give them a $50 million advertising budget, go to Saatchi & Saatchi, and that's your marketing strategy. Anybody can do that," MacLeod says. "Not everybody can walk into a kennel, get crap all over their shoes, and talk to a kennel operator about converting his clients to Iams. That takes hard work.

"With all due respect to our competitors, they much prefer the former method—the big TV budgets, the Harvard guys. It's much harder to get them one at a time. In fact, that's a barrier to entry."

Not surprisingly, Iams has been noticed. The giant competitor Ralston Purina attempted to buy the company in 1985, but Mathile wouldn't sell. Ralston Purina has since jumped aggressively into the premium market itself. Iams' main competitor in the specialty pet food market, Hill's Science Diet ($900 million in 1997 sales and 8 percent of the pet food market), was bought out in 1976 by Colgate-Palmolive, leaving Iams as the only independent player in a field dominated by mammoth food and consumer goods conglomerates like Ralston Purina, Nestlé's, H. J. Heinz, and M&M/Mars.

Competitors both large and small look with envy at what Iams has accomplished on the strength of its uncompromising devotion to quality and unconventional ability to market its brands. In most of their advertising (with annual ad budgets ranging from $40 million to $90 million), Iams' competitors promote their own products by comparing them to Iams products, thus handing Iams countless millions of dollars worth of free advertising.

"They have a better understanding of the consumer and what the market is all about," says one competitor's vice president of marketing about Iams. "And while their product quality is very good, they've done an even better job of creating the perception of selling more nutritious pet foods."

—— Unconventional Wisdom ——

All of this was nothing more than a pipe dream for Mathile when he joined Iams in 1970 as a restless, ambitious twenty-nine-year-old looking for a business to build. While Paul Iams, a world-class animal nutritionist, is credited with creating a whole new class of premium dog and cat foods, it was Mathile who bought out Iams in 1982, took control of the company's destiny, and spearheaded its explosive growth.

Mathile is a quintessential radical marketer, a natural leader who believes so deeply in his product that failure is not an option. Indeed, when Iams Company teetered on the brink of bankruptcy in 1975, Mathile chose to buy half the company from Paul Iams rather than seek other employment. While most radical marketers hire passionate missionaries—and Mathile does—he also *is* the passionate missionary that Paul Iams hired.

Mathile, who was born and raised on a farm near Bowling Green, Ohio, had a lifelong appreciation for animals and their well-being. He had no intention of joining a pet food company, however, until a friend suggested he visit Iams and meet the company's founder. Mathile was unhappy in his job as a purchasing agent for Campbell Soup, and as a favor to his friend, he drove to Dayton for an interview. Mathile was wholly unimpressed. "I thought this guy was a joke," he recalls. "The business was small, with five employees. The plant stunk, the product didn't look good, and the package was strange."

But Iams, a former Procter & Gamble salesman who was looking for help running his company, quietly played his trump card. From his P&G days selling specialty soaps, Iams knew how to win a customer. He gave Mathile a bag of his dog food to try out. Mathile didn't own a dog at that time, but he stopped by his father's farm and gave him the food for his scraggly, lethargic farm dog named Queenie. "My dad would feed anything if it was free," Mathile says. He put Iams out of his thoughts until he returned to his father's farm a month later. Out of the house bounded the dog, only this time its coat shone, its eyes were clear, and it had the energy of a puppy. "It looked like a show dog," Mathile says. "I asked my dad if he'd gotten a new dog. He said, 'No, it was that food you gave me.'"

Mathile was intrigued. What could transform an animal like that in just four weeks, he wondered? He began to investigate Iams; talking to customers and suppliers, he got the same response from all of them. Paul Iams, he was told, was a genius when it came to animal nutrition. He was a voracious student of amino acids and proteins in animal diets and believed he had created a better dog food, which he had dubbed "Iams 999" because it was "almost perfect."

Unlike Mathile, Paul Iams didn't harbor grand dreams. By the 1950s, struggling to build a profitable regional dog food business, Iams had found an opportunity to enhance his income by providing a diet supplement for minks. At that time, mink ranching was a burgeoning business, and the ranchers were constantly seeking nutritious food to enhance the lush pelts from which coats would be made. Iams formulated a nutritional supplement that was high in fat and protein, and it worked. He was soon making a nice profit selling mink food. When he visited his customers, he noticed that the guard dogs on the ranches looked exceptionally healthy and robust, with shiny coats and high muscle tone. Fifteen-year-old dogs were prancing around like puppies. The ranchers told Iams they were feeding the dogs the same food they fed the minks.

For Iams, the lightbulb went on immediately, and he began to formulate a high-fat, high-protein dog food. The conventional wisdom of the day claimed that dogs could not tolerate more than 10 percent fat and 25 percent protein. But these guard dogs were thriving on a diet of 20 to 25 percent fat and up to 45 percent protein. Over the next decade, Iams experimented with ingredients and created the first of what would become the Iams line of premium dog foods. He eschewed vegetable protein, found in most commercial pet foods, and opted instead for animal proteins, theorizing that dogs and cats are carnivores and need meat to thrive.

In an industry built on the waste products and viscera of human food producers, packaged pet foods were often filled with questionable ingredients, and some were barely palatable to dogs and cats. Iams insisted on using the highest-quality materials and supplies, and after having been burned once by inferior quality from a key supplier, he instituted stringent quality controls that became a hallmark of the company's culture.

Owing to the insistence on higher-quality ingredients—today Iams' ingredients cost $100 more per ton than those of its nearest competitor—the price of the food was high by market standards. But Iams was still able to build a small but loyal customer base for his product. By 1970, at age fifty-four, Iams had a thriving cash business serving Ohio, Indiana, and Kentucky. But he was weary and wanted someone to take over the day-to-day duties of running the company.

—— **Marketing the Mission** ——

After seeing the food's performance on his father's farm dog, Mathile was hooked. He went back to Iams and negotiated for a job. The transformation of Queenie struck a chord. "What I saw in that dog was every dog in this world who had a shiny coat," he says. "I don't know whether they'll live longer, but I guarantee they'll be happier during their life if they are fed good food."

Joining Iams turned Mathile into a radical marketer. With few resources and limited production and distribution capabilities, Mathile learned quickly that as important as it was, having a superior product was not enough. Great products cover a multitude of sins, but even they must be properly marketed. If no one knew about the food, it was nothing more than a tree falling in the forest. Paul Iams had never been as interested in building a market as he had been in creating a better dog food. Mathile, however, believed he could grow the business exponentially if he could just get dog—and later cat—owners to see what he had seen.

From the time he joined the company, Mathile followed a key radical marketing rule and spent every available weekend on the road, attending dog shows, visiting breeders, kennels, and veterinarians, and handing out samples of Iams that his wife and children had hand-packed in their basement. The veterinarians were a tough sell. Hill's, which began as a horsemeat packer, ventured into the dog food business in 1948 by partnering with a Kansas veterinarian who had created a formula for prescription diets for ailing dogs. Hill's Science Diet debuted as a commercial brand in 1968 and grabbed much of the veterinarian-endorsed market by targeting the nation's thirty-six thousand vets with product samples and healthy profit margins if they sold the brand from their offices.

But Iams, with Mathile personally leading the charge, targeted the breeders and the kennel operators, believing they were the gatekeepers—the people, other than vets, who most influenced what serious dog and cat owners fed their pets. It was a community worth courting.

Like its archrival Hill's, Iams understood the urgency of capturing a puppy or kitten's heart, mind, and appetite from the outset. Trying to switch an established diet for a finicky pet, particularly cats, can be daunting, if not impossible. By plying the breeders, vets, and pet stores with promotional packages, including free samples of the food, Iams built loyal customers before they went home with their new pet.

The company continues to seek such avenues to winning over the hearts and minds of customers. In 1996, following this tradition, Iams added animal shelters to its target markets and began sponsoring Pet Adoptathons across the country. More than seven hundred shelters participated in local promotions urging people to adopt rather than buy a pet. Iams provided starter kits, including pet food and brochures on pet nutrition, to all new owners.

Instead of resorting to expensive advertising, Iams poured resources into pioneering customer service operations that provided counsel and advice to individual pet owners. Iams, for example, was the first pet food supplier to offer a toll-free phone number on all its packaging so that pet owners could call with questions or comments. Its customer service department, which receives more than three hundred thousand calls each year on its toll-free phone lines, sends out free coupons or free samples in its "Puppy Packs and Kitten Kits" to more than 80 percent of all callers. A critical arm of the marketing department, the customer service group started with one person in 1980 and now has twenty-seven full-time trained staffers and several vets on call. The office is open twelve hours each day, six days a week, and the company has special toll-free numbers for veterinarians and breeders as well.

Though it is billed as customer service, the group is focused on consumer education: it spreads the gospel about dog and cat nutrition at every opportunity. Each caller receives a letter and nutrition literature from the company, and Iams has created a popular Website on the Internet to provide more detailed data on nutrition.

—— The Impossible as Opportunity ——

Iams, like other radical marketers, is tenacious about knowing its market and using its storehouse of knowledge as a proactive marketing tool. Despite mounting evidence that animal diet really does make a difference, Iams continues to draw criticism from some industry sectors that insist that its high-priced products are more hype than reality. A dog, critics contend, will live just as long and be just as healthy eating *Dog Chow* as Iams. So why should consumers pay premium prices for Iams? While some animal experts claim it is impossible to prove that premium pet foods have any significant impact, Iams, like other radical marketers, views the impossible as another business opportunity. The company uses its extensive research facilities to hammer at the nutrition issue, building its case slowly but effectively. Iams shares its research findings liberally in both academic and trade publications.

Having long relied on consumer education as a competitive weapon, Iams knows how to parry such negative thrusts. In early 1998, in fact, the company induced *Consumer Reports* magazine, through a barrage of irrefutable data, to retract a story for the first time in twenty years when the publication printed a misleading and erroneous report on the pet food industry.

And in a society where seventy million cats and fifty-seven million dogs are owned by more than sixty-four million U.S. households, the power of the bond between pets and owners can never be underestimated, a fact that Iams knows as well as any of its competitors. Under Mathile, Iams thinks of the animals rather than the owners as the customer. While the giant pet food makers found widespread success by anthropomorphizing both the pets and the products (Gravy Train, Gaines Burgers, Morris the talking cat), Iams simply focused its efforts on putting a better product into the bag.

Iams screens its suppliers carefully, refusing to include viscera such as ligaments or chicken heads in its products. Because of its unflinching quality assurance, Iams can claim consistency in an industry where product quality has traditionally fluctuated wildly. Indeed, Iams has been in a long-term debate with the federal government about labeling and terminology on packages; the company is currently pushing for stricter regulation of the definition of the by-products used in pet foods.

—— Innovation as Revenue ——

Part of the mystique and allure of Iams is that the company, like other successful radical marketers, has found new revenue streams by continually innovating in response to its consumers' needs. Iams, for example, pioneered the segmentation of lifestyle and life-stage pet foods, with special formulas for puppies and kittens, active and inactive dogs and cats, and large and small breeds.

And after more than forty years of extolling the virtues of dry pet food, Iams realized it had little chance of convincing the world to abandon canned food, so the company shrugged and entered the moist canned food business in 1991. Realizing that 65 percent of cat owners and 35 percent of dog owners were routinely supplementing dry food with cans of less nutritious supermarket pet food, Iams President Tom MacLeod pushed Iams into the canned food business. The seemingly obvious move took years because Mathile simply wouldn't agree until his research and product development people proved to him they could make a canned food nutritious enough to warrant the Iams label. At the very least, Iams is determined to be the canned food of choice of its own dry food users.

Because it is a core element of the company's marketing efforts, Iams spares no expense on research and development. In 1985 Mathile recruited Diane Hirakawa, a talented young researcher who had just finished her doctorate in dog and cat nutrition at the University of Illinois. Heavily recruited by competitors like Ralston-Purina, Hirakawa came to Dayton on the advice of her doctoral adviser, himself a former Purina researcher who had created the formula for *Dog Chow*. Mathile drove Hirakawa out to Lewisburg, and as they stood outside the Iams corporate office, he told her to look west at hundreds of acres of a giant cornfield.

"I own this cornfield," Mathile said. "If you come here, you can build a research facility there." Hirakawa was startled by the offer but eventually accepted the position after speaking with her adviser. "At another company, the marketing guy will come to you and say, 'Make this product and have it look like a drumstick or some cheese.' At Iams, I had a chance to make a difference in the field of animal nutrition," Hirakawa recalls. On her second day on the job, Mathile sent an architect to her office, and together they designed the first phase of the multimillion-dollar facility. Today contractors continue to visit the ever-expanding Iams campus, now on its seventh addition. Hirakawa oversees 115 researchers and support staff in a state-of-the-art laboratory that is the envy of the pet food industry.

Mathile gave Hirakawa carte blanche to shatter fifty years of conventional veterinary wisdom about animal nutrition. She says that more than

50 percent of her budget goes to long-term research, four times the indus-try average, and that R&D at Iams is driven not by business units that demand short-term payoffs but by Mathile's vision of becoming recog-nized as the world leader in dog and cat nutrition. Hirakawa, for example, has initiated research into the nutritional needs of individual breeds, a radical notion of brand extension. Iams Great Dane Diet or Chihuahua Chunks may not be far off. Great Danes, she says, have a history of bone problems, and veterinary wisdom has dictated diets heavy with calcium and phosphorous. Hirakawa says her studies showed that such a diet was the worst possible solution; indeed, just the opposite was needed, because the cure for the problem was to slow growth with less calcium and phosphorous.

—— Eukanuba: Building a Second Brand ——

As it works on new products and brand extensions, Iams continues to have remarkable success with its most radical product to date, which was an evolution of an early idea of Paul Iams. The company's Eukanuba brand flies in the face of all tenets of conventional marketing wisdom. Here is a product line with a nearly unpronounceable name (it's YOO ka nooba), an unclear product differentiation, and a market position that would seem to cannibalize the company's own flagship brand. Mathile admits that he wouldn't have created the strategy. But he has made it work successfully. Like other radical marketers, Iams celebrates uncom-mon sense and is willing to rethink the marketing mix.

Iams began producing Eukanuba in the early 1970s when Paul Iams found another way to process poultry-based proteins and came up with a richer, denser, even more nutritious formula. The product had significantly more protein and fat than regular Iams dog food.

At first, it was a company secret, manufactured with the same equipment used to make dry mink food. It was sold in small quantities in thirty-two-ounce purple-and-green milk containers. At the time, its 25 percent protein and 16 percent fat levels were far higher than those of competitive dog foods, and it sold for three times the going rate for most dog foods. Despite the pronunciation difficulty and advice to the contrary, Paul Iams insisted on naming it Eukanuba, a term he'd heard in the 1940s, allegedly coined by the composer Hoagy Carmichael to describe something "supreme."

Mathile tried to sell the product, but it met with an indifferent response. If it was going to work, Eukanuba needed to be dramatically different, so Mathile urged Iams to up the fat and protein levels. The new version hit the mark.

By the mid-1970s, Mathile personally went on a tour of American Kennel Club dog shows in six cities to introduce Eukanuba. He believed he could position Eukanuba as a high-end, specialized product for show dogs and other high-maintenance purebreds. Mathile urged the breeders to do their own taste tests with their dogs. Eukanuba won test after test. At one show in Atlanta, a Doberman that had consistently refused to eat dry dog food bit through the container and swallowed the six-ounce Eukanuba sample in a single bite.

Once word began to spread, the reaction in the market was strong and swift and surprised Mathile; Eukanuba passed the tonnage sales of Iams Plus, the popular new version of the Iams brand, in its first year. The product, especially among breeders, was a huge hit. For breeders, Eukanuba quickly became the food of choice. These owners had traditionally had to supplement regular dog food with high-fat additives such as lard or egg yolks and sometimes had to force-feed show dogs that refused to eat. The palatability of Eukanuba effectively negated the need for this supplemental feeding. Soon Eukanuba had emerged as a strong second brand for the company.

In fact, in percentage of worldwide sales, Iams and Eukanuba, sold side by side in Iams outlets, are evenly split. Nonetheless, Eukanuba continues to draw the same quizzical response from many customers: What does the name mean, who makes it, and what's the difference between it and Iams?

Mathile acknowledges the confusion and says that, in hindsight, he probably wouldn't have evolved the two brands in such a way. But he insists that Eukanuba has attracted a different yet equally important audience. Iams, he says, was built to compete everyday in the "best value" segment of the premium market; for these customers, the dog or cat is a "family member," one to whom there is often a great emotional attachment. These people want to know that the product works but not *how* it works.

Eukanuba, on the other hand, which sells for about 20 percent more than Iams, attracts "results-oriented" owners—breeders, hunters, those who show their dogs and cats, enthusiasts who want the ingredients explained in detail on the package. In fact, the company recently redid all the Eukanuba packaging to give it a more scientific look, with more nutritional data for inquisitive owners.

More important, Mathile intuitively understood the facts of market life. "If the science is known, sooner or later somebody is going to cannibalize you, attack you, so you might as well attack yourself," Mathile says. With its restricted distribution, Iams believes its two-pronged approach provides a measure of security—a safety net, so to speak—if one or the other brand falters. Like cash under the mattress, the strategy's main purpose may be simply to allow Mathile to sleep well at night. Thus far, the company has seen no erosion of either brand. "There's only one company in this business that has two big, healthy premium brands, and that's us," MacLeod says. "Our full intent is to keep them the way they are."

—— Getting Radical ——

Because he had no formal marketing training, Mathile never acknowledged the unspoken boundaries that often dictate traditional marketing programs in big companies. Iams evolved as a culture in which employees were expected to step up and be proactive in their work. When Marty Walker, an accountant, joined the company in the late 1970s, he picked up the phone because it was ringing and there was no one else around to answer it. Like everyone else, he learned marketing by talking to the customers. Walker was recently named senior vice president of sales and marketing.

Though Iams now has 1400 employees, the traditional organizational structure—with brand managers and a multilayered marketing department—is anathema at Iams. Radical marketers make sure the marketing department starts small and flat and stays small and flat, and that is how Iams has done it.

Walker recalls interviewing a young woman for a marketing position who had been a brand manager at Procter & Gamble. Though she was young, she had already managed a $60 million advertising budget for a product, which represented 80 percent of the sales and marketing budget for her brand. "We didn't hire her," Walker says. "People with classical marketing backgrounds don't fit here." Iams, he said, could never devote such spending to advertising without severely damaging its in-store promotions and channel marketing. It was her traditional marketing background, steeped in layers of brand-management bureaucracy, not the paucity of advertising dollars, that would have made her ill suited to Iams' radical culture.

In truth, radical marketers often become radical simply because they don't know any other way. Because there were only twelve employees in 1975, a phone call to the company would probably have been answered by Mathile himself. That year the marketing budget was a whopping $15,000. Mathile handled all aspects of promotion: in 1979 he put the first twenty-five-cents-off coupon on an Iams package, and in 1980 he put the toll-free number on Iams packaging. Until the mid-1980s, in fact, Mathile *was* the Iams marketing department.

—— Rethinking the Mix ——

Against daunting odds, Mathile set the company's distribution strategy. Unable to break into the crowded supermarket retail channel, Iams created its own sales channel by teaming up with breeders, kennels, dog and cat show operators, veterinarians, feed supply outlets, and pet shops. By turning to these alternative channels, Iams found not only selling space but proprietors who became evangelists for the brand, a large and effective virtual sales force of influencers who were often infected with the same missionary fervor characteristic of Iams employees.

Mathile understood at the outset that pet stores and other specialty outlets needed a product that, unlike goldfish or parakeets, would generate regular return visits from an expanding customer base. Iams offered an intriguing combination: high quality that a pet shop owner could sell proudly and brand loyalty that would guarantee regular business.

Amid the crush of competing pet foods, Mathile knew he had to stretch the limits to get noticed. Iams avoided the ubiquitous "cute puppy and kitten" graphics and embraced distinctive, colorful packaging and a warm, inviting typeface that attracted the female shoppers who accounted for 75 percent of pet food purchases. Mathile had convinced Paul Iams to abandon "the most godawful-looking purple-and-green bag I'd ever seen." To assuage Iams, he suggested putting green on Iams packaging and rhodamine red, which would become the company's distinctive signature, on Eukanuba. Working with a local two-man ad agency in Dayton, Mathile later chose yellow, a neutral color in terms of gender, for puppy food and Halloween orange for cats. As the brand was extended, the rainbow of colors grew and became a recognizable trademark for the company.

Mathile himself designed the now-ubiquitous paw-print logo on a napkin in his office in 1978. Initially, the design was used to dot the "I" in Iams for its new puppy food. But as the years passed, the logo grew in importance in all of the company's packaging and promotional material. Though he has no graphic design training, Mathile, like other successful radical marketers, can see his own company through the eyes of the customers, a vital talent. And he knows the importance of the message that Iams conveys through its unique graphics, a powerful mixture of warmth and credibility and consistency.

More recently, for example, Mathile agreed with a new variation of the paw-print logo suggested by the company's marketing department, but something about the new design bugged him. The paw-print encased in a rectangular box seemed harsh. After examining it for a few days, he suggested a minor change: round the edges of the box around the paw-print. Everyone from the board of directors to the brand managers agreed that the change was right on the money; it softened the logo in a way that much more closely fit the company's image.

In hindsight, the development of Iams packaging was classic radical marketing. With limited distribution channels and a small fraction of the resources of his giant competitors, Mathile was able to create a brand manager's dream come true: a package so recognizable that consumers knew what it was without reading the name. And even more significant, the package came to symbolize an implicit trust between the customer and the company, an attribute that giant traditional marketers routinely pay hundreds of millions of dollars to develop, often without success.

In addition, Mathile wasn't shy about trying razzle-dazzle. In the 1970s, Iams delivery trucks were painted bumper to bumper in purple, the same color as the original packaging, causing heads to turn on highways. Despite a minimal budget, Iams produced a series of television ads that ran on cable TV for just eight weeks in 1987—simply to get its retailers excited about selling the product.

And in the early 1980s, rather than beef up its sales force, Iams signed agreements with independently owned distributors that allowed it to grow from the original three-state region to a nine-state distribution area. As word of mouth generated demand among breeders outside these regions, Mathile began shipping the product direct, with orders under three hundred pounds sent through UPS and orders over three hundred pounds via common carrier freight. It was a jury-rigged system, but it propped up the company until Mathile could build an infrastructure to support national and international production and distribution a decade later.

Rather than spend on advertising, Iams put its resources into mammoth display racks that held up to nine hundred pounds of food, often convincing the shop owner to devote sixty linear feet and three shelves to Iams' expanding product line. Iams salespeople frequented the stores, doing product demonstrations, educating the sales staff, and organizing in-store promotions. "We wanted the product to shout from the racks," says Walker. "We told the owners, if you commit the space, we'll train your people, and if the product doesn't sell, we'll take it out and give you your money back."

In the early days, Iams targeted every outlet it could find, even some that were suspect, Walker says. "It was a big day at one feed dealer when we put that rack in. . . . It doubled his property value instantly," Walker says, laughing. Like most radical marketers, Iams wasn't always adept at traditional marketing methods. At one pet store, the company sponsored a promotion with an ad in the local newspaper inviting customers to bring in any empty bag of dog food and receive a free bag of Iams. "We underestimated the response and ended up giving away all the inventory in the store," Walker says.

——— To the Brink ———

As is often the case for radical marketers, Iams faced a cathartic moment, a bet-the-company crisis that took it to the brink of bankruptcy and eventually brought it back stronger than ever. It was a clear example of staying true to the brand. In 1973, not long after Mathile had taken over day-to-day operations, the Arab oil embargo set off long lines at the gasoline pumps and prompted President Nixon to impose a set of wage and price controls on American industries.

The new law froze consumer prices as well as costs of labor and raw material but exempted certain agricultural commodities, such as lard, meat, and bonemeal, from price controls. While its prices were frozen, Iams' essential commodities costs tripled: the cost of meat and bonemeal rose to $450 a ton, which was $250 more per ton than the soybean meal other pet food makers used.

Mathile and Iams faced a crucial choice: shift the formula and stay profitable or stick with the high-quality ingredients and face certain losses. Against business logic, but with the radical marketer's mentality, the pair chose to stick with what had fueled the company's success and hope for a quick removal of the price freeze.

The company showed its first loss ever in 1973. "We just about went broke," Walker recalls. "The costs were eating us alive." At one point, costs spiraled so high that it cost fifty cents more to make a bag of Iams Plus than the wholesale price of the bag.

But the financial disaster spawned something more crucial: a lesson in the value of product integrity and respecting customer relationships. "Strangely enough, it was the best thing that could have happened, although it sure didn't seem like it at the time," Paul Iams recalled years later. "Our competition cheated and used corn gluten. Breeders all over the country were in trouble. At dog shows in 1974, half the breeders were feeding out of our Iams Plus bags. We began getting orders from all over. People knew we stood for quality. It was our big turning point, but at the time all we could think of was the money we were losing."

The word of mouth spread from breeder to breeder about Iams' stance during the oil crisis and cemented its reputation among serious animal professionals. This was a company and product they could count on. Without advertising its virtues, Iams translated integrity into return on investment, and Mathile firmly planted the concept as a cornerstone of the corporate culture.

In 1975, however, after weathering the price freeze, the company was reeling. Paul Iams felt he'd taken the company as far as it could go. He had accumulated a comfortable nest egg, was in demand as a nutritional consultant in the fur industry, and felt that the wage and price control crisis had just about broken the business. He decided to close the company rather than try to grow the business any further.

Mathile went home and spoke to his wife, Mary. "I like this business," he told her. "I don't want to leave it."

Mathile convinced Iams to sell him half the struggling company, which had a book value of $200,000. He gave Iams a $75,000 note, pieced together $25,000 in cash, and for $100,000 he was an owner. This was indeed a radical move for Mathile. Interest rates were soaring; at age thirty-five, he'd burdened his young and growing family with an annual $15,000 interest payment, and his salary at the time was only $15,000.

"I had to make my money in bonuses, and my bonus was based on the company's profitability," Mathile recalls. "So I knew then we had to do something different. We had to build a plant and a research facility and borrow a helluva lot more money." But Paul Iams still owned half the company, and he detested the thought of borrowing money. A six-year-long debate ensued until Mathile bought out the rest of the company in 1982 when Iams retired to Arizona.

Unshackled by his former partner, Mathile set out to revitalize his franchise and build on the goodwill the company's name and reputation had engendered. At $16 million in sales, Iams had stagnated. But Mathile, buoyed by his success in radically marketing the company, believed he could build a $100 million business by 1990. He would actually take it twice that far, to $200 million, and at the same time enhance his personal net worth exponentially. Today Mathile is listed as one of *Forbes* magazine's four hundred wealthiest people, with an estimated net worth of $450 million.

——— Spreading the Radical Gospel ———

In 1989, despite the fact that Iams had just completed its best year ever, the company's board worried that Mathile was trying to do too much himself and thus was missing crucial market opportunities. There were signs—growth had started to slow, competitors were starting to eye the premium market more seriously—and Mathile agreed that he needed help.

Like other radical marketers, Mathile was determined to hire the best, as if the company's future depended on it. He wanted nothing less than a passionate missionary—someone like himself. Mathile chose a headhunter who specialized in high level executive searches. He uncovered three candidates, and ironically, the one who intrigued Mathile the most had the most traditional marketing background. Iams had never been an environment well suited to traditional marketers.

Nonetheless, Tom MacLeod managed to impress Mathile during a decidedly nontraditional recruiting process. Despite MacLeod's Pepsico and Sara Lee background, what impressed Mathile were his answers to questions "that seemed damn near illegal," MacLeod says. Mathile was unwavering in his requirements. He wanted someone from the Midwest, someone from a large family, someone who loved animals, and more traditionally, someone with international experience. Mathile was ready to try to replicate the Iams formula in global markets, and he needed someone who could oversee the effort.

MacLeod was raised in Kansas City, Missouri, one of six children, and he had several dogs that he doted on. He had been a marketing wunderkind, vice president of the Wilson Sporting Goods unit of Pepsico at age twenty-nine, president of Pepsico Canada at thirty-two, and president of Sara Lee Bakeries by thirty-four. Though a résumé doesn't get more traditional than that, MacLeod's success at such an early age was evidence of the emerging radical marketer within him. At age forty-one, he was growing tired of the politics and values of publicly owned companies. He was either going to a private company or starting his own.

MacLeod had no knowledge of the premium pet food industry and had never heard of Iams when the headhunter called. He spent $10,000 of his own money on due diligence, visited several pet stores, prodded the owners about Iams, and interviewed with Mathile several times. MacLeod, who knew much about human food production plants, was especially impressed with Iams' Lewisburg plant. "It was nearly cleaner than my Sara Lee plants," he says. "It was an outstanding plant, and being one of those arrogant guys from the human food side, I never expected to see that in a pet food plant. My interest was piqued."

But like Mathile twenty years earlier, MacLeod had his own epiphany when he started feeding his two black Labrador retrievers Iams during the lengthy recruiting process. His dogs' coats turned from a dull matte black to the shine of a seal's coat in four weeks. When asked what could bring a successful traditional marketer to Iams, MacLeod replies, "It was the best dog and cat food product I'd ever seen. And it said to me, from an international perspective, that this would be easy to sell. Dogs in France or Australia or Taiwan were exactly the same as the dogs in Chicago."

Ultimately, Mathile relied on his wife's intuition, "the Mary test," as he calls it, to confirm his decision. "That used to be the only criteria I'd use when I hired somebody," Mathile says. "I just took them to dinner and let them talk to Mary for a couple of hours. She still beats the psychological tests."

With Mathile and MacLeod sharing most of the key functions, Iams has tripled in size in the past seven years and continues to grow at levels well above industry average. The company now has a 3 percent market share overseas and is among the fastest-growing pet food makers in the world, especially in the Pacific Rim.

Mathile acknowledges that the specialty niche, so long ignored by the major pet food makers, is now a target. Giants like Ralston-Purina, with its Pro Plan line, and M&M/Mars' Kal Kan unit, with its Pedigree offering, have started selling premium products aggressively in the same distribution channel. With their deep pockets, they can gobble up market share quickly. But Mathile remains sanguine about these competitors because they lack the visceral understanding of this market and thus have a steeper curve to climb.

Tim Phillips, a veterinarian and editor at *Pet Food Industry* magazine, says that Purina is well entrenched in people's minds as a supermarket brand and wonders whether it can transfer that image to the specialty market. "How do you say, 'We're better than the supermarket brands,' when you've got most of your products in the supermarket?" Phillips wonders. "It's hard to be all things to all people."

Nonetheless, Iams is faced with competitive pressures it has never seen before. As Jim Koch discovered at Boston Beer Company, success brings the spotlight, along with the unwanted attention of the biggest and best marketers. One marketing vice president at a major competitor says that all the top brands must now enter the Iams market because that is where the growth is. Having brands in both the specialty channel and the super-market channel is not a drawback, he says, using the analogy of Toyota selling both the Lexus and the Corolla. Toyota doesn't highlight the fact that it sells the Lexus, but it has marketed the car successfully under its own upscale brand. Such pressure puts Iams in the hot seat.

"Just like any market that starts to get increasingly competitive, you've got to do a better job of differentiating your brand and your selling proposition," he says. "You've got to introduce more products and raise the marketing bar."

Iams has always understood that. Before the competition swung its might into the market, Iams began introducing more and more new products and variations within its brands. The company now offers a hundred different products in the United States and around the world. To its credit, Iams has found a way to raise the bar whenever a competitor ventures too closely into its territory. When one competitor created what was essentially a direct knockoff of Eukanuba, the company refor-mulated the brand, increased its nutritional content, and effectively raised the bar to outflank the invader. "We don't fall in love with our for-mulas here," Diane Hirakawa states. "We'll change if we have to."

And Iams isn't afraid to embrace traditional marketing techniques such as television advertising and market research. Competitors who dis-miss Iams as a midwestern country bumpkin when it comes to business savvy do so at their peril. The company spends significant amounts—though it refuses to provide exact amounts—on consumer surveys and market research. But like other radical marketers, it uses the research cautiously, relying more heavily on its own internal resources for setting the marketing course.

Like other radical marketers, Iams employs a surgical strike mentality in its use of advertising. In 1998 the company started to blanket cable television with a series of new ads. But Walker says the company focuses much of its marketing money on in-store promotions and will spend just 8 percent of its sales and marketing budget on advertising, which hardly amounts to a loud shout compared to the noise its giant competitors can make. In 1996, for example, Ralston-Purina alone spent more than $300 million on advertising. Still, Mathile understands that the company cannot rest on its laurels and that word of mouth may just not be enough anymore. Thus, advertising has become more of a necessity than in the past.

Iams' marketing efforts have benefited from its strong twenty-five-year commitment to corporate responsibility. In late 1997, for example, an Iams production plant in Aurora, Nebraska, refused $92,825 in tax rebate funds to which it was entitled from the tiny, financially strapped town. The production plant employs 140 Aurora residents, making it the largest employer in the community of 4,000, and the mistake that town auditors made in calculating the corporate taxes was going to have to come out of the town's school budget. The Iams plant manager contacted headquarters, and Mathile, without hesitation, approved the manager's suggestion that the money be returned.

Iams never sought publicity, but a local newspaper heard about the company's beneficence and ran a story about it that was picked up by the wire services. By the next morning, Iams was being praised on ABC's *Good Morning America* and CNN. The resulting goodwill, as evidenced by nonstop phone calls and a tidal wave of e-mail, reinforced the benefits of such corporate thinking.

Handling the Critics, —— Staying the Course ——

Despite Iams' success, skeptics still abound in the pet food universe. Generations of dogs and cats have lived perfectly content and sometimes lengthy lives on diets of *Dog Chow* or *Cat Chow*. "Nutrition is part science, part religion," says Tim Phillips. "There are lots of theories about what makes an animal healthy, happy, and causes it to live longer. But when it comes to hard scientific data, it's not there." Not surprisingly, Mathile refuses to believe the cynics. He has an intuitive sense about his customers, the cats and dogs, and what they mean to their owners. Iams, he realizes, has built more than a company, it has spawned a community around its products, a community that believes steadfastly that Iams food is better for their beloved pets.

As Iams has grown in popularity and those same supermarket chains that once spurned Mathile have suddenly come calling, Mathile has chosen to stay with the restricted distribution channel. Even the most enthusiastic grocer, with more than fifteen hundred labels of dog and cat food to choose from, is not going to devote more than six or seven linear feet to Iams products, and the company does not want to be forced to offer just two or three of its varied products.

"Which product would we put in there?" Mathile asks. "The supermarkets want the product that turns the fastest. But what about our senior diet, or the puppy diet, those brand-building, franchise-building products that wouldn't be offered?"

Mathile loves the freedom of private ownership and has no intention of going public. Iams makes lots of money, but without shareholders clamoring for quarterly returns, Mathile can focus on his vision, which is to reach a day when a majority of pet owners, asked what the best product is in the world, will reply, "Iams."

Growth, he states confidently, will continue, and nothing the competition can do will stop that. He sees no reason why Iams can't climb from 5 percent to 10 percent market share if his marketing efforts—a cumulative, well-integrated assault on the key influencers like veterinarians and the retail outlets—continue at their current pace.

"If you do the right things and make the right products and know your customer and satisfy your customer, and add to that good people, a good organization and culture, you will continue to grow," he says. "And our true objectives are not financial. We want double-digit growth, and we have financial objectives. But we are measuring against our vision, and that's much more powerful."

The National Basketball Association

Slam-Dunking a Global Market

"The thing we have learned is that
this is a living brand."
—David Stern

While dynamic, shifting markets tend to keep most CEOs awake at night, radical marketers actually thrive on the vagaries of marketplace change and instability. Indeed, because they usually started out with little more than uncertainty, doubt, and a deep passion for their product, they are not intimidated by rapid change and daunting odds; rather, they tend to demonstrate an uncanny ability to orchestrate the future rather than simply react to it.

Take David Stern, for example. The urbane lawyer and commissioner of the National Basketball Association served as host of his league's all-star weekend in New York City in early 1998. Throughout the glittery celebration, replete with movie stars, parties, and the league's brightest stars, both past and present, Stern was repeatedly pressed by many of the eighteen hundred media members to respond to the perception that the league was in trouble.

What would happen to the NBA after Michael Jordan, its signature superstar, retired? Had the quality of the game deteriorated? Would the league and its team owners, faced with soaring revenues but declining profits, reopen its collective bargaining agreement and set up a possible lockout? What would Stern do if an arbitrator overruled his decision to suspend for a year Latrell Sprewell, a star player who had attacked his coach?

What it all added up to was a broadside to sports' top brand, the NBA. Stern, the consummate radical marketer, fielded each question with both the candor and a practiced statesmanship that have marked his fourteen-year run as the most successful commissioner in all of professional sports. If he was upset that the league's annual midseason celebration, this time in the league's home city, was tarnished by such negative media focus, Stern didn't show it. No one, least of all Stern, has ignored the fact that the NBA faces pressing issues, issues that might sink a less stable corporate ship.

But Stern, who served as the league's general counsel and then vice president of business development prior to becoming commissioner in 1984, has spent more than two decades listening to doomsayers predict the impending demise of the NBA. In that time, Stern has overseen nothing less than a complete transformation of a once-foundering league into the most powerful global sports brand in the world. Under his stewardship and remarkable brand management, the NBA has flourished to the extent that basketball is now snapping hard at the heels of soccer as the world's most popular sport. Indeed, among the world's fifteen- to eighteen-year-olds, basketball has sur-passed soccer as the favored sport.

All told, Stern has overseen an incredible transformation. The numbers tell just part of the story. In 1998 the NBA took in more than $2 billion in ticket sales and television rights, more than seven times the $255 million it garnered in 1987. The big revenue genera-tors are the 150 licensing partners and 15 to 20 sponsors, relation-ships that in 1997 grossed more than $3 billion in worldwide retail sales, more than ten times the $300 million grossed a decade earlier. Not a bad haul for a basic labor force that numbers just 348, the sum of the 12-man rosters on the league's 29 teams.

In November 1997, the NBA signed an unprecedented four-year $2.7 billion television contract extension with NBC and Turner Sports Broadcasting. The league's games since the early 1990s have appeared in prime time on two different networks, one commercial, the other cable. Only a radical marketer could conceive of a plan in which Bob Costas on NBC would invite viewers to watch the NBA on a rival channel. All this is a far cry from the original cable contract the league negotiated in 1979 for $400,000, and from the early 1980s when the NBA championship series was shown only on tape delay.

To perform this metamorphosis, Stern, like other radical marketers, needed equal parts genius, serendipity, and good timing. But luck, as Branch Rickey once noted, is the residue of design. Because he inherited few of the resources now available, Stern could not rely on heavy advertising or traditional marketing methods. Instead, he simply changed the rules.

——— Nurturing a Living Brand ———

Like other radical marketers, the NBA has carefully built and nurtured a deeply emotional bond between its product and its customers, a bond and passion that transcend the game itself. The NBA logo triggers a marketer's dream reaction: respect, excitement, quality, dynamism, and fun. It is simply a club people want to join, a community in which to participate, like those enjoyed by Harley owners and Deadheads. Moreover, it is a reaction that spreads well beyond American borders.

Envisioning a global market early in his tenure, Stern started putting full-time NBA personnel in foreign cities to foment interest in the sport and the league and to cultivate local television and product sponsorships. Today the NBA has more than two hundred employees operating from offices in Taiwan, Singapore, Barcelona, Hong Kong, Tokyo, Melbourne, Paris, London, Toronto, Mexico City, and Miami. No other professional sports league, including soccer, has adopted this aggressive attitude toward building an international brand.

While foreign athletes are no longer considered exotic in most professional American sports leagues, the NBA has gone far beyond the recruitment targets of baseball or hockey and spread its recruiting net across the entire globe to attract new talent. Players representing more than twenty countries now make up 10 percent of the league's roster. The NBA is now a childhood fantasy for school-age Croatians and Nigerians as well as Americans.

Indeed, the sight of twelve-year-old boys in Bosnia or Mexico City wearing Chicago Bulls jerseys is commonplace. Even soccer, with its worldwide popularity, has nothing to compare to the NBA, a single league in which 350 of the best players in the world compete. The stunning rise of basketball's popularity in countries like Japan, which has virtually no basketball tradition or fan base, is testament to the league's marketing savvy. The NHK network in Japan broadcasts three games a week—better media coverage than what is available in some NBA cities, according to Terry Lyons, the NBA's vice president for international public relations.

"The NBA brand is the biggest sports export in the world," says Drazen Brajic, a Croatian sports reporter for *Vecernji List*, that country's evening newspaper. "Michael Jordan is the most popular sportsman in Croatia."

But precisely because of its remarkable and sustained success, the NBA has come under intense scrutiny. Every time a series of off-the-court player problems arise or a superstar retires, the media raises the specter of an NBA downslide. Recently, the negative press has escalated in light of rapidly rising player salaries and the attendant rise in ticket prices. A protracted lockout by the owners that began in July 1998 and threatened the following basketball season spawned comparisons to major league baseball's devastating strike in 1994.

Stern figures quite rightly that he has seen it all. From the time he joined the league's front office in 1978, he has heard the complaints about problems that would sink the NBA. Back then, franchises were foundering, critics loudly claimed the game was boring and undisciplined, the players were abusing cocaine, and, some pundits wrote, there were too many black players to attract a white audience. Even when the league took a decided upturn in finances and public approval, the bubble would surely burst when one or another superstar retired.

—— Driving Dynamic Brands ——

For Stern, the only way to sustain and drive a dynamic brand is to respond quickly and effectively to the circumstances that roll in like an unceasing string of thunderstorms. "The thing we have learned," Stern says, "is that this is a living brand. So if a player does drugs, that doesn't tarnish the brand. What tarnishes the brand is if there's a large hole into which the league puts its collective head."

In fact, in an endeavor in which the core product is a sneaker-shorn multimillionaire in his teens, twenties, or early thirties who is subject to injury, trades, demise of skills, and an array of idiosyncratic behaviors, a brand, according to Stern, is "not what you set out to become but rather a sum total of your responses to circumstances that you could not only not have anticipated but could not have imagined."

But while Stern's prescription sounds passive and reactive, the NBA has, in fact, been the most proactive of sports leagues, setting precedents in revenue sharing, forging television partnerships, licensing entertainment and merchandise sales, bringing harmony to a diverse group of franchises, and globalizing its product. The NBA has honed the craft of brand extension, from licensing its teams' logos to selling a popular line of videos and creating the WNBA, a women's league cast in its own image, in 1997. According to Stephen A. Greyser, a sports marketing professor at the Harvard Business School, Stern and his front-office staff exhibited remarkable vision, focusing on brand equity in the early 1980s when no other sports leagues and very few companies even understood the concept.

Though brand equity and brand management were not yet part of the business lexicon back then, Stern was the first major-league sports commissioner to recognize that his league was a marketable brand, not simply a loose collection of individual franchises. Stern has done nothing less than transform the NBA into one of the most successful and highly recognized brands in the world.

—— Embracing Serendipity ——

Today Stern smiles at the notion that he sat down in 1984 and laid out a detailed plan for success. Like other radical marketers, he orchestrated the pieces at hand and was nimble enough to embrace serendipity as it occurred.

Stern focused on building a few key alliances with both sponsors and television networks, believing that long-term partnerships strengthen and extend the brands of all parties. The league, through these symbiotic relationships with the networks and sponsors such as Nike, Reebok, Coca-Cola and McDonald's, has reaped hundreds of millions of dollars worth of marketing goodwill without spending a nickel of its own money.

The NBA brand, Stern realizes, also garnered immeasurable benefit from several sources over which the NBA had no control at all. The rise of college basketball and the NCAA "Final Four" as one of the top televised sporting properties during Stern's tenure created a unique showcase for future NBA stars. Young stars like Grant Hill, Keith Van Horn, and Tim Duncan were seen countless times on network television before ever donning an NBA jersey.

The decision in 1989 by the International Basketball Federation (FIBA), the international basketball governing body, to allow professionals to compete in the Olympics spawned the 1992 "Dream Team" of NBA stars that won the gold medal in Barcelona. The sight of Michael Jordan, Magic Johnson, Larry Bird, Charles Barkley, and other great stars playing together set off a dramatic, Beatles-like response around the world. "The Dream Team made basketball the game it is around the world," Magic Johnson said.

—— His Airness ——

Perhaps most influential was the simultaneous arrival in 1984 of Stern, Michael Jordan, and Nike. Even die-hard fans forget that it was Nike's breakthrough advertising and nontraditional marketing of the young Jordan that catapulted him into celebrity status beyond basketball itself. The concurrent rise of the NBA, Jordan, and Nike was not coincidental. Each fed off the customer value of the others and, like a Jordan slam-dunk, drove the visibility of each entity higher and higher.

Few recall that Nike was a struggling brand when it signed Jordan and introduced its first Air Jordan basketball shoe. Nike had lost money for two straight years and laid off four hundred workers prior to Jordan's rise to fame. Nike today is the dominant athletic shoe maker, with more than 44 percent of the U.S. market, and its image is tied inextricably to basketball and the NBA. In 1985 Stern helped fuel the fire, albeit inadvertently, when he and the league banned Jordan from wearing the first Air Jordans, a controversial red-and-black shoe that was unacceptable under the league's strict on-court dress code. In the wake of Stern's decision, basketball fans rushed out to buy Air Jordans, and Nike raked in $100 million in sales of the shoes in the first year alone.

Through Nike, Reebok, Converse, Adidas, and other shoe makers, the NBA garners hundreds of millions of dollars worth of free marketing that spotlights the players and the game. In fact, the marketing campaigns for the shoes, for the network telecasts, and for the league itself tend to blur together for the average fan, leaving a net positive brand image for all parties, the NBA most of all.

The league has accumulated vast experience at this brand management. Stern and his senior staff have been together for, in most cases, more than fifteen years, creating a solid knowledge nucleus that is unrivaled in most corporate settings, sports or nonsports. Indeed, most of the league's top managers have been around longer than the owners of nearly all twenty-nine franchises. This kind of stability creates buy-in for the league's radical marketing approach from its core constituents, the owners.

"We finish each other's sentences," Stern says of his top managers. "We have a group of people here who know this league, know the owners, know the teams, and therefore don't have to continually relearn or reinvent everything. If you swept us clean every four years and put in new people, the league would not be doing as well."

This collective knowledge base has carved out ambitious, well-conceived blueprints for managing its twenty-nine individual teams, as well as its 150 licensing partners and fifteen to twenty major sponsors such as Coca-Cola, McDonald's, and Nike. Just as the staff has formed long-term relationships with the owners, the same holds true with individual sponsors like Spalding, Starter, and McDonald's. Such continuity in key relationships gives the league tremendous leverage for its brand. Sponsors grow to trust that the NBA will live up to its promises, offer flexibility in cooperative marketing ventures, and remain willing to take risks to enhance the sponsor's brand as well as its own.

"David Stern is certainly the best brand manager in sports, and I'd compare him to any of the great brand managers anywhere," says David Green, senior vice president for international marketing at McDonald's.

—— Guiding Principles ——

Like other great brands, the NBA has evolved a set of guiding principles in brand identification, quality, responsibility as a business partner, responsiveness to the consumer, and creation of a mode of behavior for its players and personnel that bespeaks a responsibility to the community in which it dwells. "We tried to do things that indicated that we brought some fresh thought to each response we made," Stern says.

The first rule, Stern says, is to realize that "this is our brand and we better care for it. We might share it at times, like having joint custody, but we'd never give it up for adoption because no one would take care of our brand like we would." Radical marketers are known for their staunch devotion to their brands.

Second, like other radical marketers, Stern understood that the league's emergence and growth could not be done alone. Strategic partners were carefully selected and nurtured, and the league remains loyal, occasionally to a fault, to those with whom it does business. A long and solid business relationship with the NBA is nearly impossible to unseat as long as the business partner continues to fulfill its end of the bargain. "In most cases," Stern says, "if someone has an ongoing relationship with us, someone else just can't come in and buy them out of their position."

Green says that the NBA's relationship with McDonald's as a longtime sponsor of the league has worked so well for so long because the two organzations share very clear brand images with customers. The values they share—high integrity, high quality, consistency—ring true with customers and have been the foundation for a long-term relationship. "The great thing about long-term partnerships is that you are apt to take more risks if you know you have the same long-term goals," Green says. "With the NBA, we say, 'Let's break some rules, let's extend the brand.' It keeps things interesting."

The NBA, like other successful radical marketers, retains tight control of its brand in its most important relationships. Being highly protective of its brand, the NBA insists on having an active role in the broadcasting of its games. The league has more than a dozen executives participating in weekly meetings with NBC and Turner Sports to determine which players will be featured, which games take precedence, which new camera angles will be introduced. They stress to the teams that there is no such thing anymore as a "local" broadcast. A game broadcast in Boston one night will be shown abroad in dozens of countries within two or three days.

—— Showcase the Stars ——

The mandate is clear: showcase the stars, spotlight the brand. The league knows of the powerful reach of television. If there are twenty million admissions to NBA games during the season, that represents just five million people, says Rick Welts, the NBA's chief marketing officer. "That means that 95 percent of our fans experience the NBA on television."

In the same vein, the league works in lockstep with the television networks and corporate sponsors to direct the advertising and image that reflects on the league. Corporate sponsors must agree to advertise extensively on NBC during broadcasts, for example, and NBC provides the league with detailed sales data so that league officials can strategize with sponsors about marketing plans that enhance both the sponsors' products and the NBA. Sponsors must demonstrate "aggressive" support of the NBA brand or the relationship is terminated.

—— Fresh Answers ——

At the same time that Stern praises the virtues of longevity, he acknowledges longevity's traps. The league stays fresh by remaining open to new ideas, bringing in new people, and refusing to utter that classic credo: "We are doing it this way because this is the way we've always done it." That has, in fact, always been the wrong answer. Like other radical marketers, Stern likes to rethink the marketing mix. He has infected his staff with a fever for finding responses that suit what is currently happening in a dynamic environment and not what might have been appropriate in the past.

Critics, for example, have long predicted that outlandish player salaries would sink the league. The NBA's profitable growth and innovative revenue sharing negated that argument for years as both owners and players reaped the rewards of their game. Now, however, several young marquee players are demanding and sometimes getting stratospheric $100 million or more long-term contracts, which put a severe strain on the collective bargaining agreement and eroded profits for the owners. Ticket prices have risen to unwelcome heights, and Stern knows this situation requires answers that were simply not clear three years ago. One thing he has excelled at is creating an understanding by both the owners and the players that they can profit together or sink together.

Stern is quietly confident that a solution will be found and compromises reached. Not only is history on his side, but the quality of the NBA's response to events has become nothing short of a brand attribute. The league's executives, Stern points out, have an inherent, well-understood NBA response to the media, to the teams, to the fans, to the players' association, and to the world. Like other radical marketers, Stern has surrounded himself with a staff that shares his passion for the product and view of the competitive landscape.

When Magic Johnson of the Los Angeles Lakers announced he was HIV positive in 1989, for example, the league quickly and adamantly expressed open support for Johnson, a response that drew criticism from some quarters. The public, generally unaware at that time of the nature and characteristics of AIDS, was fearful and mistrustful of people with the AIDS virus. It was suggested that perhaps the NBA ought to take a poll of its fans before issuing a statement on Johnson. "The idea that we should take a poll was abhorrent to us," Stern says. "Our first thought was that we could do something about allaying people's fears about HIV by the way we responded to this." Though it was altruistic, the NBA's response not only raised the level of public awareness about AIDS but provided a huge boost for its brand at the same time, creating an image of the organization as a family that took care of its own.

Like other radical marketers, Stern lets ideas flow from every part of the organization, and every idea gets a fair hearing. Nothing is too outlandish, and sales goals are eschewed in favor of consistent pushing to improve the product. At meetings, ideas are tossed out like intellectual boomerangs. Someone once suggested, for example, that the league televise its annual player draft, a radical move that turned a traditionally mundane event into a highly rated live cable broadcast, hosted by Stern himself. Another suggestion called for the remake of the league's annual all-star game into a full weekend of basketball-related events, from a slam-dunk contest to the recent decision to pair men and women from the NBA and WNBA in a shooting contest.

Anything that enhances or extends the brand in a positive light is welcome. Radical marketers know that their product must be accessible—the Grateful Dead insisted on keeping concert ticket prices low, for example, and Snap-on Tools provides interest-free credit to mechanics who want to buy their tools. In 1992 the NBA created a traveling basketball carnival called Jam Session that moves from city to city, and even country to country, setting up at state fairs, shopping malls, and convention centers.

Understanding the visceral connection to the game itself for its customers, the NBA aggressively promotes grassroots participatory events for youngsters both in the United States and overseas. The rationale: a child who plays basketball at age eleven is highly likely to be a basketball fan by age twenty-five.

The NBA has a radical marketer's credo: "Never spend our own money if we can spend someone else's." The league paid for Jam Session with sponsorships and licensed product sales. Knowing that tickets to the all-star game in Madison Square Garden would be difficult to obtain for the average fan, Jam Session provided an attractive alternative, a full weekend of activities for the general public, including player practices, a midway-like carnival of hands-on basketball activities, and even a string of basketball tournaments so the fans could come and play. NBA and WNBA stars signed autographs, posed for photos, and got close to the customers. The event drew nearly one hundred thousand basketball fans who shared a common passion and obsession with the NBA brand.

—— Extending Without Diluting ——

Like Harley-Davidson and the Harvard Business School, the NBA has also become a master at brand extension without dilution. The WNBA was a natural extension based on the idea that the women's game had reached the point of quality and popularity where people would pay to watch it. By playing in the summer, the WNBA offered NBA owners another product with which to fill open arena dates. The inaugural season surpassed all expectations, with the women playing before enthusiastic, near-capacity crowds in eight cities. Better still, sponsorships akin to those of the men's game sprang up quickly, and stars were born overnight as women were featured in the sneaker ads once reserved for the men.

Stern is not afraid to take the league into businesses that stray from its core competency if doing so enhances the brand. In 1988, for example, not a single trading card company offered basketball cards. Stern believed that a key way to build brand loyalty among young fans was to have them trading and collecting basketball cards the same way they traded baseball cards. So he took the NBA into the trading card business, creating a joint venture with a distribution company. The league took the photos, produced the cards, and swallowed the investment costs because of the value of the brand enhancement. Today the league has licensing agreements with four major trading card makers.

In late 1998 the NBA opened its first NBA Store on Fifth Avenue in New York—the first retail establishment owned, operated, and merchandised by a North American sports league. The 15,000-square-foot store sells NBA and WNBA licensed products, includes an interactive, multimedia attraction culled from the league's video and photography archives, and even has a basketball court for games and special events.

The NBA will also venture into the restaurant business as a partner with the Hard Rock Cafe. Starting in 1999, the partners plan to open NBA Cafes at Universal Studios in Orlando, Florida, and nine other locations around the world over three years.

The NBA acknowledges its weaknesses and is willing to tweak the product if it improves the response to the brand. Over the years, the league has adopted new rules concerning the three-point shot, shorter time-outs, and tougher officiating to curb violence in the game. Other than the ten-foot basket, nothing is untouchable, says Bill Daugherty, the league's vice president for business development.

Stern smiles when he hears criticism of the game itself. People once complained that the game was too fast; today it is too slow. They wanted the twenty-four-second clock changed to thirty seconds, but today it should be pushed down to eighteen. Radical marketers believe in the essence of their product, and Stern is no different. He calls himself a basketball conservative and resists wholesale changes to a sport that has flourished for half a century. The lesson is to know how and when to respond.

"You respond, but in bits and pieces," he points out. "You deal with hand-checking, flagrant fouls, taunting, the things that tarnish the traditional game that gets played. We have a competition committee, people who really love this game, and they know it's less about consumer preference and more about keeping the machine pristine."

—— Staying Close to the Customer ——

Like Clay Mathile of Iams visiting dog shows and kennels on weekends and EMC's Dick Egan hosting customer dinners night after night, Stern is a radical marketer who knows how to get close to his customers. In essence, he owns the marketing function himself. Being a die-hard basketball fan, Stern sits among the fans—not perched up in a commissioner's skybox—at countless games throughout the season. He is, like other radical marketers, his own customer. Though NBA fans cut across a wide demographic, Stern believes that the game itself is the common ground for the community of fans. He makes a concerted effort to find the value proposition from a fan's point of view for every product or service the league offers.

"Stern is special," says Bill Walton, an NBA Hall of Famer who now announces games for NBC. "He loves the game itself, and he is on a first-name basis with everyone in the league. He's not isolated in some castle."

Like other radical marketers, he built an organization of passionate missionaries—extremely smart and aggressive people who share his love of the game. This gives the league a visceral connection to its customer base. Even back when its resources were tight and prospects gloomy, Stern and his staff believed deeply in the inherent value of the product and viewed the impossible as just another business opportunity.

But it was a daunting transition. The NBA, when Stern took over, was not a serious business; it was just another sports league. "We didn't have a lot of self-respect, because we had nothing to compare ourselves to," Stern recalls. In fact, the NBA back then was akin to today's National Hockey League, an eager entity searching for an identity upon which to build a brand. (Not surprisingly, the NHL hired its latest commissioner from the NBA's front office.) Both the National Football League and major league baseball had built strong brands through savvy television deals and licensing arrangements, models Stern would carefully study. "We were very much the poor cousin," he says.

Stern insists that he had no grand plan to turn things around. But like other radical marketers, he initiated a series of emerging principles focused on creating and building a brand. An organization run by lawyers would be likely to look for historical precedent, but the NBA that Stern envisioned had no precedent. The league, up to then, had enjoyed some national popularity, but not on a broad scale. Only serious hoop fans embraced the league and its evolution of stars like Bob

Cousy, Bill Russell, Wilt Chamberlain, Jerry West, Elgin Baylor, and
Julius Erving. During the Boston Celtics' remarkable domination of
the league, for example, when it won eleven championships in thirteen seasons between 1957 and 1969, the team averaged just over
eight thousand fans per game in the Boston Garden, which held
nearly fifteen thousand for basketball.

—— A Content Play ——

But Stern, like other radical marketers, saw something in his product that others did not. He took over the league at the outset of the
cable television revolution, and he understood quickly that all these
channels needed programming and would shift the focus from a ratings battle to a pure content play. And he did indeed have the content. He saw basketball as a balletic, telegenic sport tailor-made, with
its soaring slam-dunks and rapid-fire action, for television. He also
saw dazzling young athletes, perhaps the best and most talented pure
athletes in the world, who were not hidden under football helmets or
baseball caps. These emerging stars, properly marketed, Stern
believed, were more than athletes, they were entertainers capable of
bringing fans to their feet as enthusiastically as Sinatra, Streisand, or
Baryshnikov. The league quite consciously decided to market its athletes as heroes and entertainers.

People love stars, and the NBA has been blessed with generations
of them. Walton, who played on two championship teams himself,
says the fans have a special relationship with the players, much like the
feeling Grateful Dead fans have about the band. "Neither the games
nor the concerts can happen without the fans," says Walton, a serious
Deadhead. "The Dead knew that, and the players know that. The
performers will never reach that ultimate level of productivity without
the energy and passion of the fans. You can't go into an empty gym
and play a phenomenal level of basketball, just as the Dead could not
capture in the studio the same magic they achieved on the stage."

Stern inherited the league just as Larry Bird and Magic Johnson
were embarking on storybook careers that no Hollywood scriptwriter

could have invented. The Boston Celtics and Los Angeles Lakers became the perfect antagonists throughout the 1980s, and their two brilliant stars lit up the marquee and captivated a swelling basketball audience. Waiting in the wings was Jordan, who quickly served notice that he would take the game to new heights. Cynics would argue that Stern and the NBA owe their success to these larger-than-life heroes. But that argument misses the point. Great stars played before these heroes and could not pull the league up. If this generation of players became the stars, Stern and his team built the stage and wrote the script for their achievement.

A vociferous reader and student of other related businesses, Stern ingests everything from *Daily Variety* to *Direct Satellite Business* and other industry trade publications. He turned to other sports leagues like the NFL to learn about merchandising operations and to Major League Baseball for its production capabilities. He found analogies in the Olympics as well, spotting the benefits of a global brand that sought to attach its name to sponsors, events, and licensing opportunities.

—— Lessons from the Best ——

But more than that, Stern's models were in the entertainment business, Walt Disney in particular. From early in his tenure as commissioner, he believed the NBA had the potential to become an entertainment conglomerate that would more resemble Disney, Six Flags, or Time Warner than the NFL. Today he tells people the NBA "is like Disney with twenty-nine theme parks."

In fact, what Stern developed was perhaps more difficult than Disney, something unique in business: a multifaceted sports and entertainment business built on a *single* brand. Disney might have *The Lion King*, theme parks, and Buena Vista television. In the broadest sense, they are all Disney, but they are diverse brands.

"We have a hard goods business, an apparel business, a sponsorship business, a trading card business, an event business, an arena business, a cable and network business, and it all revolves around one single brand, the NBA," he says.

Thus, everyone in the organization, all six hundred employees, are constantly reminded of the impact each business function and each person has on various aspects of the brand. Hammered home is the radical marketer's theme that, regardless of whether you are in player programs, security, finance, or human resources, you are managing the brand. If not everyone is doing his or her job, the brand suffers. If security fails or the windbreaker a fan bought falls apart, the brand is damaged.

In this way, the NBA brand—and perhaps more important, its culture—evolved. Stern can list by name his top managers and their respective lengths of tenure with the league. He doesn't presume that other businesses can expect such loyalty and longevity, but he takes full advantage of its existence in his office. Most particularly, the longevity has spawned a synchronicity of thought on issues, from how to respond to Magic Johnson's revelation that he was HIV positive to Dennis Rodman kicking a cameraman, to Latrell Sprewell's choke-hold on Coach P. J. Carlisimo at practice.

"Essentially, you are the sum total of your responses," Stern states. "And that's a little bit truer with a business that deals with people rather than objects. It would be nice sometimes to have cartoon characters. There's no record of Bugs Bunny ever kicking a cameraman if the animator didn't want him to be kicked."

—— Managing the Franchises ——

Stern's most challenging task in building and managing the brand was to pull together the teams, a loose collection of individual franchises, and get them on board as believers and evangelists of the NBA brand. Whereas other professional sports leagues are characterized and often hindered by ego-driven, grandstanding individual team owners, the NBA has forged a strong alliance of its franchises by exerting tight control and superior support for the teams.

"Part of the reason they have such control is that the teams have given it to them," says Ed Levin, a Citibank vice president and former consultant who has done work with the league. "Stern had some early wins and rallied the owners around him." The owners have bought into the idea of letting the game and the players shine while they and their egos remain in the background.

The organizational structure, in some respects centralized, in others highly decentralized, has served to promote and protect the brand. While the league is a confederation of twenty-nine independently owned franchises, each with its own identity and marketing organization, the NBA provides a unifying and stabilizing influence not seen in other professional sports.

The league itself retains tremendous control but also expects and encourages strong local presence by each franchise in its own market. The league negotiates and oversees all national and international television rights, sponsorships, and license relationships, with revenues shared equally among the teams. Such sharing, now more common in other sports, fostered unprecedented stability for NBA franchises, allowing teams in smaller, less glamorous markets like Sacramento, Milwaukee, and Indianapolis to remain competitive with those in major ones. As a result, no NBA franchise has relocated in more than fifteen years.

In 1994, when the Minnesota Timberwolves' ownership was teetering on the brink of insolvency and contemplating abandoning the market, the NBA sent dozens of its top legal and marketing managers to Minneapolis for several months to shepherd a sale of the franchise to local investors so that it would stay in place. To their credit, the team owners recognized the goose with the golden eggs Stern was hatching and poured their resources and support behind him as he negotiated a breakthrough revenue-sharing agreement that enriched both the owners and players.

And the league has a team services department dedicated to supporting the individual franchises in everything from selling local radio and television rights to designing the skyboxes and courtside advertising in a new arena. The league actually sends out two thick binders twice a year to each franchise listing every service, activity, and promotion available for the teams to use. Stuart Layne, executive vice president for marketing for the Boston Celtics, has worked in other professional sports franchises and says no other sport offers such franchise support.

Much of the support is focused on revenue-creating opportunities. Welts, the NBA's chief marketing officer, points out that each team succeeds by how well it markets its local television and radio rights as well as by how well it fills its arena during NBA off-dates. The NBA understands the sports entertainment market better than other leagues and has encouraged its owners to expand their horizons and view themselves as multidimensional entertainment outlets in order to keep their arenas in use for 250 to 300 dates per year. During Stern's tenure, teams have gone from selling 40 percent of their seats to 92 percent, including expensive luxury boxes; as a result, revenue growth can come only from raising ticket prices, making better television and radio deals, or venturing into other activities.

Thus, NBA owners have bought into other sports, such as arena football, indoor soccer, and even baseball and football, to create an unprecedented collective payoff. Incredibly, during Stern's tenure, every franchise in the NBA has moved into either a brand-new or completely refurbished arena. By dovetailing their marketing with the wide reach of the NBA brand, most of the individual teams have thrived. And conversely, the teams produce massive quantities of content that the league can repackage and sell overseas.

——— Finding Residual Value ———

Like other radical marketers, the NBA understood immediately the residual value of its product. Companies trying to build global market share envy the NBA's model. For example, the NBA has built the most widely distributed televised sports property in the world and is now seen regularly by more than 600 million viewers in 196 countries. More than 1,100 NBA games are broadcast each year, but only 120 are aired on national commercial and cable television. That leaves nearly 90 percent of the broadcast content available to be repackaged and broadcast to an insatiable global audience.

"If you think about trying to introduce a new product internationally, it is tough," says Welts. "But we have no manufacturing, no new costs of production. We already have eleven hundred episodes and ten thousand hours, and all we need is videotape." Welts foresees a huge audience in China, for example, and says the league can roll out its product on television before it sends personnel to open an office. "Once we're established on television, the consumer products will flow," he says.

Once they get a taste of the product, foreign broadcasters want more. At courtside during the NBA all-star game and championship games are television broadcast crews from all over the globe, from Iceland to Macedonia.

The league also recognized that in order to sell a lot of recorded music, you must perform a live concert every once in a while. So through its long-term partnerships with sponsors like McDonald's and Coca-Cola, the NBA has held both exhibition and regular season games in foreign countries. Knowing that Mexico City, for example, is an NBA hotbed, several regular season games have been played there, and Stern has targeted it as a possible expansion city. The NBA has also raised awareness of its brand by pushing joint marketing efforts, such as the McDonald's Championship, held every other year in a foreign city and involving that year's NBA championship team.

As the impresario orchestrating this vocal chorus, Stern must be as well versed in satellite broadcasting and the structure of major product endorsements as he is in the game of basketball itself. His varied diet of reading material exercises his mind, he says, and creates an ever-expanding puzzle of subjects that might touch and improve his product. "If you are living in a dynamic world and you don't know what that world is until it hits you over the head, then you can't respond," Stern states. "The questions may remain the same, but the answers change. The answers are different in 1998 than they were in 1983."

The league, for example, faced the retirement of Julius Erving, its first telegenic superstar, but then along came Larry Bird and Magic Johnson. When Bird and Johnson retired, doomsayers arose, but there was Michael Jordan to pick up the slack. Jordan's inevitable departure will be overwhelming. After Jordan led Chicago to a stunning sixth NBA title in June 1998, *Fortune* magazine featured him on the cover and estimated that he has single-handedly generated more than $10 billion worth of revenues for the league, for companies whose products he endorses, and for the wide circle of entities that feed off the NBA.

The *Wall Street Journal* noted that the league's revenues have risen more than tenfold to $2 billion since Jordan joined the Bulls in 1984. And the television ratings for Chicago Bulls games on NBC in 1997–98 were 60 percent higher than for other nationally televised games. Bulls' merchandise sales account for nearly 20 percent of total sales, and Jordan's NBA-produced video has sold more than one million more copies than Shaquille O'Neal's, the second-most-popular video. The Bulls are the league's hottest attraction, regularly selling out opponents' arenas when they come to town.

But Stern is a student of change and change management. He addresses the Jordan issue head-on. "Can a league like ours say that losing the greatest player of all time, perhaps in any sport, will not have some negative impact? I'm not going to stand here and fool you. Of course it will." But Stern then points out that NBC and Turner Sports invested $2.7 billion in a television contract whose duration will certainly go well past Jordan's retirement because they believed deeply in the product and its continued growth. The league makes no pretensions as it grooms a host of talented young players like Grant Hill, Kevin Garnett, and Kobe Bryant to fill Jordan's extraordinary shoes.

Stern understands that business is cyclical, that some of the greatest corporations, like General Motors, IBM, and Xerox, have experienced breaks in their cycles of success. But he uses Jack Welch, chairman and CEO of General Electric, as a role model. "I watch GE, and when Jack Welch says he wants to be number one or two in every industry in which they compete, and the company continues to succeed, I think, 'Why not? Why can't we be like that?' "

Radical marketers fear nothing more than the status quo, the inertia that often paralyzes big organizations. Stern echoes the memorable line from a character in the hit play *Rent*: "I'm a New Yorker, fear is my life." Stern has driven this fear of complacency deep into his organization, making it a working tenet. In its frenetic Fifth Avenue offices, the NBA staff hears Stern's admonition: "We had a great day yesterday, but obviously it's going to be a terrible day today unless we do something better, different, unless we respond." Moving into the meteor showers in the thin atmosphere of success, "you'd better be prepared to duck and weave and speed up to get some distance between you and whatever you are running from, or you'll fail," Stern says.

8

Snap-on Tools

A Mobile Army of Dealers and
Eight Decades of Brand Equity

*"We don't have our customers wasting their
time figuring out what they need. We bring
the product to them."*
—*Robert A. Cornog*

Anyone can sell a ratchet wrench or an electric drill. But a radical marketer understands that a customer is buying a solution, not just a tool. So when Snap-on Tools sells a wrench, it is really selling a tightened bolt, and when it sells a drill bit, it is actually selling a hole.

A radical marketer like Snap-on also understands that selling the solution is merely a conduit to the actual value proposition. The real value is in the customer relationship; the embrace of the brand that spawns a lifetime of committed buying and a belief that, until proven otherwise, the solutions will always flow.

To achieve these kinds of relationships, an organization requires more than vast advertising budgets and layers of brand management. The best relationship-oriented brands emerge from a relentless and consistent commitment to innovation and staying close to the core customer base.

It would be hard to find a company closer to its core customer base than Snap-on. Since its founding in 1920 in Milwaukee, Snap-on has followed a simple two-pronged strategy: make the very best quality tools, and make them as accessible to the customer as possible. The customers, in Snap-on's case, are the one and a quarter million automobile, truck, and airplane mechanics in the United States and overseas who firmly believe that Snap-on is the tool of choice. Bringing them these tools is an army of franchised Snap-on dealers who navigate their ubiquitous and distinctive Snap-on vans, every week, right to the customer's doorstep.

The formula has been highly effective. Snap-on Inc. is a $1.7 billion giant with record earnings of $150 million in 1997 and a 60 percent market share in the $3 billion mobile van automotive tool market. Though the company's growth slowed in 1998, forcing layoffs and restructuring changes, Snap-on remains the dominant player in its market. Its closest competitor, Mac Tools, a division of Stanley, holds just 13 percent. Indeed, approaching its eightieth anniversary, Snap-on has achieved legendary brand equity in its category. "Snap-on is to tools what Xerox is to copiers," says Tom Morabito, the owner and head mechanic at Amtruck, a small independent garage in Boston that services trucks.

Like the emotional attachment of a Harley-Davidson or the fanatic devotion of a Deadhead, Snap-on's mystique is found in its relationships, in its ability to provide value in what some would deem an outmoded selling proposition—face-to-face. Snap-on has never spent a dime on brand-based advertising, preferring, like other radical marketers, to let its intimate customer relationships market its products.

In the age of the digital revolution, with the advent of a raft of faceless marketing techniques, from telemarketing to the World Wide Web, Snap-on has thrived because of the devotion of its dealers, who get up five mornings a week, climb into their white Snap-on vans, and visit each of between two hundred and three hundred customers on a detailed route once every week. "We don't have our customers wasting their time figuring out what they need," says Robert A. Cornog, chairman and chief executive of Snap-on. "We bring the product to them."

If Snap-on is a retail company at heart, as Cornog calls it, it is by retail measures among the most successful in the world. Retail companies measure by sales per square foot, and Snap-on, with an average 160-square-foot van producing upward of $400,000 in revenue, far surpasses the likes of Bloomingdale's or Sears. "It looks archaic," Cornog says. "But instead of real estate on the corner with the fixed costs of people, taxes, overhead, we have a very powerful business out there at the point of sale."

It is a radical business model, difficult to emulate today and a significant barrier to entry for potential competitors. Despite its unique approach, however, Snap-on offers lessons to other would-be radical marketers that can translate across many industries.

——— The Dealer as Pied Piper ———

Snap-on's distribution methods, for example, may indeed seem archaic in a wired world. But they in fact strike a deep chord with customers. These rolling retail stores stocked with more than $100,000 worth of Snap-on merchandise—hand tools, power tools, tool cabinets, and diagnostic equipment—are a throwback to a bygone era of ice cream trucks, milkmen, and physician house calls, and are greeted by Snap-on customers with childlike enthusiasm.

"When the Snap-on guy comes, he is like the Pied Piper," says Ray Magliozzi, a garage owner in Cambridge, Massachusetts, and cohost with his brother Tom of the popular NPR program *Car Talk*. "His van is filled with those great things that make you happy. For those of us who fix cars for a living, the Snap-on visit is a treat, and the tools are like toys." Indeed, if people have a personal physician, accountant, lawyer, and hair stylist, why not, Snap-on cleverly reasoned, a personal tool supplier?

With this time-tested formula, Snap-on, like other great radical marketers, built a culture along with the brand. While other tool-makers shipped their manufacturing offshore, Snap-on continues to make all its tools in American factories. The company pioneered the concept of a lifetime warranty on its hand tools, but its quality level is so high that the warranty has been rendered nearly irrelevant. The tools are ergonomically designed and built by hand using the highest-quality metals to ensure durability and comfort. Mechanics routinely report that they continue to use intact sets of Snap-on tools they purchased twenty-five years earlier. Like Harley or Iams or Boston Beer, Snap-on understands that people are willing to pay a premium price for owning the best. There is more impulse buying in this business than one might expect, and much of that impulse stems from the tool being a Snap-on.

Like other radical marketers, Snap-on has stayed true to the brand. Despite the lure of increased volume and additional revenue streams, Snap-on has never discounted the brand, never offered a "Snap-on Lite" or off-priced version of the tools simply to gain market share.

Snap-on has also created a community of consumers. To a mechanic, Snap-on is one of the symbols of professionalism that separates him from the weekend motorheads armed with Sears wrenches or Black & Decker screwdrivers who tinker in the garage with the family Ford. Visit a mechanic's service bay anywhere in the United States, and you will see the trademark red Snap-on tool cabinet filled with a wide sampling of the company's fourteen thousand products.

For the shop owner and his veteran technicians, Snap-on is the mark of excellence, the status symbol of the trade. Their tool collection is a valuable lifetime investment built slowly over time with the pride of a collector of fine art or rare books. Garages generally don't supply tools for mechanics; they must outfit themselves. Most mechanics spend upward of $30,000 or more on Snap-on tools over a career. For the young mechanics, Snap-on is an aspiration, a transforming talisman of the wanna-be. Mechanics engrave their initials on their Snap-on tools and shine their Snap-on tool cabinets with the same affection with which they'd wax a vintage Corvette.

"They've employed a very straightforward philosophy: they make the best stuff and solve the problems," says Magliozzi. "They charge the heck out of you, but the tools really work better."

In the 1960s, for example, Snap-on engineers, responding to a request from the U.S. Navy, designed a new kind of wrench that grabbed the flank of a nut or bolt rather than the corner. The new wrench, therefore, wouldn't round off the corners of stubborn bolts and nuts, as conventional wrenches always did. This patented "flank drive" concept offered a dramatic performance improvement for mechanics, who quickly embraced the new tool. When the inevitable copycat products hit the market, mechanics learned painfully that flank drive works only if the tool is made of the highest-quality steel and tolerances for exacting measurements are maintained. In other words, Snap-on had a lock on the market.

"We can tell who uses good tools and who doesn't," Cornog says. "Those who use cheap tools have skinned knuckles and cut hands. They don't get their work done because their tools don't fit into the spaces. And they swear a lot."

—— Celebrating Uncommon Sense ——

Like other radical marketers, Snap-on does not make its products elusive or exclusive. Snap-on tools and equipment are expensive—at least 10 percent above competitor's prices and sometimes double what one would spend at Sears. But to its customers, price is rendered moot by the company's long-held philosophy on credit.

To a mechanic, the Snap-on van is not simply a rolling retail store but a mobile bank as well. Individual dealers understand that many of their customers can't afford the pricey tools. Some have neither access to credit nor even a checking account. So the dealers encourage the customers to buy Snap-on tools today and pay them off, bit by bit, week by week, without interest. Snap-on has its own financial services division, which finances or leases large equipment purchases with market-rate loans and liberal credit checks. But most of the company's $1.7 billion in annual sales are accumulated in the crumpled ten- and twenty-dollar bills handed to the dealers each week by the legion of grateful mechanics.

Snap-on dealers augment this flexible receivables program by taking trade-ins on used Snap-on tools for partial payment, while encouraging young mechanics to trade up to the top of the line. The dealer himself pays to have the company refurbish the used tools, which he can resell.

It is a fascinating business relationship built entirely on mutual need and trust. For young mechanics with $200 weekly salaries and dreams of someday owning their own garage and creating a business, the Snap-on dealer represents an opportunity to build a foundation for the dream. Conversely, Snap-on dealers acknowledge that the system has inherent risks, and they report losses to the occasional deadbeat who makes off with the tools without paying.

But the losses are negligible, they say, a small percentage of their sales. The vast majority of the customers are highly reliable and conscientious about paying off their debts. Snap-on, they quickly understand, helps them make a living, and it is not a relationship they want to tarnish. The auto service community in any given city or town is generally tightly connected, and word spreads quickly about the deadbeats.

Snap-on believes that credit is the most important factor in the relationship between the dealers and customers. The credit and convenience Snap-on provides, often with no credit check, bespeaks the trust and long-term bond that has been the foundation of the Snap-on experience in the marketplace. Many mechanics would simply not be in business today were it not for a Snap-on dealer who extended them the credit to buy their tools.

Celebrate the Customers, —— Honor the Dealers ——

Snap-on, after nearly eight decades in business, has established a deep, visceral connection to the automotive community and prefers to celebrate its customers and their profession. Radical marketers love and respect their customers, and Snap-on is no exception. Rather than spend hundreds of millions of dollars on advertising to promote its brand, Snap-on instead has focused its resources on extolling the virtues of its customers and supporting its six thousand dealers.

With great radical marketing instinct, for example, Snap-on decided that it could heighten its own market presence by turning the spotlight on its customers rather than itself. Though its advertising outlays are negligible compared to those of such giants as Sears, Black & Decker, and Stanley, Snap-on decided to spend some money to thank its customers.

In 1994 the company launched a $2 million "tribute" campaign honoring "auto technicians." Believing its customers were unfairly maligned and stereotyped by Hollywood and the media as unsavory, unintelligent, and unscrupulous rip-off artists, Snap-on won widespread goodwill with a series of print ads with tag lines like, "When did you first learn the value of a good mechanic?" and, "It takes a lot to be an auto technician." Even the most cynical and wisecracking auto mechanics appreciated the gesture. Framed copies of the ads are now commonplace in auto shops and service bays around the country.

—— Only Passionate Missionaries ——

If its devotion to the customer is strong, Snap-on's relationship with its dealers is even more impressive. Despite its decentralized structure, Snap-on has built a dynamic corporate culture that incorporates dealers as well as employees. Dealers must spend upward of $150,000 to get a franchise on its feet, including inventory and the cost of the van, and the massive financial and emotional investment puts intense pressure on the relationship between the company and its dealers. Dealers who succeed are therefore deeply committed.

Snap-on has carefully nurtured this intensely loyal dealer network. Though, unlike Harley employees, they haven't taken to tattooing the company logo on their bodies, most dealers take immense pride in being associated with Snap-on, and many are second- and even third-generation Snap-on dealers. One St. Louis dealer drove his route for fifty years before turning it over to his grandson. In 1997 Snap-on was voted by *Entrepreneur* magazine the number one mobile franchise and fifth overall out of more than eight hundred franchise-based organizations.

Snap-on recognized long ago that its dealers are entrepreneurs—independent businessmen with a desire to dictate their own financial security. Because the dealer network is the backbone of the company, the company fostered this independent spirit and backed it up with extensive training, an army of support technicians and direct sales reps, a supportive pyramid structure of regional field managers, and a disciplined focus on quality and commitment to a single market segment.

Despite extremely limited daily contact with the company, Snap-on dealers feel remarkably close to it because of the commitment and level of support they receive in everything from creating customer routes to sending out technical experts to help sell complex technical diagnostic systems. Snap-on has made dramatic improvements in its manufacturing and distribution processes in recent years and, at the same time, installed a new information system that allows its dealers to tie into regional distribution centers via laptop computer to track inventory, receivables, and market trends.

"You realize you are only as good as the company that is backing you up out there," says Joseph Holmes Van Mater Jr., a Snap-on dealer in New Jersey, for the past sixteen years. "If you don't have support or technical backup, you're not going to survive."

The forty-four-year-old Van Mater, one of Snap-on's top dealers, has been on delivery trucks almost all his life. His family ran a 365-acre dairy farm in New Jersey and Van Mater, as a teenager, delivered milk to many of the dairy's three thousand customers. After college, he set out on a business career and landed a job with Chrysler. Four years later, he was laid off. "It was devastating," he recalls. "I never wanted that to happen again."

Van Mater returned to the retail delivery route life, this time as a Snap-on dealer. His father had sold the farm, gone into the trucking business, and become a Snap-on customer. The younger Van Mater decided that Snap-on gave him the chance to create his own business, work his own hours, and be his own boss. Once his son was a dealer, the elder Van Mater joined Snap-on as an employee.

Sixteen years later, Van Mater is one of Snap-on's most successful franchisees. In 1997 he recorded sales of more than $600,000. He buys his tools wholesale from Snap-on and sells them at retail prices to customers on his carefully scripted route, which includes not only auto mechanics but a bicycle repair shop, a plumber, airplane mechanics at Newark Airport, and an importer of exotic woods.

"My customers can set their watch by me being there," Van Mater says. The company helped set up the route, and then Van Mater tailored it and grew it on his own. He learned radical marketing from the parent company and has created his own reward program for his customers, giving out stylish Snap-on jackets and taking his best customers to a day at the racetrack. He carries more than two thousand different items in his van at any given time—from a 75¢ spark plug gapper to a $40,000 diagnostic system—and says that the inventory on hand is the differentiating factor.

"The tool industry is unique," he explains. "You can't order off a Website. In a garage, when a car is half torn apart and the mechanic needs that tool right now, I usually make the sale because I have the tool on the truck or can get it there within an hour."

Van Mater echoes the sentiment of countless Snap-on dealers who call the working relationship "a family atmosphere," despite the fact that daily contact with the company might be no more than a few e-mail messages received on the dealer's laptop computer in the morning.

Snap-on has resisted branching into other markets such as home improvement or construction (though it does sell a line of medical instruments) and has avoided retail distribution channels that would funnel sales away from its dealers. Throughout Snap-on's history, the company has nixed any corporate decision that might undermine the dealer.

At the same time, Snap-on looks for growth opportunities. The company is experimenting, for example, with a Snap-on retail outlet and product demonstration center in Albuquerque, New Mexico. This is a radical departure for Snap-on, but the company felt that with the burgeoning growth in sales of its high-technology diagnostic equipment, Snap-on vans simply weren't big enough to fulfill that need. Dealers needed a place to send customers for training and demonstrations of the new digital systems. Snap-on also wanted to test its brand equity with consumers. Cornog says that dealers are credited with commissions on all sales at the center, and retail sales from walk-in traffic go into a pool and are distributed to the area dealers.

What Albuquerque and two other planned centers will demonstrate is how far Snap-on can extend its brand without diluting it, according to Cornog. It is a bet worth making, says James C. Lucas, an analyst who tracks Snap-on for NatWest Securities. Lucas says such centers will fill a need as more and more products are made available, particularly on the diagnostic equipment side. The key is to bring together the customer and Snap-on's brand clout as often as possible. "Don't underestimate the power of ego when marketing to male-dominated industrial workforces," Lucas says. "Testosterone does sell."

—— "Five Do the Work of Fifty" ——

T ied inextricably to the automotive industry, Snap-on can track its evolution alongside America's growing love affair with the automobile. Despite its reputation as a conservative midwestern company, Snap-on has made the bets of a radical marketer: calculated risk based on a deep understanding of its core business.

As Henry Ford revolutionized American industry with the assembly line and flooded the market with suddenly affordable and accessible automobiles, the secondary markets began to emerge. In 1919, as different models of cars began to filter into the marketplace, Joseph Johnson, a young manager at a Milwaukee tool company, noticed a trend. Not only was there a need for people to repair these vehicles, but because there were so many models and few standardized parts, they would need more flexible tools than the market offered to work on these cars.

Mechanics' socket wrenches, for example, were one-piece units, with the socket tightly and permanently affixed to the handle. A mechanic had to buy many sizes and handle patterns to work on different machines. Johnson saw an alternative. What if a mechanic could buy five different handles and ten sockets that could be attached and detached as needed, thus providing him with the flexibility of fifty different combinations?

He and a coworker, William A. Seidemann, decided the concept was too good to ignore. They left their jobs, made a prototype of their idea, and, since the sockets snapped onto the handles, called their nascent company Snap-on Wrench Company. The first marketing slogan was "Five Do the Work of Fifty."

Realizing this radical new product could be appreciated only if it was seen, Johnson and Seidemann sent their first two salesmen, Stanton Palmer and Newton Tarble, out on the road. Believing they had a premium product to sell, the pair took a swatch of green pool table felt, laid it on a table in the auto repair shops along Chicago's Michigan Avenue, and displayed the shiny, innovative tools to awestruck mechanics. They sold 650 sets in their first 16 days.

The young company thrived, and when the Great Depression hit in the 1930s, Snap-on, like all good radical marketers, adapted to serve the customer. Snap-on salesmen asked mechanics to compile "wish lists" of tools they would buy if they had the money. The company decided to extend credit to these struggling workers, knowing there wasn't much value in keeping the tools wrapped up in boxes.

By supporting their customers, allowing those who couldn't afford to make a full payment to pay in small weekly increments, Snap-on created a huge base of goodwill, built market share, and got its products into the hands of far more customers than the competition. The concept produced unexpected results, like exiting the Depression with a modest profit, along with the creation of route lists, purchasing records, and data for territorial sales statistics. It also created a sales model for the future.

After World War II, when shortages from the war turned into pent-up demand for an exploding American economy, Snap-on found another radical approach to selling its wares. So hungry were nonmilitary customers for tools that the company started releasing excess stock to its salesmen, who promptly loaded their cars and station wagons with tools and headed directly to customers' garages.

This method served two key needs that became a tenet of Snap-on's business model: it delivered the product directly to the stressed and overworked mechanics who simply couldn't take time to shop for tools, and it increased the salesman's earnings, thus giving him an incentive to develop direct delivery routes to every customer.

All along, Snap-on stayed focused on making the highest-quality tools—all of them handmade, using only the finest metals and alloys, in American factories. The equation was clear: these tools were being used eight to ten hours a day under the most stressful conditions. They needed to fit the hand comfortably, they needed to work well and flexibly, and they couldn't break. Through this, Snap-on sent the message that its customers were professionals, as crucial to the American culture and lifestyle as doctors. Like doctors, they deserved the best equipment with which to perform their jobs.

—— Back to the Future ——

Snap-on, now headquartered in Kenosha, Wisconsin, has managed to ride that difficult dual path that characterizes the best radical marketers: it has held true to the original vision of the company while successfully adapting to the myriad changes and shifts in its target industry.

As the automotive repair business has shifted dramatically in the past decade—from conventional tune-ups and oil changes to complex diagnostic repair on increasingly technology-laden vehicles—Snap-on has become a high-tech company, forging a dominating presence in the diagnostic equipment and information technology side of the business.

The world's automakers have filled their vehicles with not only complex high-tech parts but model- and make-specific parts that require specialized tools. From one year to the next, models change significantly, and cars today have more onboard computers than the Apollo moon rockets. While this change has had a major impact on service departments at car dealerships, it has wreaked havoc on the independent garages that service all makes and models and need an ever-increasing array of tools to cope with the changes.

In 1990 just 18 percent of all systems on new vehicles were computerized. Today nearly 90 percent are computerized, and Snap-on has adapted. Through acquisition and in-house development, the company quickly grabbed a leadership position in this market and has alerted its dealers that the future is in microchips as well as chisels.

Today nearly half of the products Snap-on sells have a software component, and the company has positioned itself well to remain the provider of choice to automotive technicians. Innovation fuels its growth in the diagnostic area. In 1998, for example, the company started selling ShopKey, an integrated, software-based shop management system that brings together its diagnostic capabilities and management information products into a single computerized system. By pushing hard into high-tech diagnostic equipment, Snap-on has extended its brand and its traditional revenue stream as well. While these new systems find the problem, hand tools and power tools are still required to fix the problem. One business simply builds on the other, and in the end Snap-on wins. "Not a day goes by without learning something new," Magliozzi says, "and new tools are required all the time."

—— Rethinking the Marketing Mix ——

For Snap-on, the successful move into electronics has put pressure on its traditional selling model. "You don't sell a diagnostic system or integrated information system the same way you sell a wrench," says Marty Silverman, a consultant with Booz-Allen & Hamilton in Chicago. "It's no longer about the feel of the tool in your hand and the fit and finish. It's about functionality, and you have to get the dealers to understand this different kind of tool."

To respond, Snap-on has put more than three hundred additional vans on the road driven by trained technical representatives who visit customer sites at the dealer's request to provide sales backup and training. Judging from the numbers, Snap-on dealers have successfully made the transition. Indeed, the increased complexity in automobiles, with everything from antilock brakes to computer-controlled sensors in virtually every internal system within the engine and chassis, has driven more and more sales.

After sixteen years, the New Jersey dealer Van Mater keeps expecting his customers to have all the tools they need, but it simply never happens. "I sell something new to at least one hundred people every week," Van Mater says. "The range of what a small independent garage runs into now is phenomenal: transmissions, shifting sequences, line pressures—everything is computer-controlled. There are three or four sizes of oil pressure sensor sockets, and a mechanic might not have even seen it before."

Though the increase in automotive complexity has complicated the lives of auto technicians, it has raised the stakes to the game for tool companies. The days of selling just wrenches and screwdrivers are long gone. The higher-ticket items, like computerized diagnostic systems, lead to recurring revenues, not just for tools but for software and related technology. Snap-on, Cornog says, has always believed that it can sustain its success if it can ensure that its products help its customers make money. That has been the key value proposition from the outset.

This sounds simple and perhaps obvious. But in a marketplace flooded with buying options, Snap-on understands viscerally the thought processes of an independent auto mechanic who has a customer's five-year-old Toyota on the lift, it's 3:00 P.M., and the car's engine is inexplicably wheezing and chugging like an asthmatic goat. In an independent shop, where time is money, where hourly repair rates have skyrocketed and still don't scale as high as at the dealerships, the mechanic might spend half a day tracking down the problem and end up at 5:00 P.M. with a very angry customer.

Into this scene comes the Snap-on dealer, who pulls up in his van and suggests a solution: a motorized fuel system vacuum that pumps a cleansing liquid through the fuel injectors to flush out the engine. The dealer demonstrates the system on the Toyota, and it runs like a brand-new car. The grateful shop owner buys the system on the spot, worrying about the financing arrangements later.

It sounds far-fetched, and yet Magliozzi says such stories are true and happen with great frequency. Magliozzi recalls a now-retired Snap-on dealer named Tony Pino who serviced his garage and epitomized the Snap-on sales style.

"He was never in a hurry," Magliozzi recalls. "He'd see you struggling with some part under the hood, and he'd lean over and say, 'We have a tool that makes that a lot easier.' And it would work, and you'd buy it. You wouldn't even ask how much it was." In the more than twenty-five years he has been in the auto repair business, Magliozzi estimates he has bought over $100,000 worth of Snap-on tools, and he still uses the wrenches and screwdrivers from his first toolbox.

Steve Pino, Tony's son, is also a Snap-on dealer, and he spends his week visiting three hundred garages and car dealerships in the Allston-Brighton section of Boston and the nearby suburb of Watertown, where he grew up. For Pino, Snap-on is more than a company, it is like a family member. Pino's father drove a Snap-on van for thirty years, and Pino's brother, brother-in-law, and father-in-law have all been Snap-on dealers.

Pino, like Van Mater, is a sixteen-year Snap-on veteran, and he has built a successful business for himself on his twenty-foot white van. In good years, he has generated between $7,000 and $9,000 in sales a week from the back of the van, which holds more than $150,000 worth of Snap-on inventory.

Pino spends up to sixty hours a week in his van, cruising the back streets and industrial parks of this blue-collar section of Boston. He has had to adapt to a changing demographic, and his clientele is now an ethnic rainbow. Mechanics from Jamaica, Thailand, Vietnam, Ireland, and Africa climb into the van at each stop and gaze longingly at the interior, which is filled to capacity, including the ceiling, with every manner of tool and equipment.

Even as the mechanics hand him tens and twenties to pay off a past purchase, they are eyeing the next socket set or ergonomic screwdriver with the wistful looks of a child in a Beanie Baby store. The passion for the tools transcends the pragmatic and becomes personal. "It's jewelry, it's adornment," Magliozzi says. "It enhances your own self-image and impresses your customers."

At each stop, Pino checks his laptop computer for each customer's personal account. He not only monitors accounts receivable but creates a needs list for each mechanic so he can remind them which tools they coveted in previous visits. In the shop itself, Pino trades barbs with the wisecracking mechanics, hands out new socket sets or wrenches for his customers to fondle, and sells an impressive number of new tools before lunchtime.

Pino embodies the Snap-on brand to his customers. His competitors, like Mac or Matco, SPX or Cornwall, simply do not have the dealer network and blanket coverage of Snap-on, and so mechanics do not create the relationships with those salespeople that they have with Pino. Intensely proud, auto mechanics will spurn the brand if they feel disrespected by the dealer. Pino's success bespeaks his rapport with the customers and his own emotional attachment to the tools.

"I'm a tool junkie myself," he says. "I really like the stuff I sell."

—— Finding New Revenue Streams ——

Snap-on competes with a variety of companies across several different product lines, but none of its competitors have the breadth of market coverage of Snap-on. Snap-on management, though conservative, has not been afraid to make acquisitions to buy into new markets and extend market share. And Snap-on has successfully exported its business model overseas and intends to build that market share. Already

Snap-on is the second largest hand-tool manufacturer in Europe; by making all its tools in the local market, the company incorporates features and price points that work within that market.

But CEO Robert Cornog acknowledges that within five years Snap-on must push into new markets in order to extend the brand and fuel growth. Like Harley-Davidson and the NBA, Snap-on has licensed its brand for peripheral merchandise like T-shirts, hats, and jackets. The company is also pursuing other brand extensions with the notion that these will not dilute the brand. Though it is unlikely that a Snap-on Café will open in Manhattan anytime soon, the company is unafraid of brand extensions that fit the model. The company made a licensing deal with the National Football League, for example, to put team logos on its popular ratcheting screwdriver. In another deal with a major automaker, Snap-on sold a commemorative tool cabinet in the colors, finish, and design of a classic 1957 Chevrolet Bel-Air.

But a major revenue stream may well lie in finding ways to extend Snap-on's brand equity into related professional fields, such as home building and contracting. Though Snap-on sees a natural path to the home improvement, do-it-yourself building market, Cornog doesn't believe that market is the right fit. Like other radical marketers, he understands the soul of his own business and doesn't relish straying too far from it. "We understand people who make a living with our products, with tools," he says. "And that is much more attractive for us than the do-it-yourself focus."

The allure of great brands, such as Rolex, Mercedes-Benz, or Armani, stretches across most boundaries, and Snap-on knows the cachet it holds. The goal is to make its brand more accessible without undermining its dealer network.

"Most of us want to buy the best of anything we can afford, whether it's cars, watches, suits, or tennis rackets," Cornog says. "Most people can't afford the best in most things, but one exception is tools. You can buy the very best tool and feel good about it. In that sense, Snap-on is a reasonable consumer product, and our job is to figure out how to make it available."

9

Virgin Atlantic Airways

A Passion for the Impossible

"Richard Branson is the Don Quixote
of business: the bigger the windmill,
the more he wants to go after it."
—David Tait

As we pointed out in Chapter 2, the first rule of radical marketing is that the CEO must own the marketing function. As passionate as other leaders profiled in this book are about personally pushing their brands, none take that conviction as far as Richard Branson, chairman and CEO of Virgin Atlantic Airways.

Branson, the forty-eight-year-old British billionaire and founder of the vast and far-flung Virgin empire, is nothing less than an "image wizard," according to *Time* magazine. A flamboyant iconoclast who roared on to the British and later international business stage by ignoring conventional wisdom and taking on entrenched giants in a diverse array of businesses from music to cola, Branson is the P. T. Barnum of twenty-first-century commerce, a charismatic pitchman whose show-business flair is coupled with a razor-sharp business sense.

As Barnum once said, "In order to get noticed, you've got to wiggle your ears." Since 1969, when Branson, at age nineteen, started Virgin as a mail-order record business in London, he has been wiggling his ears furiously in a virtual nonstop marathon of publicity that has built Virgin into a $4 billion conglomerate. Virgin now ranks among the upper echelons of international brands. Indeed, as *Time* pointed out, Virgin may be the most recognizable brand to emerge from Great Britain since the Rolls-Royce.

Perhaps more than any other brand, Virgin epitomizes its founder and leader. The more than twelve thousand Virgin employees are as likely to say they work for Richard (no last name is necessary) as for Virgin. In the United Kingdom, Branson is nothing less than a national icon, admired widely by young and old alike for his personal style as much as for his business success.

Like Branson, the Virgin brand connotes a sense of irreverence, rebellion, and fun that cannot be simulated on Madison Avenue. Perhaps even more remarkable, most brands built on such ephemeral characteristics fade quickly, but Branson has found a way to sustain and market the spirit for nearly thirty years. He is a relentless modern master of the staged publicity stunt, turning his clever antics into hundreds of millions of dollars' worth of free advertising for his brand. When he launched Virgin Cola in the United States in the spring of 1998, for example, Branson steered an army tank down Fifth Avenue in New York and earned interviews on each of the network morning TV shows as a result.

Virgin, however, is more than just hoopla and hype, and in Branson's passion and remarkable agility as a businessman, there are lessons in brand building for every company, large and small.

Branson has succeeded in an eclectic variety of businesses—from cola to condoms, financial services to wedding gowns—seemingly through sheer force of will and his extraordinary personal dynamism. But there is much more to the continued success of the brand. Unlike most fixed brands, says Branson, Virgin is constantly evolving with each new business venture regardless of how unusual the marketplace. "The brand is regenerated, rather than extended in the conventional sense, by each business we become involved in," Branson wrote in an essay on building brands. "We are in essence an unusual venture capital organization: a branded one."

Rather than offering financial backing in the strict sense of venture capital, Virgin offers a powerful branding and management resource to the stagnant organizations that Branson acquires, such as British Rail, or the start-ups seeking growth, in which Virgin takes an equity position and to which it lends its name. To ensure the brand's vitality and integrity, Virgin usually retains a minimum 51 percent control of all Virgin-branded businesses, and Branson insists on a highly decentralized and flat management structure, with no Virgin headquarters and minimal hierarchy throughout the organization. The only requirement is that each business adhere to four core values—quality, competitiveness, innovation, and fun.

Perhaps none of his dozens of businesses epitomizes the Virgin brand as much as Virgin Atlantic Airways, the $1.5 billion crown jewel in Branson's empire. In fact, much of what Branson brings to his new business ventures are lessons he learned creating Virgin Atlantic.

Of all his businesses, Virgin Atlantic is one of the few wholly owned by Branson, and the one on which he dotes. Having sold Virgin Records to Thorn-EMI for nearly $1 billion in 1992, the airline has become the focus of most of his attention—some say because it, of all his myriad business ventures, was the furthest afield and the most likely to fail.

Instead, the highly profitable Virgin Atlantic has soared beyond all expectations, particularly those of Branson's closest business partners, who were outraged, at the time, that he would risk all of Virgin's stable of companies on such a far-flung venture. Now the second-largest long-haul carrier in Britain, Virgin Atlantic flies to New York, Newark, Orlando, San Francisco, Los Angeles, Miami, Boston, and Washington, as well as South Africa, Hong Kong, Athens, and Tokyo. It has won a long list of travel awards as one of the world's top airlines from a variety of travel publications, such as *Condé Nast Traveler*, *Travel and Leisure*, and *Executive Travel*, and along the way it has become an agile competitor to that venerable old English institution British Airways.

In fact, Virgin Atlantic's success demonstrates clearly that Branson is far more than just a public relations expert. (Though it certainly didn't hurt that his good friend Princess Diana wore a Virgin Atlantic sweatshirt to her daily aerobics class when the airline was first launched.) Like other radical marketers, Branson has an uncanny ability to spot business opportunities that others don't see, to hire strong managers who share his values to run these businesses, and to keep the workforce inspired by making employees and customers his top priority.

Virgin Atlantic also served to refocus the Virgin brand for Branson. Up until the airline's launch in 1984, Virgin had established itself as a friendly brand with broad cachet in the United Kingdom. It was the move into airlines that created the basis for Branson's "big bad wolf" theory of marketing. "We began to target markets where the customer had been consistently ripped off or underserved and the competition was complacent," he wrote in *Brand Warriors*, a 1997 collection of marketing essays. He calls these bloated competitors "big bad wolves."

"Wherever we find them there is a clear opportunity area for Virgin to do a much better job than the competition," he says. "We introduce trust, innovation, and customer friendliness where they don't exist. It is a successful formula and ensures that the brand gets stronger with each new launch." In this way, Virgin Atlantic quickly began to represent quality and value for the money and to become "the people's champion."

In the emerging digital era, when entrepreneurial ventures are springing up daily in the new globally connected network of business, Branson's example is no longer outlandish. Indeed, in a landscape of virtual corporations, Internet-based business models, and a growing frenzy of alliances and acquisitions, Branson's management style is becoming more and more acceptable to mainstream executives. CEOs may not want to pilot hot-air balloons or speedboats across the Atlantic for publicity, as Branson has done, but they can well embrace his core business tenets: offer quality, be competitive, be innovative, and make it fun. Further, they can emulate his devotion to firsthand customer contact and his fervent tenacity.

Branson honestly views the impossible as simply another business opportunity. As is the case with great athletes or scholars, the admonition that something can't be done is stimulus enough for Branson to leap into the fray. David Tait, head of Virgin Atlantic's U.S. operations, calls Branson "the Don Quixote of business: the bigger the windmill, the more he wants to go after it."

Like other great entrepreneurs, Branson is unafraid of failure. But unlike many other successful business leaders, he refuses to stay within the confines of a single core business. Rather than "sticking with what you know," Branson's credo is: "If you know one business, you know any business. If you can run a record company, you can run an airline, you can run a bank; if you run a bank, you can run a soft drink company."

Though Branson's move into the airlines business in 1984 may have seemed brash and headstrong, Branson took a radical marketer's view and turned around the equation. From a businessman's perspective, the idea was foolish: others more knowledgeable than Branson in the airline industry had failed. But from the customer's point of view (the only way a radical marketer can see it), there was opportunity.

Branson told *Airways* magazine in a 1997 interview:

> As a businessman, I traveled a lot. Almost without exception, the experience was not pleasant. Traditional airline people see themselves in the transportation business. Coming from the entertainment industry, I saw it differently. If you're spending twelve hours on an airplane, they can't expect you to just stare at a blank wall the entire time, except when they drop a piece of chicken in your lap. The airline needs to entertain you, to make the experience fun, to give you options on how to spend the time. In a sense, when we started Virgin Atlantic, I was trying to build the perfect airline for myself. If you try to build the perfect airline for yourself, it will be appreciated by others.

In this way, Branson typifies the radical marketer's mindset. He has no formal marketing training and has never worked in a hierarchical company of any kind. Thus, he is not burdened by marketing formulas and conventional wisdom. He believes in stirring the marketing mix, eschewing market research for a "screw it, let's do it" attitude, and relying on uncommon sense.

He is an intelligent, relentless, occasionally ruthless businessman who has created a unique business formula for building upon the Virgin brand. Yet most important, he has a visceral connection to his customers because, despite his riches, he retains an empathic bond with consumers, a bond that stems from his unerring ability to view the world through the eyes of a "regular bloke." This ability to see things as his customers see them is a common characteristic of great radical marketers. It is real and powerful and cannot be faked or garnered through market research and focus groups.

In Britain, which loves nothing as much as a good underdog, Branson has embraced that role with relish in the business community. Both his dress and his manner are casual and friendly, an appealing counterpoint to the prototypical stodgy British business tycoon. Like Clay Mathile at Iams or Rich Teerlink at Harley-Davidson, Branson thrives on customer contact. When he first set up the airlines, he had a policy of calling fifty customers every month to chat and get their feedback. Even as his personal fortune swelled past $1 billion, he never isolated himself within layers of marketing bureaucracy. He refuses to rely on market data or focus groups or the stock market to monitor how his company is doing.

One of the reasons he has resisted offering Virgin Atlantic shares to the public is that he doesn't want to have to explain his idiosyncratic ideas to shareholders. He prefers to spend his time with customers. On his frequent Virgin Atlantic flights between London and the United States, Branson is a blur of motion, serving drinks, shaking hands, querying passengers with a folksy "How'm I doing?"

David Newkirk, a London-based consultant with Booz-Allen & Hamilton, tracks the travel industry and initiated some benchmark studies on consumer insights. The most insightful executives connect directly with their consumers, the study concluded, and few come close to Branson in this regard. "He talks to his customers all the time," Newkirk says. "Lord help you if you are on a plane with him. You'll never get any sleep."

Branson stories abound and have become the stuff of legend. One flight attendant told *Airways* magazine: "He was on one of my flights when a passenger reported that a toilet was broken. When I finally made it up there, I found Richard lying on his back, soaking wet, fixing the toilet."

When a Virgin Atlantic flight is badly delayed, Branson often shows up at the arrival gate to apologize personally to the weary travelers and hand them a gift certificate to a Virgin Megastore or a discount on future travel.

Although it may sound as if Branson is flying the planes, serving dinner, and unloading the baggage all by himself, in fact, the six thousand Virgin Atlantic employees operate in the Branson mold. They have become missionaries for the brand by emulating the characteristics upon which Branson built the Virgin empire. If the flight attendants laugh and joke with passengers far more than their British Airways counterparts do, it is because they actually enjoy the job, love the company, and get paid to make sure the customers are entertained as well as transported.

"Direct connection to the customer is the way to get the greatest innovation," Newkirk says. "When P. T. Barnum was out front, he was also talking to his customers all the time and understanding them."

—— Transforming the Product ——

The core of an airline is a fleet of metal tubes flying from one point to another loaded with people who, for the most part, would prefer to be somewhere else. Like on the ground. At their destination. Unfriendly ground personnel, grouchy flight attendants, bland food, a bad movie with painfully uncomfortable headsets, and dismally cramped seats do little to improve the overall customer demeanor.

While most airlines either don't understand this customer experience or refuse to acknowledge it, Virgin Atlantic built its entire value proposition around it. If most air travel is aggravating, scary, tiresome, expensive, and unreliable, Branson reasoned, Virgin Atlantic would mitigate those negative attributes by making it fun. Virgin would sell better entertainment, better onboard perks, and a better total travel experience on the ground and in the air. Prices would be competitive, but Virgin wouldn't compete on price. Back in 1984, an era of discount carriers and price wars, the concept was radical. In fact, it still is.

Though it was a sketchy premise upon which to build an airline, Branson simply knew no other way to operate. The philosophy was at the heart of all his Virgin businesses. He'd become Britain's "hippie capitalist" during the 1970s with his innovative Virgin Records. He signed unknown artists whom no other label would touch, like Mike Oldfield, whose *Tubular Bells* album sold five million copies as Virgin's very first release in 1973. The stable of artists grew from Oldfield, the Sex Pistols, and Boy George to include the Rolling Stones, Phil

Collins, Peter Gabriel, and Janet Jackson, thus making Virgin one of the six largest independent record companies in the world.

Branson's thrill, however, came from starting new businesses, not simply running existing ones. In 1983 he was approached by Randolph Fields, an American attorney living in England, to make an investment in a new transatlantic airline that would travel the coveted London–New York route. Branson was intrigued and jumped in over the loud protestations of his business partners.

As their involvement deepened, Branson and Fields met with David Tait, then a young airline industry consultant who had worked for the ill-fated Laker Airways, which had gone bankrupt in 1982. Tait told Branson it couldn't be done. "Great, that's what I hoped you would say," Branson replied. "Let's do it then."

And it was Sir Freddie Laker himself who brought out the Barnum in Branson. "Freddie Laker sat me down and said, 'If you are going to take on Pan Am, TWA, and British Airways, you've got to use yourself and get out there and realize that if you dress up in a captain's outfit when you launch the airline, you'll get on the front page. If you turn up in ordinary business clothes, you'll be lucky to get a mention. Remember, the photographers have got a job to do; they'll turn up to one of your events and give you one chance. If you don't give them a photograph that will get them on the front page, they won't turn up at your next event.' "

On February 29, 1984, Branson and Fields, wearing World War I era leather flying gear, announced the formation of Virgin Atlantic Airways. The British newspapers ate up the story, running photos and features that assured the stripling airline of massive free publicity. Few of the readers that day realized that the "airline" had yet to secure an actual plane. If competitors were watching at all, it was with bemusement at this amateur effort that seemed doomed to fail.

Tait had not been impressed with Fields, but Branson, then a bearded hippie living on a houseboat in London, was a different story. Tait thought, "This guy might just be crazy enough to make this thing work, and if he doesn't, we'll have a helluva lot of fun trying." Tait was prescient enough to see that though Branson knew nothing about the airline business, the skills required to make an airline successful heading toward the 1990s would be marketing-based, not transportation-based. Great service, clever and innovative perks, and enthusiastic flight crews would win the day. If anyone could ignite the fire and passion, it would be Branson.

Tait signed on as Virgin Atlantic's first U.S. employee and agreed to run North American operations. From the outset, the picture was clear. Virgin Atlantic couldn't compete with the likes of British Airways by being the same. Radical marketers disdain the copycat method. British Caledonian, a longtime competitor to British Airways, had recently resumed its London–New York route with the promise that it would be just as good as British Airways. "If you're only going to be as good as your competition, what's the point?" Tait says. "Why would I choose you? I'll go with British Airways rather than someone trying to mimic British Airways." Not surprisingly, British Caledonian was eventually acquired by British Airways.

Virgin Atlantic, though it touted itself as a low-cost airline, couldn't compete solely on price. Sir Freddie Laker had tried that and failed. Virgin Atlantic would have to be different, innovative, outrageous. Eliminating first class completely, Virgin Atlantic would offer a first-class experience at business-class fares. If the airline could win over the business flyers, their fares would supplement the back of the plane and allow the innovations to be spread to coach-class customers as well. Branson called his business class "Upper Class" and had to be convinced by colleagues not to name economy class "Riff Raff."

After a fierce battle to secure gate positions, Branson could only get permission to fly from Gatwick, London's other, more distant airport, to Newark, New Jersey, rather than JFK in New York. The first plane, an old Boeing 747 that had once been leased to the Argentinean national airlines, was not secured until eight days prior to the first scheduled flight and didn't arrive in London until June 18. Engine trouble was not resolved until the day before the inaugural flight. And the new airline didn't receive permission to sell tickets in the United States until the day before the first flight.

Nonetheless, on June 22, 1984, five months after its conception, Virgin Atlantic's first flight took off with the bright red Virgin logo splashed across the huge tail of the plane. The 440 "guests"—friends, celebrities, and, of course, the media—were greeted on board by a brass band, waiters from Maxim's in white tie and tails, magicians, singing groups, Branson's father, and seventy cases of champagne that flowed freely. Madonna's new hit song "Like a Virgin" blared loudly around the plane. According to Tim Jackson, author of *Richard Branson, Virgin King* (1996), Branson forgot his passport and nearly wasn't allowed off the plane in Newark.

The airborne party received international press coverage, and without spending a dime, the fledgling airline garnered millions of dollars' worth of attention. Virgin did run a newspaper ad in the New York newspapers a few days later: "Eat, Drink and Fly with an English Virgin. To London. For $159." Tickets could be purchased through Ticketron. It was an auspicious start and set an irreverent tone that has not changed significantly in fifteen years.

Behind the scenes, Branson displayed the canny business mettle that is a key part of his success. According to Jackson, Branson could not work with the volatile and confrontational Fields, and soon after, through cagey maneuvering, Branson edged Fields out of the business and took over the operation himself. Virgin Atlantic had not been Branson's idea, but it would succeed or fail as Branson's baby.

—— Filling a Void ——

If Virgin Atlantic was radical outside the plane, it was *inside* the plane that the airline got really radical. Dogmatic conventional airline wisdom was challenged quickly and continuously. Branson questioned everything with childlike persistence. "Why does it have to be this way?" he would ask when confronted with traditional meal service or in-flight entertainment. To a radical marketer, the answer "That's the way everyone does it" is simply unacceptable.

Radical marketers see opportunity in businesses where competitive success is based solely on the fact that no one is doing it better. The consumer may accept such providers grudgingly but will never become loyal or viscerally attached to the product or service. Rather than being scared off by a competitor's size, Branson simply sees a bigger, softer underbelly that he can attack. As an upstart in such a market, Virgin was able to cash in on the lack of consumer loyalty and quickly make a favorable impression simply by focusing on the customer's needs. To that end, Virgin Atlantic's service needed to become an experience that customers would talk about at cocktail parties, in the executive suite, and around the water cooler.

The innovations began on that first flight and have never stopped coming. For example, while competitors offered a single in-flight movie on their six- or seven-hour flights, Virgin Atlantic took advantage of new projection and video technology to offer movies, music videos, sitcoms, and other video programming for nearly the entire flight. While passengers on other carriers suffered with inferior and uncomfortable headsets, Virgin, following the new Sony Walkman trend, offered comfortable padded headsets and even invited passengers to keep them when they deplaned. Tait studied the issue and realized it actually cost more to recycle the used headsets than to give them away. In so doing, Virgin Atlantic appeared not only innovative but extremely generous as well. Travelers love nothing more than a good deal.

Free wine was served throughout the plane, not just in business class. Instead of a choice of chicken or beef, as on most airlines, Virgin Atlantic added a pasta dish as a third choice. "It didn't cost any more," Tait says. "It just took a little more thought."

All these changes were for economy as well as business-class passengers. Tait points out that most airlines view economy passengers "as a bunch of cattle" for whom price is all that matters. "To an extent, that's true," Tait says. "But there are enough people who are discerning enough to know that if the price is the same, they'll go where they're going to get something better for the money."

In recent years, as technology has progressed, Virgin Atlantic became the first airline to install video screens on every seatback and offer nonstop entertainment, including programming and video games for children, throughout the flight. While most flight crews shudder at the sight of children boarding a plane, fearing the noise and the extra toil involved in serving them, Virgin Atlantic embraced young travelers, giving out Virgin backpacks filled with in-flight activities and goodies and offering video games as part of the entertainment package. "We love children," Tait says. "The nice thing about children is that each one generally brings a couple of big people along with them."

—— Up Front ——

The true Virgin experience, however, is found in Upper Class. Up in the front of the plane, Branson discovered he could really have fun. By marketing first-class service at business-class fares, Virgin Atlantic early on began to attract business travelers who reveled in the innovative service. As Tait said, "We viewed it as entertaining guests at thirty-five thousand feet, as opposed to transporting passengers from point A to point B."

Indeed, Branson "cracked the code" on what business travelers really want, says the Booz-Allen consultant David Newkirk. Most businesspeople work so hard that they view an airplane flight, not as a place to continue working, but as a chance to unwind and relax. Virgin Atlantic, by making the flight more fun and more relaxing, tapped into that need and milked it effectively.

Much of what Virgin Atlantic pioneered, such as sleeper seats, has since been copied by other long-haul carriers. Upper Class passengers are treated to fully reclining seats for sleeping and are handed duvets and complimentary sweatsuits to slip on prior to falling asleep. A sixteen-channel, interactive seat-arm video and audio player provides dozens of movie and video choices throughout the flight, and besides the *four*-choice meal option (including vegetarian), ice cream and hot scones are served during the flight as well.

A bar and lounge, where passengers may gather and socialize, is set up on the lower level of the fleet's 747s, and an in-flight beauty therapist offers manicures, head and neck massage, and aromatherapy for passengers. Virgin Atlantic's flight crews number three or four more attendants than those of any competitors and are thus able to lavish more attention on passengers. "Virgin's business class is better than anybody else's first class," says Frank Lonergan, a San Francisco business executive who travels extensively to Europe and Asia. "It's the only flight I actually look forward to."

Not to be outdone, Virgin Atlantic ordered sixteen new Airbus A340 jetliners in 1997, and when they arrive in 2002, they will include private bedrooms with double beds, showers, an exercise area, and even hot tubs for passengers. "You can do it on cruise ships and trains. Why not on planes?" Branson told the *Wall Street Journal* in an article about the increasing sexual activity of passengers aboard airlines. "We're not the kind of airline that bangs on bathroom doors," he added.

Branson and Tait were also radical enough to realize that, depending on the length of the flight, up to 40 percent of travel time is spent on the ground. While competing airlines ignored this aspect of the trip, taking responsibility for customers only after they'd checked in at the gate, Virgin Atlantic decided to buck conventional wisdom and expand its customer service literally from door to door.

Virgin Atlantic decided early on to not contract out passenger check-in services, as some airlines do. "We found that to control the level of service, we had to have our own people doing it," Tait explains. "We spent a lot of money on training, and we insist on some revolutionary things, like eye contact or a smile at the passenger."

Upper Class passengers are entitled to a free limousine (usually a new Range Rover) or chauffeured motorcycles, called LimoBikes, from their home or office to the airport. Using fast-food restaurants as a model, Virgin Atlantic unveiled "Drive-Through Check-in" at selected airports. A passenger en route to Heathrow, for example, gives his ticket to the driver, who radios ahead the passenger's name, flight number, and destination. Upon arrival at a special Virgin Atlantic satellite check-in station at the airport, a clerk comes to the car, takes the passenger's passport, ticket, and bags, and returns with the passport, boarding passes, and directions to the Virgin Club, the innovative Upper Class lounge. The driver drops the passenger at an entrance near the lounge, and the passenger need never lift a suitcase or go near the check-in counter.

The lounges extend the in-air Upper Class experience to the ground. Virgin Atlantic opened lounges at all the airports it serves and turned them into spas. Besides the usual complimentary drinks, Virgin Atlantic offers full meals, massages, manicures, haircuts, showers, a special sound room for listening to music, a putting green, a quiet, librarylike conservatory, and more. When the flight is ready for boarding, an announcement is made, and the passenger simply wanders over to the gate and boards, where the pampering continues.

When the plane lands, yet another car is waiting to take the passenger to his or her final destination. Competitors have scoffed at Virgin's use of free limos, claiming that most business travelers can expense their airport ground transportation and don't need this perk. Tait says that corporate travel offices are starting to notice the free limos, however, and as business travel has grown prohibitively expensive, many are opting to fly Virgin Atlantic in part because of this feature. More important, Tait says, the limo service has made a dramatic dent in the number of no-shows for Virgin Atlantic. Passengers who don't think twice about not showing up for a $2,500 seat on a plane, he says, feel guilty about turning a limo driver away from their driveway. The limo company, however, can call in a cancellation on the passenger's behalf.

Never missing an opportunity for consumer feedback, Virgin greets arriving passengers with a phone call while they are in the limo. "Hello," says a friendly voice, "I'm calling on behalf of Richard Branson. How was your flight?"

—— Consistently Radical ——

Because radical marketers are such control freaks and sticklers for details, size and consistency matter a great deal. In an industry dominated by giant behemoths such as British Airways, United, and American, Virgin Atlantic has quite purposefully stayed small. After flying just one plane for the first two years, the airline began slow and controlled expansion, adding new planes and destinations carefully. Today there are twenty-two planes in the entire fleet, with six thousand employees and more than three million passengers annually.

"We went for routes that would sustain a daily widebody operation year-round, and we've stuck with that," Tait says. "We haven't jumped into seasonal markets, and we've stuck to our core brand values. A lot of carriers stray from their core business, and customers don't know what they are getting. We've stayed very consistent with our product."

In fact, Tait says, despite conventional wisdom and a trend toward consolidation among the big players, staying small has been a huge advantage for Virgin Atlantic. "The *QEII* has a stopping distance of six miles and a turning radius the size of Rhode Island," Tait says. "We can change direction on a dime, which makes it very difficult for our competition to keep up with us."

For example, it is impossible for British Airways to change its in-flight offerings on just the routes it shares with Virgin Atlantic. It must copy Virgin Atlantic on all its flights or none of them; otherwise, a British Airways passenger flying from London to Jakarta would receive different treatment than one flying from London to New York. Consistency is key in the airline business, and unmet expectations are a source of many complaints from frequent travelers.

Virgin Atlantic ventured into domestic service in Europe in 1996 by buying a Belgium-based carrier and renaming it Virgin Express. Tait says the company is also eager to begin domestic flights in the United States as well, but is stymied by U.S. laws that prevent a foreign carrier from having a controlling ownership of an airline in the United States. While Branson loudly fights what he calls "archaic" laws, Virgin Atlantic may find an American carrier to become its partner in such a venture.

But will such a move compromise Branson's time-tested formula as well as the Virgin advantage? Short-haul flyers tend to choose the carrier based on time and price rather than airline preference, and thus it becomes a frequency and loyalty game rather than a frills and service play. Branson's ability to deliver his product might be diluted. The question a radical marketer must ask himself is, how big can he get without going beyond the boundaries of his formula? And if he does, will it break?

"The best marketers have rigorous boundaries on what they choose to do and venture outside it only at some risk," Newkirk says.

Of course, those are just the kind of challenging words that set Branson in motion. Virgin Atlantic actually sees its attributes as extendable to all routes, long or short. In an era of consolidation, the British upstart is thrilled with each new alliance, according to Tait.

"If you can only fly three airlines in the U.S., do you think they are going to continue innovating or try to get better? Why should they?" Tait declares. "They're carving up the country very nicely—'You take this part, we'll take this part,' and what can you do?

"So that's great news for us. It makes our service levels look that much better. It opens the door to us coming in as a domestic carrier very nicely." Tait believes that "people will flock" to a different, high-quality service.

——— It's the People, Stupid ———

Radical marketers tend to hire passionate missionaries who perpetuate the brand with their loyalty and deep belief in the product. A Virgin Atlantic flight crew, from the pilots to the flight attendants, is no less than an extension of Branson himself. They tend to love their jobs—to covet them, in fact—and they become evangelists for the brand.

Branson's pecking order is clear: employees, customers, shareholders. "If you don't have a happy and highly motivated workforce, customer satisfaction goes out of the window," Branson says. "And if you don't have satisfied customers, you don't have a business." Satisfied employees and customers ultimately lead to happy shareholders, he adds.

Branson pays more than lip service to his devotion to his employees. He gives out his home address to all employees and encourages correspondence about everything on their minds. On his desk every morning, amid a mountain of mail, is a pile of letters from employees, which he reads first.

Though Virgin does not give stock options, it has a generous profit-sharing plan and health benefits plan, enough to keep employees from seeking work elsewhere. But speaking with Virgin Atlantic pilots and flight attendants, the discussion always comes back to Branson's personal touch with employees. They talk about his annual summer parties at his home in Oxfordshire and about how he rides the crew bus and stays at the same hotel as the flight crews when he travels. He inevitably takes that crew out to dinner and turns the evening into a long party.

Branson told *Airways* magazine, "How could the chairman send a message to his employees that the hotel his company puts them in is not good enough for him? Besides, I always have eighteen delightful people to go to dinner with this way; that's always fun."

And one would be hard-pressed to find another chief executive who takes more than a dozen rank-and-file employees with him on vacation, but Branson does each year. Exemplary Virgin employees, whether they are cleaning ladies or Virgin Atlantic pilots, are invited to Necker Island, Branson's private Caribbean resort, to vacation and to schmooze with the chairman.

It may sound corny, but fun is actually a core attribute of the Virgin value set and the brand. "If you aren't having fun doing business, your people aren't going to have fun, and at the end of the line your passengers aren't going to have fun either," Tait says. "It's an incredibly important ingredient in the mix."

In an industry where turnover is high, especially among flight attendants, the Virgin Atlantic atmosphere and reputation as a fun place to work are tremendous lures. Because Virgin Atlantic is a non-union shop and a relatively young airline, it can keep its costs contained better than most competitors. Flight crews are paid competitively, but their salaries are far from the top of industry salary charts. Nonetheless, a flight attendant's job on Virgin Atlantic is highly coveted and tough to get. Virgin Atlantic flight attendants tend to be much younger than their counterparts on other airlines because seniority issues are not as paramount. And personality is a crucial factor in the selection process. Dour and serious types need not apply.

Despite its irreverent image, Virgin Atlantic refuses to cut corners on safety and maintenance and has among the toughest safety training standards in the industry. But Branson's notorious sense of humor trickles down; the flight crew just flat out seems to be having a good time. In fact, British Airways has taken to working with its flight crews to drop some of its British correctness and show some personality. Radical can be learned.

—— Surgical Strikes and Finding the Mix ——

As with all of Branson's businesses, outward appearances are only the tip of the iceberg. The companies succeed because they are built on sound business principles and a deep understanding of the market. A long-term commitment to building the brand and keeping it at Virgin standards is at the heart of Branson's success.

For Virgin Atlantic, the new realities of air travel create stressful challenges that a fun experience alone cannot resolve. While the fares for economy travel to Europe have stayed remarkably stable since the airline began to fly in 1984, business travel costs have soared. Business-class fares, says Tait, are higher today than first-class fares were ten years ago. Because of this, it is the business travelers who are subsidizing the folks in economy class.

Thus, Virgin Atlantic must find the right passenger mix. Revenue management is now the name of the airline game. A carrier can fly with a 100 percent load factor and still go out of business. To address this challenge, Virgin Atlantic created a "premium economy" class, a full-fare economy ticket that is cheaper than business class but offers more comfortable seats and preferential treatment for coach-class passengers. And Tait points out that Virgin Atlantic budgets to lose money certain months of the year and offers what he calls "silly fares" in order to get travel agents into Virgin Atlantic seats.

"Our biggest challenge is initiating trial," Tait declares. "Seeing is believing, and word of mouth is our greatest advertising vehicle." Virgin Atlantic also battles the ubiquitous frequent-flyer programs that hold business travelers captive and the "devil you know" factor that keeps many business travelers from experimenting with a new product. Because its own mileage program can't compete with the huge networks of its competitors, Virgin Atlantic, like any great radical marketer, changes the rules.

Periodically, for example, the airline contacts its top twenty frequent flyers in a given city and sends an invitation saying, "Richard Branson would like to invite you to dinner in the hottest restaurant in town." Branson personally escorts the customer to dinner at an exclusive local eatery, and word spreads quickly around the office the next day that the CEO of the airline personally takes frequent flyers out to eat. Virgin Atlantic's cachet increases proportionately.

Though its advertising budget is a drop in the bucket compared to that of its competitors, Virgin Atlantic spends nearly $50 million a year on advertising in the United States and the United Kingdom. Because its name does not indicate where it flies to, Virgin Atlantic must continually remind customers of who it is. But like other radical marketers, Virgin Atlantic uses the surgical strike approach to advertising rather than the usual shotgun method of its competitors.

Airlines, Tait says, take themselves way too seriously. Advertising campaigns tend to sell the airline as the end product in and of itself, which he says is ludicrous. "Have you ever heard anybody say, 'Hey, let's go get on U.S. Airways and fly around for a while'?" Tait asks. "The thing people look forward to the most when getting on an airplane is getting off." Tait is also amazed at campaigns for the product in which the airplane seat is featured. He says, in a popularity contest, airline seats would be "right up there with dentist chairs."

Instead, Virgin Atlantic uses its advertising to underscore its irreverent image and boast of its perks. Though it does a small amount of television advertising, the airline spends most of its advertising budget on print ads. "If Concorde passengers had massages, manicures, personal video screens and sleeper seats, maybe they wouldn't be in such a hurry to get here," read one such advertisement.

"You sow the seed of interest by having advertising that is as different as your product is," Tait says.

To cut through the clutter, Virgin Atlantic looks for unique opportunities. The airline scored the ultimate "product" placement in 1998 during both the season finale and the season premiere of the hit NBC comedy *Friends* by flying the show's characters to London on Virgin Atlantic as part of the story line. Branson himself was given a cameo role in the episode, and to ensure blanket coverage, Virgin Atlantic ran a commercial during the show. Whatever the cost of the commercial, the airline received millions of dollars worth of free publicity.

Realizing that its markets are limited in the United States, Virgin Atlantic created specific ads targeted for individual markets. When the airline was about to launch its San Francisco service, it conducted local focus groups to ask travel agents and frequent flyers what was unique about San Francisco. Instead of replies like "Fisherman's Wharf" or, "The Golden Gate Bridge" most respondents identified two elderly ladies, identical twins named Vivian and Marion Brown, who dress up in their Sunday best each day and shop and stroll around the downtown area. The entire Virgin Atlantic campaign was built around the theme: "Virgin Atlantic, the official airline of Vivian and Marion."

It was a huge hit, Tait says, and the ultimate tribute came from a local sales manager for British Airways who spotted Tait at lunch one day and complained that she had suggested a similar idea to her advertising people when British Airways was launching a double daily service from San Francisco to London. The response: "We're not going to do regional advertising. Are you crazy? Do you know how much that would cost?"

In fact, one of Branson's great pleasures is tweaking British Airways at every opportunity. In the early 1990s, British Airways initiated a surreptitious campaign to discredit Virgin Atlantic, and when Branson found out, he filed a libel suit, which he later settled for more than $900,000. Branson gave the money to his employees and sent out a note: "Thank you all for your help in our defense. After all, a Virgin's honor is her most prized possession."

In the long run, Virgin Atlantic's success will depend on how well Branson has imparted his lessons to the rest of the company. As is the case with other great radical marketers, it may be that Branson's most important asset is his insatiable curiosity and willingness to learn. As he told *Time*, each new business is a new trip to school.

"In the first three months, I treat it like a university education," Branson said. "I completely immerse myself in the new business. I try to find out why other people are doing it so badly and how we can get in there and do it better. Shake up the industry and offer the public a better product. In a sense, it's that learning process I find the most fascinating part of my job."

10

EMC Corporation

Beating IBM at Its Own Game

"Here an idea goes from point to point, not through six marketing guys. . . . At IBM, an idea would have had to stop at fourteen places along the way."
—Dick Egan

The world of high technology is filled with radical marketers, past and present, from Hewlett-Packard, Dell Computer, and Apple to the latest Internet-based pioneers like Netscape, Yahoo, and America Online. Lightning-fast product cycles, unceasing technical breakthroughs, unprecedented wealth creation, and an ever-shifting business landscape make high technology an industry well suited to the frontier mentality of radical marketers.

But the evanescent nature of success in this dynamic environment often turns yesterday's radical marketer into tomorrow's irrelevant museum piece. In a fierce Darwinian struggle for product pertinence, market share, and profit margins, sustained success is often an elusive target. Market forces are so intense that they can stagger even a giant as imposing as IBM and focus attention on the tiniest start-ups, which can find themselves with multibillion-dollar market caps before they even ship their first product.

In such an environment, radical marketers willing and able to stick to the core attributes that made them radical in the first place tend to maintain their success. Richard J. Egan, the cofounder and chairman of EMC Corporation, is one of those.

Amid the many highly publicized names in high technology, Egan's EMC, based in Hopkinton, Massachusetts, is an obscure player in an arcane market niche, at the outer reaches of Massachusetts' Route 128 high-tech region. But since 1990, under Egan and CEO Michael Ruettgers, EMC has quietly transformed both itself and its industry and turned conventional high-tech wisdom on its ear. EMC did nothing less than convert computer storage into a huge, fast-growing strategic business while unseating none other than IBM as the dominant player in that market. For decades, data-processing professionals lived by a simple mantra: "No one ever lost their job by buying IBM." EMC, by parlaying an uncanny ability to listen to its customers and provide the new and potent technology that these customers yearned for, rendered that statement an anachronism.

Since 1992, on the wings of its Symmetrix storage products, EMC has increased its sales tenfold from $386 million to close to $4 billion, with profits soaring from under $30 million to nearly $700 million in 1998. According to *Business Week*, among major technology companies, only Microsoft, Intel, and Cisco Systems had higher net profit margins in 1996 than EMC.

More impressive, in 1990, IBM owned 76 percent of the mainframe storage market and EMC had no measurable share at all. Today EMC is the dominant player, with 50 percent market share to IBM's 27 percent. In the total worldwide external storage market, EMC has eclipsed IBM and now holds nearly 30 percent of the $10 billion market. It is number one in all high-end storage, and when *Business Week* published its list of the top fifty "best performing" companies in 1998, a list that crossed all industry boundaries, EMC counted forty-four of the fifty among its customers.

With analysts expecting computer storage sales to soar to $35 billion or more by the year 2002, EMC is growing at 30 percent a year and is likely to become a $10 billion company in less than five years. Though few, including IBM, have conceded EMC's future success, analysts are already suggesting that EMC has become a "franchise" brand, along with Intel, Microsoft, Cisco, and Oracle among the pillars of the high-tech community.

EMC fashioned this remarkable market shift by doing what most great radical marketers do: viewing the impossible as just another market opportunity. The radical marketers at EMC ignored tradition and the status quo, envisioned the market as they believed it should be, found the crack in the firmament, and staked a claim. Most important, EMC stayed passionate and focused on its market while its competitors' vision was clouded by a diversity of businesses and attendant distractions.

Of course, great products that were doomed to obscurity by marketing failure mark the history of high tech. EMC had a better idea, but there was no guarantee that the company could sell it. In 1990 EMC was recovering from a two-year downturn, and from the outside it seemed that mere survival was the focus of the company's agenda. But like all radical marketers, EMC believed so deeply in its product that failure was not an option. With a few simple yet radical concepts, it would change the storage world.

At EMC, for example, the CEO as well as the chairman continue to own the marketing function, and they get out of the head office and face-to-face with customers as much as any senior executives in the high-tech sector. Not only has EMC showed great respect for a customer base that IBM virtually ignored, but in so doing, EMC created an ever-widening community of users committed to the brand. In a market cluttered with a cacophony of marketing promises, EMC has reshuffled the mix and stayed steadfastly true to the brand.

—— Outflanking Goliath ——

More than anything else, EMC used its visceral understanding of its core customer—the information technology professional—to build a product line that focused with laser accuracy on that customer's needs and desires. In so doing, it outflanked its giant competitor, IBM, and, without massive advertising or promotion, stole large chunks of market share in record time.

To grasp the magnitude of how completely EMC changed its market, one has to consider a bit of history.

Data storage, since the 1960s, had been controlled by the individual computer vendors. Companies like Digital Equipment Corporation, Sperry, Honeywell, NCR, Data General, and Prime Computer all sold the storage devices to accompany their own proprietary computer systems. IBM sold the giant mainframe computers used by most corporations and thus dominated the market for mainframe storage devices— little more than bulky electronic file cabinets that were a necessary peripheral to complete the system.

IBM's brand was sacrosanct in the data center. It made no more sense to look elsewhere for storage than to buy a washer without the dryer. In the complex world of computing, storage was a paradox: on the one hand, these devices held the "family jewels"—the corporate data such as payroll, accounts receivables, inventory, and personnel files that were the corporate lifeblood; on the other hand, storage was a dull and arcane add-on peripheral, like printers and fax machines. When a company used up its capacity on one storage device, they simply called the IBM sales rep and bought another.

For years no one thought to compete with IBM in mainframe storage, but when competitors began to realize that Big Blue was reaping 70 percent gross margins or higher for these mundane devices, a market sprang up. Competitors like Hitachi and Amdahl saw an opportunity and began to sell clones of the IBM devices, competing on price and a few add-on features. From a technology standpoint, the direct-access storage device (DASD) generally doubled in speed and capacity every eighteen months, but no one at IBM saw the strategic business value of storage. It was just a market, albeit a lucrative one, driven by deep brand penetration. In the vast Armonk empire, storage was a cash cow milked effectively enough to give IBM a 76 percent market share by 1990.

In the computer wars, data storage was a quiet front, and IBM and the other computer companies liked it that way. Data-processing managers had little leverage—to haggle on price, the best tactic was to strategically place the "million-dollar" Amdahl coffee mug on your desk when the IBM sales rep arrived. Seeing a competitor's presence in an account might just knock a million dollars off the IBM price.

After more than three status quo decades, an unexpected shift happened, virtually overnight. As often happens in the computer industry, the change was driven by a new technology vision. IBM had always improved the speed and capacity of its storage devices by writing millions of lines of complex microcode to run these wheel-like disk drives. But in the late 1980s, engineers at tiny, obscure EMC came up with a simple yet radical new concept. Rather than writing more and more code, which had caused IBM's products endless problems, why not build storage devices made up of literally hundreds of small, off-the-shelf disk drives, make them work together with a simple bit of microcode, and put them in a package that would be smaller, cheaper, faster, more powerful, and inherently more reliable than IBM's products?

And further, if you could build a device like that, you could actually tailor it far more specifically to a data center's needs, offering higher performance, higher availability systems at higher prices for the most important data, and less expensive, less powerful systems for archival data not needed on a daily basis. IBM had built its franchise on a "one size fits all" philosophy, but information technology managers had long been frustrated by this restrictive technical approach.

When EMC introduced its Symmetrix product line in 1990, it flew so directly in the face of conventional wisdom that, initially, competitors simply scoffed at the concept. "They went through denial," Ruettgers says. "It was just the lunatic fringe that bought our boxes." At the product introduction in New York, only six analysts and reporters showed up. If IBM was watching, there didn't appear to be much to worry about.

But the competitors' smirks disappeared almost as quickly as their customers did. There was little money for advertising, so EMC, under its marketing vice president, Bob Ano, fashioned a sales offensive that was clearly radical in the storage world.

The first priority was to build a track record and establish credibility. To get in the door, EMC salespeople offered to install these million-dollar systems for free on a trial basis. They called it a "puppydog sale"—once the customer had the cute puppy at home for a few days, the dog would never come back to the pet shop. Only the very largest companies could request such "loaners" for benchmark testing from the likes of IBM. EMC gladly installed its machines for three to six months' trials in customer accounts of all sizes; few of the machines came back.

One converted customer, a large insurance company, used the free trial to process its year-end data, a massive number-crunching effort that traditionally took two full weeks of computer time. Using EMC's Symmetrix, the company completed the task in three days. A catalog sales company was able to keep its books open and take orders up to three days longer at Christmas using the new storage system. It was this type of demonstration that got people hooked, a metaphor Egan likes to use.

"It was like cocaine," Egan says. "Once they saw what this could do, there was no going back. We had the needle in their arm."

Initially, EMC targeted smaller companies where the IBM bias might not be as strong. There was a pragmatic value as well. "Frankly, if something was going to blow up, it would be better happening someplace where people wouldn't hear about it," Ano says. But EMC left nothing to chance. Incorporated into its systems is its "Phone Home" link back to headquarters, an automatic internal diagnostic test system that detects errors and, via a laptop PC and modem, alerts EMC engineers that a problem looms. In most corporate accounts, EMC service engineers will show up, fix a potential problem, and leave without the customer realizing that anything out of the ordinary has occurred.

EMC, analysts say, gives away service as part of its products, taking in only around $15 million each quarter on service revenues. Having barely survived a two-year run of product failures in the late 1980s, EMC would rather send an army of service technicians to a customer site than risk technical problems.

EMC offered superior price performance as well as lower energy costs and a far smaller footprint, which was a godsend for companies with data center space at a premium. Like an auto dealership, EMC even offered to trade its equipment for IBM equipment, which it resold through brokers on the open market.

—— Making Storage Strategic ——

And most important, EMC began the reeducation of the corporate computing market, building an impressive case that data storage could have a dramatic strategic impact on a business. Rather than pouring resources into advertising, Ano set up a series of seminars for information technology (IT) managers and chief financial officers to make the case that access to information, made faster and easier by EMC's new storage systems, was directly tied to revenues.

EMC would feature a well-known industry figure as guest speaker to lure attendees. Then, using data gathered from real customers, EMC researchers made the case that faster access to information, through better storage systems, paid off in sales and earnings for a company. This was a powerful message and "got us into selling opportunities with customers," Ano says. It was also a radical departure: recasting storage as a strategic business opportunity for competitive advantage was a concept that would have drawn derisive laughter five years earlier.

Like other radical marketers, EMC simply didn't have the money to throw at advertising—based on percentage of revenues, the company remains one of the smallest in the industry in terms of advertising expenditures. Like other radical marketers, EMC believes in surgical strike advertising rather than massive spending on vast campaigns. In 1998, for example, EMC spent less than $10 million on advertising, a tiny drop in the bucket compared to the $300 million spent by IBM in 1997. But Ano points out that EMC's systems, which sell for between $200,000 and $3.4 million, "are big-ticket items with a targeted audience. We don't need the whole world to know who we are."

EMC also quickly learned to target its resources where they would do the most good. From their collective experiences visiting customers' offices, EMC executives saw a broad interest in golf, so the company sponsored a series of golf tournaments around the country and invited key customers and potential accounts. Each of the forty events attracted one hundred people and cost between $25,000 and $40,000. Ano would speak to the gathering first, and then EMC salespeople would golf with the prospects, thus garnering a captive audience for four hours. "We reached four thousand potential customers with the same message," Ano says, "and it was cheap compared to a quarter-page ad in the *Wall Street Journal.*"

The lesson, Ano says, is "to keep on message, repeat the same basic themes over and over again." Such consistency won converts faster than even EMC thought possible.

From a storage standpoint, "we had been all IBM for ten years or more," says Rich Malone, chief information officer of Edward Jones, the $1 billion financial services firm based in St. Louis. "I'd never heard of EMC. But they came to us with a better idea of our company, our philosophy, and our direction than anyone else. They took the time to understand our business and how their product would help our business. We're 100 percent EMC now."

——— Creating a New Market ———

Like other great marketers, EMC upped the ante before its competitors could react. While IBM, Hitachi, and Amdahl sought an answer to Symmetrix, EMC, under Ruettgers and his crack engineering staff, had a vision that would jolt the data storage industry yet again.

The stunning proliferation of corporate data, the vast sprawl of corporate networks, and the increasing popularity of the Internet fueled an insatiable need for computer storage in the early 1990s. It is a trend that will keep growing well into the next millennium. Storage became the tail that wagged the dog, now dictating, even more than the CPU itself, how fast a system could crunch numbers. In this light, EMC created "open" storage systems. Not only would Symmetrix systems work with mainframe computers, they could now couple with all other computers, from personal computers to workstations and midrange computers, running all types of software throughout a corporation.

This was a case study in marketing savvy that stemmed directly from the relationships that Ruettgers and his executives had formed with customers. EMC's top executives, particularly Egan and Ruettgers, spend hundreds of days each year meeting with customers, listening to their needs and taking their calls when a crisis arises. For a customer set that endured decades of frustration dealing with IBM's multilayered bureaucracy, the attention of EMC's senior-most officers is highly prized.

Not diverted by the market research and bureaucratic layers that most companies use to interpret customer needs, EMC actually listened and understood its customers' most important issues. During the 1980s, the advent of personal computers had pushed corporate computing power out of the glass-house data center into departments and business units. Called "decentralization," it was a revolution that wreaked havoc on corporate computing.

Business users had no concept of how difficult building and running computer networks could be. After years of frustrating system crashes, unkept promises, and lost data, the trend came full circle and contrite users have begun to return to the data centers for help.

Ruettgers recalled a meeting with the IT manager at John Deere. When he asked if this manager saw distributed systems coming back into the data center, the manager nodded, and then his face grew red and a vein bulged in his forehead. "I told those assholes not to do this," he raged. "Now they want me to take it back again. As far as I'm concerned, those guys are going to have to crawl on their hands and knees over a hundred yards of broken glass before I take them back." For Ruettgers, it was an epiphany. He had struck not only a nerve but a vein of gold as well.

Here was a huge business opportunity, a platform upon which EMC could build its brand. EMC, incredibly, was the first storage company to offer this open storage approach, which would help solve the IT dilemma. Even more important, EMC was able to use its technology to upgrade its older systems so that customers would not have to buy entirely new systems. The product a customer bought three years ago is better today through upgrades than it was the day he bought it, which is a radical marketer's dream concept. "Customers end up with more value than they had initially," Ruettgers says. "That makes us unique. I know for sure that my Jaguar hasn't gotten any better since I bought it."

In 1995, when Ruettgers predicted that EMC would sell $200 million worth of these open systems in the first year, even his own staff thought he'd lost his mind. But Ruettgers had heard the pain of these exasperated customers and he knew they would pay almost anything to make that pain disappear.

In fact, they were willing to pay a lot, more than the cost of EMC's mainframe storage. Even charging double what other storage vendors were asking, EMC couldn't keep up with demand. The open storage concept caught on like wildfire, fueling EMC's steep ascent since 1995 and building a two-year gap between EMC and its nearest competition.

——— A Street Fighter's Passion ———

For Dick Egan, a sixty-two-year-old, chain-smoking engineer with a salty sailor's vocabulary, EMC's success is heady stuff. If his personal $350 million net worth hasn't validated his radical approach to business, then EMC's rush to the head of its class certainly has. Indeed, Egan is provocative, aggressive, and volatile, but he is also an eager raconteur who remembers vividly the minefield that is EMC's history, including a close brush with chapter 11 bankruptcy, so he stays a long step or two removed from arrogance. EMC watchers, who acknowledge Egan's business tenacity and vision, are quick to point out that it has been Ruettgers' management savvy and operational skill that has fueled much of EMC's growth in this decade.

But EMC is nothing if it is not a mirror of its chairman's volatile, street-fighter personality. Soon after IBM named James Vanderslice as head of its struggling storage division in 1995, Vanderslice sent an exhortative memo to his employees claiming that IBM would soon "stick EMC in the eye with a hot poker." Not surprisingly, the internal memo found its way into EMC's offices and Egan read it. He immediately sent a brass fireplace poker to Vanderslice via Federal Express with a note: "I understand you've implored your troops to stick us with a hot poker. Enclosed is the poker; rest assured we'll supply the heat."

Egan also found inventive ways to torment IBM customers who refused to consider another vendor. He calls them "dinosaurs" and sends them blue underwear with "IBM" stenciled on the bottom, a ploy that either enrages them or gets a laugh and a chance to pitch EMC.

Though some of his lieutenants cringe at such provocations, Egan's aggressiveness rubs off on EMC's employees, particularly the sales force, a group of young, intense former jocks who don't take no for an answer.

According to a front-page article in the *Wall Street Journal*, EMC has always taken an unorthodox approach to sales. There is no cap on compensation for the sales force, and most representatives get about 65 percent or more of their pay in commissions, compared with about 25 percent at IBM. EMC says its six hundred or so reps earn an average of $250,000 a year, making them among the best-paid salespeople in any industry. Last year five top performers pulled in more than $1 million each.

In an industry where most of the salespeople were fifteen-year veterans in blue suits, Egan thought like a radical marketer and early on decided, owing to lack of resources more than anything else, to hire inexperienced but passionate and eager young people right off local campuses like Boston College and Northeastern. He looked for attractive former athletes from blue-collar backgrounds, people who'd been on teams, who knew about what it takes to win, who weren't jaded by past experience or awed by the prospect of taking on a seemingly unbeatable competitor like IBM.

Then he housed them in an old telephone center, a big room in which they could do follow-up sales calls in a group setting. When a sales rep made a sale, he would rush over and ring a big cowbell that Egan had installed in the room. He called that experience "EMC University." After a few months on the phones, he'd send them out into the field.

Like their chairman, EMC salespeople were aggressive and tenacious, refusing to be turned away. They were EMC's missionaries and evangelists.

"One of the best advantages we had with these kids was that they didn't know how tough IBM was or how much the market was dominated by IBM," Egan says. "They'd bang their head against the wall and then go do it again. I'd get two or three calls a week from customers saying, 'Would you get this salesman off my back? He just won't stop!' I'd say, 'Jeez, I'm sorry, I'll get on this right away.' And I'd call the salesman and say, 'Way to go, Joe!'"

Finding a way to contest every sale, even after the competition wins, is a radical and potentially dangerous approach, but EMC found a way to make it work. As with other aspects of the market, in this regard EMC simply changed the rules. Ruettgers points out that in the early days of the storage market, a gentleman's agreement—conceived and sanctioned by IBM—made clear that once a customer made a decision, the selling was over. "We never believed that," Ruettgers says. "We believed you ought to continue to contest this thing until the customer finally gave you the order." Like other radical marketers, EMC understood that having a great product wasn't enough. To gain credibility, prospects had to be turned into believers, and if you are trying to move aside a mountain as imposing as IBM, you'd better be prepared to push hard.

Ruettgers recalls a dinner with a customer in Buffalo who talked about his decision to buy EMC. On the day he was going to make his decision, his secretary came in and said the EMC salesman was on the phone again. The customer, leaning toward IBM, had been trying to duck this salesman for a week and a half. His secretary said, "He's in his car in the parking lot. He just wants fifteen minutes, and he'll sit and wait until you are ready." The salesman had driven from Rochester, an hour away, without an appointment. The executive, out of excuses, let the salesman in and eventually chose EMC.

On many occasions, with a sale in the balance, Ruettgers or Egan would visit the customer personally and approve some price adjustment to swing the deal in EMC's favor. Jim Mayer, executive vice president for technology infrastructure at Chase Manhattan Bank, vividly recalls the 1994 meeting in which Chase decided to make EMC its favored storage vendor over Hitachi and IBM. When the EMC sales team came in with its final bid, Egan was with them, a fact that greatly impressed Mayer. But Mayer hesitated; the price was still not where he wanted it to be to commit an untested player like EMC.

When Mayer said he'd need time to consider the deal, Egan picked up his cellular phone, called his son Jack, then the vice president of sales and marketing, back in Hopkinton, and told him he was cutting the price in order to sign the deal on the spot. "That action, that kind of CEO support and flexibility, won EMC the deal hands down," Mayer says. "Both Hitachi and IBM were too bureaucratic to make a deal that way." Despite the fact that Chase is among the five largest banks in the United States and spends $2 billion annually on information technology, neither IBM's nor Hitachi's CEO had dropped in personally, as Egan did.

Let Your Customers Be Your
—— Marketing Department ——

By concentrating its sales and marketing efforts at a few key accounts, like the giant banks, and blanketing those customers with service, support, and even free use of its systems to win them over, EMC went from a virtually unknown entity to a trusted storage vendor in eighteen months. Against all odds, EMC is now the safe bet that IBM once was. And EMC has embraced a most effective radical marketing philosophy: let your customers do the marketing for you.

For Denis O'Leary, Chase Manhattan's former CIO and now executive vice president of national consumer services, EMC is not just a radical marketer but a high-tech marketing model for the next millennium. EMC's penchant for staying close to the customer is at the root of the company's success. "If we have a problem in storage at 3:00 A.M., I know I can get Mike Ruettgers on the phone and he isn't going to ask why I'm calling," O'Leary says. He says Egan and Ruettgers epitomize a new CEO-centric selling model that has started to pervade the high-tech sector, a model that puts CEOs of high-tech companies in constant touch with customers. Both Egan and Ruettgers are true road warriors—jetting off to dinner with a single customer in Washington one night, in Hartford the next, and Chicago the next. "It's not a once-a-year visit, it's how they do business," O'Leary says.

More important, EMC, like the noted bank robber Willie Sutton, knows where the money is and follows it. O'Leary notes that the nation's nine thousand banks spend nearly $20 billion on IT each year, but that the top five—Citibank, Chase Manhattan, NationsBank, Bank America, and First Union—represent nearly 40 percent of that spending alone. All are EMC customers. In fact, all of the top twenty-five banks are EMC customers. "In the new high-tech business model, you don't spent your time on the last five thousand banks," says O'Leary. "You cover the top twenty-five really well, and the rest will come to you."

Unlike the traditional marketing paradigm of Procter & Gamble, EMC understands that it doesn't have to cover the entire world. Rather, it tunes its value proposition to the fact that major industries like banking, communications, and media are consolidating and now the big institutions set the standards. EMC, O'Leary says, has been outstanding at "credentialing" itself and letting CIOs spread the word to each other. "The most effective marketers let their customers do the marketing," O'Leary says. "If you get your footprint onto the future leaders, the bigfoots of the millennium, they'll do your marketing to the rest of the industry for you."

Monny Zerbe, for example, senior vice president for technology operations at Paine Webber and a thirty-year information technology veteran, has become an EMC zealot since he joined Paine Webber in 1995. When he arrived at the financial services firm, the data center was 100 percent IBM, mainframes and storage. Within two years, Zerbe had replaced nearly all of the IBM storage devices with EMC products.

For Zerbe, the decision to switch to EMC was driven by technology, price, and an ability to work with the company on a level he had never experienced with IBM. Over dinner with the EMC marketing representative, for example, Zerbe proposed an unusual purchasing arrangement in which he would agree to buy a certain volume of storage over a six-month period for a specially calculated discount.

EMC not only agreed to the arrangement but enthusiastically incorporated the plan into its relationship with several other customers. Zerbe was able to get a price so aggressive that he didn't feel the need to put the deal out for bids. "IBM would not have made a deal like that," says Zerbe. "They are just not capable of doing that."

—— Loving Your Customers ——

Like most radical marketers, those at EMC found that their first brush with success only fueled their passion. Resting on laurels has no place at EMC. When Egan and his marketing vice president Bob Ano saw the early stages of success unfolding, they simply pushed even harder. When the first few salespeople earned commissions over $1 million, Egan had their W2 statements framed and displayed at a company meeting to get everyone else pumped up. "When someone gets a commission check of seven figures, you want to let people know it is possible," Ano says. "You have to stress success."

All EMC's senior executives keep a "favorite customer" list, a group of customers that become their individual responsibility. Other than dinners and phone calls, each executive has his or her own style of maintaining personal contact. Egan, for example, is a voracious reader, a keen student of people and motivation, and one of his personal trademarks is to send books he likes to customers and business contacts. When Frank McCourt's prize-winning memoir *Angela's Ashes* was published, Egan checked his list of customers, found all those with Irish surnames, and sent each a copy of the book as a gift.

Such personal touches from the chairman of a $3 billion company don't go unnoticed. And even as EMC fortunes have soared, Egan remains tuned in to EMC's customers' businesses on a daily basis. When the stock market plunged in October 1997, Egan called the head of domestic sales and ordered him to call the CIO of every brokerage house that EMC did business with—which was nearly all of them— and offer assistance, directly from the chairman, with any systems problems caused by the tidal wave of electronic orders and transfers that had strained the computer systems of Wall Street.

Egan also learned quickly who his customers listened to. Early on EMC had identified key industry analysts whose opinions shaped the market, and the company aggressively set out to shape those opinions. EMC focused a steady stream of faxes and e-mails at these analysts about EMC products, customers, strategic decisions, and sales. "No one is better at stating their case to me than EMC," says David Vellante, a veteran storage analyst at International Data Corp in Framingham, Massachusetts. "They give you a healthy dose of EMC every chance they get. They are even more aggressive than Oracle, Microsoft, and Sun."

Egan is indeed tenacious, with the zealous nature and commitment to the long term common to radical marketers. Peter Lynch, the stock market guru and former manager for Fidelity's Magellan Fund, was an early and enthusiastic investor in EMC. At his behest, Fidelity owns 8 percent of EMC's stock. Lynch describes Egan as a "billion-kilowatt dam" with "the-power-of-seven persistency."

At Northeastern University's graduation ceremony in 1997, Lynch and Egan were seated next to each other on the stage, both being awarded honorary degrees, when there was a break in the ceremony.

"Egan went down into the audience where the engineering graduates were sitting and started recruiting," Lynch recalls. "He interviewed four graduates and got at least one hire out of that group. He just never stops." Indeed, analysts all have Egan stories. IDC's Vellante remembers speaking about an IBM storage customer at an obscure technology conference. After he concluded, Egan, who'd been sitting inconspicuously in the audience, rushed up to the stage and pumped Vellante for the name of the customer so he could send his salespeople calling.

—— It's the Products, Stupid ——

Most important, Egan grew up in the data-processing world and understands viscerally the oft-ridiculed techno-wizards, the information technology managers who are now EMC's core customers. In his office, amid the usual executive mementos, is a small blue cardboard sign that Egan shows to visitors. IT'S THE PRODUCTS, STUPID! the sign says, and Egan is quick to credit this bit of wisdom for EMC's rise. Information technology professionals understand performance, reliability, service, and failure. For them, "the product" is at the core of their experience.

A radical marketer like Egan, however, also understands their pain: IT, a profession long under siege, is corporate anathema and has found itself in the unenviable position of being the most crucial yet least understood function of modern corporate life. For the past three decades, the pressure has mounted continuously for IT to deliver value, real business value, for the trillions of dollars that have been spent on it. Chief information officers, besieged by angry CEOs seeking return on their investments, buffeted by endless technology shifts and product innovation, and rocked by the evolution of volatile global markets, have struggled mightily to survive the onslaught.

CIOs average less than five years at each job and thus are a cynical and conservative group, not prone to putting their careers on the line for unknown companies with unproven products. Computer vendors have targeted them as customers but rarely have actually listened to their needs. When EMC showed up in the form of a young salesperson, barely out of college, asking a CIO to put this new, radically different product out into his data centers to perform a highly critical business function, most doors closed loudly and swiftly.

From a marketing perspective, therefore, EMC had no choice but to be radical. Ano, whom Egan hired from the foundering high-tech giant Wang Laboratories to head up EMC's marketing efforts in 1989, summed up the situation. "We had no track record on the mainframe disk drive side of the business, and we were coming in with a radically different product to the most conservative guys in the world . . . and we were trying to replace IBM," Ano says. "We had a slight credibility problem."

Ano set up focus groups in four cities, bringing in IT managers and explaining the EMC concept to them. The older participants, the veteran IBM bigots, were skeptical. The younger ones, weaned on personal computers, the Internet, and new technologies, thought the concept more promising. Neither was ready to buy. Presentations to industry analysts like the Gartner Group or International Data Corporation yielded more skepticism. "I felt like a ten-year-old who tells his father he plans to be president of the United States," Ano says. "The dad says, 'Sure you can, son,' in a slightly condescending way. The attitude was, 'It's all very interesting, but no one will buy this.'"

And even Egan and his cohorts grudgingly understood why. EMC had had a checkered and colorful history since Egan, an ex-marine and former Intel executive, and his college roommate and partner Roger Marino (the M in EMC) founded it in 1979.

"No on the Storage, How About —— Some Office Furniture?" ——

When Egan and Marino set up their nascent data storage company, the world of information technology was on the verge of massive change and unparalleled growth. Back then, IBM's control of the computer universe was first being challenged by the radical marketers of the day, the innovative minicomputer companies like Digital Equipment Corporation, Data General, Wang Laboratories, and Prime Computer, which were also raking in huge profits by selling smaller, less expensive, but powerful computers that challenged IBM's supremacy for the first time.

Unlike these pioneering ventures, EMC was a pilot fish, a tiny start-up looking for a product, for a way to feed off the sharks and whales that dominated the new marketplace. In its earliest days, EMC sold other company's products, even office furniture that was being manufactured by an old Intel colleague in California. Egan still uses one of these particleboard desks and laughs when he remembers pulling $400,000 a year out of the furniture business.

EMC's first internally developed products were solid-state memory cards that plugged into the minicomputers that had grown so popular. Companies like Digital and Prime made their own memories and charged monopoly prices for them. EMC could build them cheaper and compete on price as a third-party vendor. Even then, Egan was a radical marketer. Customers, he recalled, worried that EMC's products wouldn't work with their computers. Egan installed what he called a "comfort switch"—a small toggle switch with a light. "We told the customers, 'If you think our product is causing a problem, throw the switch.' Between you and me, all that switch did was turn off the light."

Because the memories were solid-state, they were inherently reliable and highly unlikely to fail. But his switch gave EMC a differentiated product. For Egan, it was a marketing lesson he'd remember: find the customer's objections and eliminate them, whether they are real or imagined.

The big computer makers sponsored annual "user group" meetings in which their customers would gather and view upcoming products, hear presentations, and see what other computer makers were selling in that market. Egan decided that EMC needed more visibility, so he rented space at Prime Computer's annual user meeting in New Orleans. In the exhibit hall, Prime had the largest booth, but Egan rented a big space nearby. He called his son and daughter, asked them to take off a few days from work and school, dress sharply in business clothes purchased for the occasion, and help him man the EMC booth.

"We had this big booth, and we looked crisp, sharp, and professional, and people thought we were some big-deal company," Egan recalls, laughing. "Prime was blindsided. They didn't know much about us, but by the end of that show the whole Prime universe knew who we were."

Prime no longer allowed EMC into its shows, but that one show jump-started the start-up, and it began to grow.

—— Averting Disaster ——

Throughout the 1980s, EMC showed strong, steady growth in the add-on memory business. While in the midst of a public offering in 1986, the company began to build a different kind of storage device using arrays of small, inexpensive disk drives that increased speed and performance. In a price-based selling model, Egan realized he could enhance profits by buying key components of his products rather than assuming the expensive development and manufacturing costs in-house.

He bought fast disk drives from NEC, the Japanese electronics giants, for the heart of a new storage device that EMC was marketing. But the quality control in the NEC clean rooms turned out to be faulty, and dirt particles allowed to get into the drives became tiny time bombs that, in a few days, months, or years, would crash the systems.

It was insidious, and testing did no good. A drive could run satis-factorily for months and then, without warning, it would crash. With 10 to 20 percent of its systems failing, EMC plunged into a maelstrom, trying to find the problem, get new systems to outraged customers, and stay out of bankruptcy all at the same time.

"Roger and I spent day and night on this," Egan says. Every other call was from an angry customer, and Egan and Marino would person-ally go and help take out the old equipment and put in a new system, meanwhile feverishly searching for a second source for the disk drives. "We did everything we could, but it brought us to our knees," he says.

EMC had raised $60 million in its initial public offering (IPO). By the time the disaster was over in 1989, the company had blown through $55 million of its cash, leaving it on the edge of chapter 11. EMC nosedived into five consecutive losing quarters. "I remember an analyst saying it would take seven quarters for us to get back on our feet, and I didn't believe it. But it turned out, he was right," Egan says. "I felt terrible for our customers. These guys had put their jobs on the line for us and trusted us to move away from IBM."

Fortunately for EMC, disk drive crashes, mostly of IBM systems, were not uncommon, and customers in the storage market were more forgiving. Egan and his executives visited every customer, gave away product, soothed damaged relationships, and never lost a customer. Still, EMC was battered, stalled in the market, and reeling from the quality crisis.

In 1988, in a prescient move, Egan realized the company needed professional management. He hired Mike Ruettgers—a Harvard MBA who had high-level operational experience at companies like Raytheon—to come in, put in much-needed controls, and create a solid organization.

Ruettgers engineered a stunning organizational turnaround, overseeing nothing less than the reinvention of EMC as a company. Ruettgers had spent thirteen years in engineering management at Raytheon, at one point overseeing the development of the Patriot missile. He knew how to execute against a plan and how to get "all the wood behind one arrow," says one analyst.

Like other great radical marketers, EMC also relied on luck and timing as well as management savvy to turn its fortunes around. At the time the company was starting to eye the mainframe storage market as a potential sweet spot, Egan met a computer engineer named Moshe Yanai, a former Israeli tank commander, who had a radical idea about computer storage. Yanai and his development team had been working for Nixdorf Computer in nearby Waltham, Massachusetts. Nixdorf had been trying to build an IBM-compatible mainframe but decided to kill the project. Egan offered Yanai and his team a job at EMC.

It was Yanai who conceived of the idea of building a completely new and different type of mainframe storage device, the seed of what later became EMC's Symmetrix product line. And later, it was Yanai, prompted by Ruettgers's vision of the coming marketplace, who engineered the open storage systems. As all radical marketers come to realize, everything flows from great products; marketing, radical or traditional, ultimately comes up empty without product excellence.

"Moshe has made a number of key technical calls which flew in the face of conventional wisdom but were spot-on," says IDC's Vellante. "The company would not be where it is today without Moshe."

—— The Humility of Failure ——

EMC's product set has won rave reviews, but the high-technology landscape is littered with great products that failed because they were not properly marketed. Major players, from Xerox to Apple to Digital Equipment, have provided example after example of great technology rendered irrelevant by an inability to make a strong marketing presence felt.

Information technology is unlike other industries: successes generally come in short bursts, with momentum carrying a company only so far. The moment a company gets comfortable, it is already on the way to obsolescence. In an industry where product cycle times are a good five times faster than in any other industry, EMC knows it could lose its lofty position in twenty-four months. IBM, for example, has retargeted storage as a critical market and feels the hunger of a tiger ousted from its favorite domain.

In fact, this is what keeps Egan awake at night, even as his net worth soars. EMC has invested more than $1 billion in software development and plans to invest another $1 billion by the year 2000, believing that the future of the storage industry is in software, not hardware. Several new and innovative products, such as data management and disaster recovery software, which provides the ability to automatically mirror all data on two physically separated systems simultaneously, have fueled rapid sales growth. But Egan wants more and more ideas from the company's eight hundred engineers.

To that end, EMC built a state-of-the-art customer briefing center at its headquarters and hosts more than one hundred customers every month who meet one on one with the company's top engineers. These customers—the senior technical people whose jobs rely on quality products and support from vendors—present their technology wish lists, which EMC engineers actually incorporate into products. Four of the company's last six major software products were built from customers' suggestions.

Egan loves to tell stories of reluctant customers he brought up to the briefing center and sat down with the company's engineers to share their wish lists for new products. It is from the customers, he believes, that most new ideas will emerge, and as long as EMC facilitates that connection between engineering and the marketplace, the steady stream of new products will flow. "Here an idea goes from point to point, not through six marketing guys," Egan says. "I traced the process through with one of our people, an ex-IBMer, who figured that to do the same thing at IBM, an idea would have had to stop at fourteen places along the way."

Ano tempers Egan's enthusiasm by pointing out the natural animosity between engineering and marketing that is felt in most high-tech firms. It simply isn't possible to incorporate every customer request into product development, he says, and engineers often believe that if they've spoken to one customer, they've talked to them all. So marketing must step in and translate, aggregate, and prioritize what the customers are saying. The truth, Ano says, is that most customers don't really know what they want and radical marketers must continually ask questions, digging deep into understanding a customer's business in order to find out what they require. After that, marketing must translate all this for engineering. "EMC is very good at that," says Ano, who retired from EMC in 1996.

But, he cautions, "you can't presume to have all the answers. Grand plans hardly ever pan out." EMC itself has had several grand plans, most of which have not worked as they were expected to. The business grew much more rapidly than anticipated, so they found what worked, leveraged it, and kept trying new ideas. The curse for most high-tech companies is that when they test their plan and find that the facts don't support it, they simply stop testing. Most high-tech companies don't correct their plans, Ano says; they stick with them and assume the customers are wrong. "A lot of the big computer companies around here stuck to visions that didn't work for far too long," he says.

Complacency and arrogance are rare at EMC because most of its senior executives have worked at other area companies that failed. Currently, the Route 128 high-tech region is humming with high employment and hundreds of entrepreneurial start-ups, but the empty office space formerly occupied by the likes of Digital Equipment, Data General, Wang Labs, Prime Computer, and Apollo Computer provides a stark reminder that once-dominant companies are now defunct, acquired, or shells of their former selves.

EMC is aware that another EMC may lurk out there somewhere, waiting to do to them just what they did to IBM. The company launched a broad and traditional marketing campaign in 1998 with a three-page ad in the *Wall Street Journal* announcing "The EMC Effect," an undisguised nod to the "Intel Inside" campaign that has successfully built Intel's brand recognition.

But EMC spent less than $10 million on the campaign, a tiny drop in the ocean compared to giant industry expenditures in advertising and promotion. Egan and Ruettgers believe that the burgeoning investments in corporate knowledge management, the proliferation of the Internet, and a growing spotlight on enterprise computer systems will push storage revenues ever higher, with EMC rising on a higher tide than its competitors. Its brand will become a respected member of the pantheon of high tech's most noted brands by retaining its most radical marketing methods.

"We always knew our product was good," Ruettgers says. "But the high-tech world is filled with good products. The key here was to have the patience to play this hand out and to listen really closely to what our customers say."

11

Harvard Business School

Radical Marketing to the Highest Degree

*"Our challenge is to be able to expand our
range without diluting the brand. But the
risk on the other side, the risk of sitting still
and doing nothing, is equally as great."*
—Dean Kim Clark

Turning a brand into the gold standard of its industry has usually been the result of superb traditional marketing. Coca-Cola, Walt Disney, Kodak, IBM, and McDonald's are world-class traditional marketers that have used quarry-deep pockets and massive advertising and promotion to achieve envied status for their products as some of the world's most recognized and respected brands.

Occasionally, a brand ascends to similarly lofty heights at the hands of radical marketers, reaching the summit of an industry or market niche without spending heavily on advertising or pouring resources into marketing budgets. Harvard Business School, for example, not only created the market for graduate schools of business, but after ninety years it continues to reign as the most successful and respected brand in its class. Generations of top business leaders and an unending flow of influential management theory have emerged from HBS, shaping not only the American business landscape but the global economy over the past half-century. Like Boston

Beer Company with handcrafted beer and Iams with premium pet food, Harvard defined the MBA and built a lucrative market around it.

Since its founding in 1908, the "B-School" has thrived by adhering to a consistent theme among radical marketers: stay focused on a clear mission, understand and remain close to the core customers, and maintain nothing less than relentless brand control. Like other radical marketers, Harvard Business School has not only created markets but remained focused and flexible enough to respond when these markets shifted.

The B-School is itself an enormously successful nonprofit business entity. Its $820 million endowment is by far the largest of any graduate business school, as is its $200 million operating budget. Its vast, immaculately landscaped sixty-acre campus is the envy of the competition, and most important, its alumni directory is a who's who of global business leaders, chief executives, entrepreneurs, consultants, and venture capitalists.

Recent Harvard Business School graduates earn average starting compensation of more than $145,000 per year, higher than any other business school, and its publishing unit is fast becoming the L. L. Bean of graduate business education, with a mail-order catalog of seventy-five hundred products—from best-selling business books to case studies to a host of interactive, computer-based teaching tools. Its executive education program, a pioneering example of successful brand extension, generates more than $50 million in revenue each year. And its vaunted *Harvard Business Review* remains the bible of management theory and yet another highly successful extension of the brand.

Despite a natural tendency to dismiss Harvard Business School's branding capabilities as nothing more than the power and influence of the name "Harvard" at work, the B-School has, in fact, opted for radical approaches to creating, extending, and protecting its brand throughout its history. There are lessons here for even the most traditional corporations.

—— Staying on Top ——

Indeed, like other great brands, Harvard Business School has been elevated to icon status, a seemingly impenetrable position at the top of the business school heap, impervious to occasional attacks from critics and remarkably facile at recovering from upheaval within its ivy-covered walls. From the outside looking in, it all seems easy; a well-endowed, tradition-rich institution cranking out an endless stream of exceptional graduates who move quickly into the highest, most influential positions in the global economy. Their crimson-lettered sheepskins ensuring top jobs with astronomical salaries, these grateful alumni fuel a self-perpetuating cycle, sending their donations as well as their protégés and children off to the B-School, where they too co-mingle with the best and the brightest. (The admissions office, however, while giving special attention to the children of alumni, will not admit them automatically if they don't measure up; maintaining the integrity of the brand is paramount.)

But like EMC, Providian, Harley-Davidson, and other radical marketers, the B-School engineered its success quite purposefully. Its market position has less to do with serendipity than with a consistent focus by its leaders on sustaining the luster and reputation of the brand. From the earliest days, the B-School's managers focused intensely on the quality of the product and felt a deep, visceral connection to its customer base, from the time the customer entered the school as a student to his or her continuing relationship as an alumnus.

The B-School has succeeded on three fronts that characterize all great brands: (1) the substance and quality of the product itself has stayed consistently at the top of its market, recognized as such even by those who have no connection to it; (2) a community was created and nurtured around the product—a vast network of alumni who support and open doors for each other throughout their lives; and (3) it has earned a pedigree, a cachet that raises the value of not only the product itself but everything related to it.

While some radical marketers rely on a single dynamic individual to drive the brand, like Richard Branson at Virgin Atlantic or Clay Mathile at Iams, Harvard Business School's brand has been shepherded by a succession of innovative deans, most of whom trained either at the B-School itself or at Harvard University. More than brand managers, the deans have served as keepers of the mission, guardians of the trademark, and each has found ways to extend the brand without diluting its value. Like a CEO, each has owned the marketing function and refused to delegate it down into layers of bureaucracy. The brand managers, in fact, are the nearly two hundred faculty members who understand viscerally the culture and ideology of the brand and, on a day-to-day basis in the classroom, attend to the growth of that brand.

Gifted young academics who clamor to get an offer from the B-School are drawn to the brand. "I had two offers, Harvard and Berkeley, and it was a no-brainer," says the Harvard Business School professor Susan Fournier, who specializes in relationship marketing and brand loyalty. "I knew if I came here, I'd learn things that I'd never learn anywhere else. There's an understanding that this is the best brand in the business; I'd call it a classic. It has an incredible heritage, lineage, and has been managed deftly to keep true to the essence of the brand."

—— Tracking the Community ——

Harvard's brand management extends well beyond the classroom. The B-School alumni office keeps close tabs on most of its sixty-six thousand living alumni, tracking their careers, their earning power, their families, and their civic and social contributions. It is a big club, but an elite club whose membership generally ensures access to limitless earning power and major influence in the business community.

In 1997 HBS grads were offered an average of four jobs upon graduation, tops among business schools. A steady program of well-attended dinners and business meetings, sponsored by individual alumni clubs in cities around the world, keep the alumni closely connected to the brand. In recent years, for example, the alumni clubs began sponsoring a series of luncheon/teleconferences in which a B-School professor at the Boston campus delivers a presentation that is beamed, via satellite, to dozens of cities. For $100, an alum can mingle with his or her fellow grads, learn something new, and express a continued commitment to the brand.

Indeed, the alumni directory is a more powerful testament to a brand than a spot on *Fortune* magazine's "most admired companies" list. Check the academic credentials of top management in companies in any industry, and Harvard will be better represented than any other business school. Steve Kaufman, the fifty-six-year-old CEO of Arrow Electronics, a $7.7 billion electronic components supplier in Melville, New York, is an example of the Harvard Business School "product."

Kaufman is a member of the HBS class of 1965. Among his classmates were Louis V. Gerstner Jr., now chairman and CEO of IBM, and Arthur Martinez, chief executive of Sears. Kaufman, a Boston native with an undergraduate degree in engineering from MIT, worked at a small manufacturing company in Michigan, joined Kennecott Copper for a short stint, and then spent eleven years at McKinsey & Company as a consultant. In his steady upward climb, he joined Midland Ross for three years before being recruited to Arrow fifteen years ago. He was named CEO in 1986 and chairman in 1994.

For Kaufman, the B-School has remained a potent force in his life, even more than thirty years after graduation. He has been back to the school eight times for executive education courses and plans to teach there part-time when he retires. He credits the school with shaping his business life and experiences.

The course work itself created a framework for problem solving—a "mental ability to synthesize and focus down" on a problem—that he continues to use on a daily basis, he says. His B-School education taught him to think within this framework, define the problem, and identify the key factors and issues that need to be resolved. Being exposed to more than five hundred cases about companies in every industry gave him a "database" of knowledge that he has applied, as needed, throughout his career.

In addition, the contacts he made with people like Gerstner and Martinez provided a network of information, introduction, and lifelong friendships that continue to have an impact on his professional and personal life. Most ethereal, but real, is the reputation that accompanies a B-School diploma. "Whether it's right or wrong, fair or unfair, the fact is that many people make judgments based on pedigree," Kaufman says. "The Harvard Business School has a terrific pedigree, and when people find out you went there, their opinion of you goes up just a notch. And quite frankly, it is helpful."

From the "Organization Man"
──── to the Entrepreneurial Elite ────

Like a high-powered consulting firm or investment bank, the nearly two hundred deans and faculty members at the school form a dynamic partnership in which information moves quickly and debate and introspection drives out most tendencies toward arrogance. Any Harvard Business School dean or senior faculty member will assure you that success is not a birthright, nor is it inevitable. "You can't have a first-rate MBA program with a second-rate research program or third-rate library," says Linda Doyle, president and CEO of the Harvard Business School Publishing Unit. "The constant theme is that we must be the best, and a whole, integrated process makes the brand very strong."

Like any business, the B-School has ridden the cyclical sine waves of the marketplace, sometimes having to reengineer entire pieces of the curriculum or internal structure. Though the B-School once produced the vaunted "Organization Man," funneling a steady stream of gray-flanneled graduates into big corporations, the school has also been a spawning ground for innovative new pursuits. Such fields as venture capital and management consulting, for example, were essentially created by members of the Harvard Business School faculty. In recent years, the school has poured resources into major initiatives in entrepreneurship and information technology, both areas where there had been a lack of academic presence.

While literally hundreds of alumni like IBM's Gerstner, Martinez at Sears, Kaufman at Arrow Electronics, and Raymond Gilmartin at Merck maintain Harvard's presence in the chief executive's suite, today 40 to 50 percent of HBS graduates eventually start their own businesses or run start-ups. A majority of others head into consulting, investment banking, or venture capital. If there is arrogance at the B-School, it is among the students who, knowing they are the best and the brightest, are impatient to make the big score.

In 1980 the school had one faculty member teaching one course in entrepreneurship. Today, under B-School Dean Kim B. Clark, there are eighteen full-time faculty and another dozen doing research devoted to entrepreneurship. In 1997, 185 B-School graduates took jobs in the San

Francisco Bay Area—nearly as many as from Stanford's Business School, which sits in the heart of that entrepreneurial region. At the same time, Harvard Business School opened a research center in the Silicon Valley to further study the business of the high-technology sector.

Simultaneously, the curriculum, through course structure and case studies, has become much more international, reflecting the globalization of business. New case studies focusing on women-run businesses have been introduced into the curriculum, reflecting yet another trend. As is the case with other radical marketers, the integrity of the product remains high because change is welcomed, not shunned. But the brand endures because change is always run through the same consistent filters.

The B-School's Clark says that ensuring the quality of the brand is a paramount concern; in fact, it is the driving force behind most decision-making. Extending but not diluting the brand is a hallmark of radical marketers. Great radical marketers stay true to the brand. Because of the lure of the Harvard name, for example, the B-School is the target of an endless stream of potentially lucrative proposals, from books and products to customized courses. Most are turned away.

Clark describes a tempting offer from a prestigious consulting firm to use the HBS executive education program to conduct a customized, eight-week educational program for its entry-level people. It was an extensive and extremely lucrative assignment, one that would have generated a recurring revenue stream for years. "If you ran the numbers, it was a gold mine," Clark says. "But it would have been exactly the wrong thing to do."

In the mid-1990s, when the executive education program decided to offer customized programs for individual companies, Clark insisted that the choice to enter that market not be dictated by a desire to fill the school's already bulging coffers. A custom course had to build the faculty's knowledge base and provide opportunities for the faculty to work with company leaders on difficult and challenging problems. An assignment had to result in a broader and deeper understanding of a particular business, or it would be rejected. The consulting firm's proposal was simply a diluted version of the Harvard MBA, a boiling-down of its core curriculum, and Clark didn't hesitate to reject it.

─── Sharing a Center of Gravity ───

Tenure may breed complacency in some academic institutions, but few among the 193 Harvard Business School faculty undervalue the brand they represent. In fact, teaching excellence is the brand's focus. The classroom, says one professor, is the "keel that drives the ship forward." Just as it attracts the cream of the student crop, the B-School has long been a magnet for the top academic minds. But intelligence is not enough. Harvard, with its vaunted "case" method of teaching, long ago established an intractable demand for teaching excellence that permeates the school. In a radical departure for a graduate academic institution, the B-School's professors' priority is teaching excellence before research.

"They put the highest emphasis on the art of teaching of any academic institution I've come in contact with," says Kaufman. "There is a huge emphasis on classroom capability, intellectual brilliance, and the art of teaching. It may be the most important part of what makes the brand so special."

New professors are themselves subject to rigorous teacher training, signing up for teaching seminars the summer before the fall semester and attending more seminars on a weekly basis throughout the school year. Teaching groups are formed and colleagues meet several days each week at 6:00 A.M. to prepare for classes that begin at 9:00. In addition, each new professor is assigned not one but several mentors, one for academics, one for publishing, and one simply to acculturate them in the "Harvard Way."

A culture that has evolved for nearly a century creates a powerful structure for the brand. "Everybody has the same center of gravity," says Susan Fournier. The passion for excellence is pervasive. When a snowstorm is forecast for the Boston area, for example, B-School professors spend the night in their office or in faculty dorm rooms. Missing classes, whether because of inclement weather or consulting assignments, is taboo.

Like other successful radical marketers, the B-School's managers have tended to the brand with worshipful, almost neurotic attention. "The brand is carefully nurtured and protected," says Benson P.

Shapiro, a marketing consultant, 1965 HBS graduate, and faculty member for twenty-seven years, "because people judge us by everything we do, from how we answer the phone to the landscaping on the campus." The school is so obsessive about its brand that it published a twenty-page brochure solely to advise people on the correct use of the Harvard Business School shield.

—— Rethinking the Mix ——

Even when the school has missed a crucial market trend—and it has missed several—it has the firepower and resources to recover quickly and find a leadership position.

Throughout the 1980s, competitors such as Stanford, Wharton, and the Kellogg School at Northwestern took direct aim at Harvard, reexamining curriculum, restructuring entire programs, and grabbing market share, while hammering at Harvard's reputation for innovation and leadership. Indeed, the B-School, because it is such a bellwether for graduate business education, has come under relentless scrutiny, especially in recent years.

For example, in *Business Week*'s biannual rankings of the top business schools, begun in 1988, Harvard has never ranked number one. The business media have written extensively about the school's shortcomings, lobbing broadsides at perceived weaknesses in its curriculum or questioning the management strategies that guide this pillar of American capitalism. Yet even John Byrne, the *Business Week* reporter who tracks the business school market, acknowledges that the surveys and critical essays have had little impact on the brand.

"The brand is so strong, its power can more than offset any number of strategic mistakes," Byrne says. "Ten years of polls showing it is not number one has, by and large, had no corrosive impact on the brand."

Harvard takes the various polls seriously enough; a second-place finish in 1988 and a drop to third in 1990 in *Business Week*'s survey stung and set off an intensive internal reevaluation of the school and a revamping of its strategic direction in 1993. But the B-School has always done its own internal assessment, making a science of evaluating its product.

The quality of its applicant pool, for example, remains unparalleled, with test scores, work experience, and leadership quality as high as it has ever been, according to Clark.

—— Brand Power ——

How powerful is the brand? The school simply can't keep up with the demand. More than 50,000 requests for applications come in annually. Nearly 7,500 students formally applied for the 880 seats available in 1997. The school admits 1,000, and nearly 90 percent come, making it the highest yield in the business school business. Not content to rest on its laurels, the school actually tracks the 10 percent who choose not to attend to find out why. Clark says that a few attend a rival school, but the majority decide to stay in the workforce, usually opting for a better job.

Students who do attend are monitored closely throughout their two-year stay and even after they graduate. Like fine wine, the B-School graduate increases in quality and value as the years pass, with the true measure of each class coming about twenty years after graduation. The class of '95 therefore should be dominating the business world of 2015.

Although it is an institution subject to the bureaucratic paralysis characteristic of academia, the Harvard Business School has managed to move, for the most part, in lockstep with real business practice and current management concerns. In creating the original market, Harvard was not afraid to defy conventional wisdom. Among the radical policies that bespoke its visceral connection to its customers was the B-School's early encouragement of its faculty to consult with companies and stay involved with actual business issues.

Indeed, its closeness to real-world practice has always run against the academic grain. While most graduate-level academics concentrate on highly analytical, narrowly focused research in their respective fields, Harvard took the unique and radical approach of making its business education practical, applicable directly to everyday business rather than to lofty academic scholarship only. Its renowned case studies, produced by faculty members and research associates, track current businesses and the operational or economic crises they face. As a result, the B-School, through much of its existence, has been the subject of ridicule and scorn within the academic community; professors who sought true academic legitimacy went to Chicago or MIT or Stanford, where they could pursue theoretical research.

Harvard nonetheless attracted an all-star lineup of faculty, from Robert McNamara during World War II to Michael Porter, Robert Kaplan, and Rosabeth Moss Kanter in more recent years. The brand, as radical as it was, held tremendous allure for academics who wanted to push the limits of management theory and have their ideas tested in the real world.

In an academic environment where revenue-producing ventures have traditionally been anathema to institutional mores, the B-School has found pioneering ways to extend its brand in everything from book publishing to Internet-based education. Indeed, the B-School's care and feeding of its brand offers lessons that apply directly to a wide range of corporations, many of which are run by its graduates.

—— A Delicate Experiment ——

Though Harvard University, with its vaunted medical and law schools, had a history of establishing professional education as a justifiable academic pursuit, the idea of a graduate-level business school at the turn of the century was indeed a radical concept. Joseph Wharton, a Philadelphia ironmaster, gave $100,000 to the University of Pennsylvania in 1881 to finance the first undergraduate business program. Dartmouth College opened the first graduate business school, the Amos Tuck School, in 1900. But it was Harvard's entry into the market eight years later that put the stamp of legitimacy on what was then considered an outlandish idea.

In an era of robber barons and shopkeepers, the words *business* and *education* were rarely used in the same sentence. Though a spate of independent business schools had sprung up around the country by the turn of the century, universities were loath to consider granting degrees in such unscientific, nonacademic pursuits. Businessmen learned through apprenticeships, on-the-job training, and the blood, sweat, and tears of the workweek. Classrooms might teach the principles of accounting, but business leaders started off by entering through the gates of the factory or corporate office and clawing their way upward.

Nevertheless, Harvard Medical School and Harvard Law School had long since become pillars of their respective academic fields, proving that professional graduate education worked. Under President Charles W. Eliot and the government professor (and later president) A. Lawrence Lowell, the idea of establishing a similar graduate-level program for business had been percolating at Harvard for nearly a decade. Several Harvard professors and students had begun to make a strong case that the study of management and business theory, particularly in the dominant industries such as railroads and textiles, had merit.

An early radical marketer, Lowell understood the controversy he might set off. In 1907 he wrote: "I think we had better do things nobody else does; but we had better do them under the conditions that will be most likely to ensure success."

To that end, the new school would grant Harvard master's degrees in business to those already prepared with liberal arts or science and engineering degrees. The goal would be to train and educate leaders and eschew the specialists. It would not be a school of marketing or finance or operations. It would be a school for general managers.

Even more radical, Lowell envisioned a school where the faculty was closely involved in the practice of business itself. Could you create, Lowell wondered, a school that not only offered a valuable professional education, with faculty that were deeply knowledgeable about real business practices, but at the same time coexisted at Harvard and was academically credible and respectable? The mixing of business and the lofty ideals of academic research and pedagogy was nothing less than heresy at the time. No wonder Lowell called this "the delicate experiment."

Nevertheless, with fifteen faculty members (including instructors from several corporations) and twenty-four full-time students, the Graduate School of Business Administration opened in the fall of 1908. For the first time, a group of students were gathering exclusively for graduate business studies at Harvard.

From the outset, the new school had to fend for itself both financially and academically. At Harvard University, the long-held tradition was that each school was a "tub on its own bottom," and though the Harvard name was no small marketing advantage, the entity had to grow and gain financial stability and acceptance on its own.

—— Staking the Claim ——

What Harvard had, more than any other advantage, was a virgin market being tested by a growing cadre of intellectually strong and spirited professors and students. While most other top universities ignored the graduate business school market for decades, Harvard was able to hone its product, capture market share, and take risks that would otherwise have seemed imprudent.

The MBA would remain a relatively obscure and arcane degree well into the 1950s. But by then, Harvard would claim nearly 25 percent of all the MBAs in the marketplace, giving it brand leverage accorded to such market-share giants as Coca-Cola and General Motors. In 1949, for example, there were only 3,900 MBAs granted from 100 business schools in the entire country, and Harvard accounted for one of every six. In coming decades, the MBA, like the American economy, would skyrocket in value.

In 1997 alone, more than 85,000 MBAs were granted from nearly 1,000 business schools. Harvard granted 882 MBAs in 1997, and though its market share was down to 1 percent, it still turned out the single largest class. By essentially being the first in the market, Harvard carved out market share that has never been equaled. With more than 66,000 living alumni (a figure which includes graduates of several of its flagship executive education programs) and 110 alumni clubs, the Harvard B-School network is more than six times larger than those of most of its prestigious rivals.

This hugely influential network of chief executives, chairmen, and powerful movers and shakers extends the brand on a daily basis in boardrooms and executive suites around the world, reflecting back the success of the institution without costing a dime for advertising and promotion.

Business Week's Byrne used to compile a list of the corporate elite, the leaders of the five hundred largest companies and their educational background. "Harvard always topped the list and always led by a lot," Byrne says. "If you look at their alumni directory, it's incredible. The people who go to Harvard are incredibly bright and diverse."

Of course, like other radical marketers, Harvard built this platform of accomplishment slowly, stumbling here and there, even to this day. Much of Harvard's early history is characterized by the fits and starts of a new institution in search of an identity.

—— Shaping the Product ——

But in the 1920s, under the visionary Dean Wallace B. Donham, an early radical marketer, the B-School coalesced and began to take shape as the icon of American business education. In 1925, with a $5 million gift from the banker George F. Baker, Donham began building the vast neo-Gothic B-School campus on a tract of Boston marshland, directly across the Charles River from Cambridge and the main Harvard campus. It was hubris perhaps, or a great act of faith in the brand. Today, with twenty-nine buildings, on sixty acres, its own library, dining halls, athletic facilities, dormitories, and chapel, the B-School boasts the most dynamic business school campus in the world, bigger than many entire universities, and no small selling point when recruiting top students.

Donham also inaugurated the vaunted "case" method of teaching, which he based on his own law school education. Dissatisfied with the dry, lecture-style teaching that was prevalent in the B-School, Donham's shift to an interactive verbal wrangling among students and faculty over specific business problems from real companies was a radical departure that became a hallmark of the B-School brand. Donham, ever the radical marketer, began effectively extending the brand with the publication of the *Harvard Business Review* in 1922.

During World War II, the B-School shut down operations in order to become a training center for production management and supply logistics for the military. With HBS training, the crucial statistical control of military aircraft, for example, was handled with such efficiency that it played a major role in the outcome of the air war against Germany.

Even while focusing on the war effort, however, radical marketers within the B-School began designing ways to further extend the brand by creating the early beginnings of the school's executive education program, a resourceful way to fill increasing demand and simultaneously increase the alumni network. The first such effort, in 1943, brought seventy businessmen, including a dance studio manager and an artist, to Harvard to learn management skills for the war effort.

—— The Class the Dollars Fell On ——

Despite all that the B-School had accomplished since its founding, it was only after the war that the school burst onto the scene as an international brand. Returning to the B-School campus were a legion of young war veterans, seasoned leaders at age twenty-five who'd literally saved the world and were now eager to try their skills on the new battlefield—the American marketplace. Tough-minded, confident, and battle-tested, this new generation of business school graduates would transform the MBA from an obscure, undervalued degree into a passkey to prosperity and success.

In 1986 the author Laurence Shames wrote *The Big Time,* a book about the B-School's remarkable class of 1949. In it Shames wrote:

> Professional management, at the time, was a subject, which to the average joe, was only slightly less abstruse than quantum physics, but which seemed a good deal more important. An MBA guaranteed penetration into a body of almost sacred knowledge, and it did so at a historical moment when the prestige, as well as the commodity value, of management skill had never been higher. Faith arrives in a flash; skepticism takes time, and in 1949 faith in modern rational management— *American* management—was new, axiomatic, and utterly untarnished.

Thus, as the postwar boom began to sweep across the United States, Harvard Business School suddenly held an unparalleled allure. Harvard, no pun intended, was in a class by itself. The veterans who entered in the fall of 1947 made up a group so filled with talent that it would eventually send dozens of its members to the executive suites of major corporations like Xerox, Johnson & Johnson, Capital Cities, and Bloomingdale's. The class of '49, during its twenty-fifth reunion in 1974, was dubbed "The Class the Dollars Fell On" by *Fortune* magazine because of the remarkable accumulated wealth and power of the group.

It was only the beginning.

In subsequent decades, the B-School's power and influence grew with the fierceness of a strong bull market. Business became the most dynamic force in society, driving change, spurring development, reshaping the world. A measurable percentage of the movers and shakers leading business had come from the B-School. While most of its current competitors were only just entering the business school market, Harvard had forged a competitive advantage that remains insurmountable. In the process, the B-School achieved a marketer's nirvana and became *the* brand, the name that defined the market and was mentioned in the same reverential tones as Rolex watches and Mercedes-Benz automobiles.

The advantage was the product, and the product was an HBS graduate. The alumni made the brand known in every corner of the globe. According to Kim Clark, half of Harvard University's sixty thousand alumni living outside the United States are graduates of the B-School. Harvard B-School and its faculty served as a model for and helped create more than a dozen foreign business schools, such as Insead in France.

Not surprisingly, Harvard tracks its alumni carefully: what jobs they take, how long they stay at each position, what contributions they make both in business and in society. Clark acknowledges the various surveys and ratings of business schools, but for the B-School, "the alumni are the measure of the school."

Leveraging the Brand:
—— Executive Education ——

Radical marketers excel at creating product line extensions without losing brand integrity. For Harvard Business School, its executive education program has been the consummate brand extension— leveraging a complementary product line perfectly, generating growing revenue, adding luster to the brand without diluting it. Since the executive education program began in the 1940s with the pioneering Advanced Management Program, Harvard has leveraged its strong reputation to lure experienced, senior-level business leaders back to campus to learn new business practices for a hefty fee. The AMP today, a revamped, shorter program than the original (now nine weeks rather than thirteen), costs $40,500 in tuition, and the 160 seats are filled for every spring and fall session.

Nondegree executive education in the United States has grown into a $4 billion business, with the strong global economy of the mid-1990s fueling demand. Business schools, which once dominated the market, now control just 25 percent, with internal corporate training units, private training companies, and consultants making up the rest.

The dramatic changes in the market provided a stern test for the HBS brand. The B-School lost market share by ignoring obvious market trends and opportunities in executive education in recent years. While CEOs made it clear, for example, that they didn't have thirteen weeks to spare for going back to school, Harvard stubbornly stuck to its long program while competitors began luring CEOs with four-week offerings. Indeed, whether because of intellectual snobbery or a misguided effort to protect academic integrity, the B-School came under fire in the early 1990s for not aggressively marketing its executive education programs.

When the market for customized courses—specific programs designed for individual companies—began to flourish a decade ago, for example, Harvard looked the other way, worrying that such commercial work might compromise the integrity of the school. While the faculty, most of whom had flourishing consulting businesses, debated the merits of customized courses, rival business schools, such as Wharton, Northwestern, and Duke, were able to grab market share with aggressive marketing of their programs. "Harvard could have had the whole market to itself," states Byrne of *Business Week*.

Like other radical marketers, however, the B-School had a different agenda. Economics was not the determining factor, an ironic twist for a business school. In this case, the mission of the school, and thus the brand itself, was the barometer. If a program didn't enhance the mission, it was not adopted. The B-School refused to compromise quality for quantity; courses would be taught by B-School faculty, not hired guns from outside the campus. Courses had to bring executives to the Boston campus because the lure and power of the brand lay in the direct interaction between the faculty and the students. Pure distance learning, therefore, was out.

—— Stretching the Limits of the Brand ——

Knowing when to be a pioneer and knowing when to let others take the arrows in the back requires wisdom drawn from decades in business. When Clark became dean in 1995, the growth of the MBA program was a priority item. There were so many outstanding candidates unable to get in that discussions got under way about expanding the number of students admitted to the MBA program, from 850 to perhaps 1,200. Clark eventually rejected that idea and turned instead to W. Earl Sasser, an HBS management professor and senior associate dean of executive education, to expand executive education.

Sasser brought in McKinsey & Company, the consulting firm, which laid out a portrait of the marketplace. Clearly, the school's general management courses, long the backbone of the program, were no longer in the sweet spot of the market. Growth was in customized courses and in shorter, more directed programs that provided measurable payback to a company.

New programs have been offered. One, called "The General Manager," brings newly minted general managers to the campus for three weeks, sends them back to their business units with specific problems to work on for two months, and then brings them back to Harvard for three more weeks to review the work experience and focus on implementing change.

Intent on enhancing the international flavor of executive education, the school introduced the "Program for Global Leadership" in 1998. Similar in structure to "The General Manager," the new course has students spending three weeks of study in Singapore, then two months back at their respective offices—where they work in virtual teams for two months—and it concludes with a three-week segment at the B-School campus.

The B-School has quietly forged ahead into the customized course market with clients like Compaq Computer, Novartis, and the World Bank. Sasser points out that the rules for customized courses are stringent. The B-School won't take on an assignment without CEO commitment and senior-level executive participation on the part of the client. The course needs to be global in nature and has to offer an opportunity for the faculty to develop course material and do research. As pointed out earlier, the school doesn't hesitate to turn away work, even extremely lucrative work, if these criteria aren't met.

The B-School is limiting its customized work to fifteen clients at a given time. Executive education accounted for $50 million in revenues for the B-School in 1997, up 40 percent in just two years. But Sasser still spends much of his time worrying about the brand.

"I ask myself every day, 'Have we reached the limit?'" Sasser says. "Every day I think about the brand, about the dilution of the brand, who the client is, what they are asking for, what other institutions are involved as partners on a given project. I don't want to appear arrogant when we turn people down. But we have to think about how much faculty time we can devote to this."

—— The Business of Business Schools ——

Radical marketers constantly rethink the marketing mix and celebrate uncommon sense. In fact, visionary leaders at Harvard, like the former dean John H. McArthur, have understood intuitively that access to the B-School was limited, even on a campus as spacious as Harvard's. There were just so many seats in so many classrooms. With the regular MBA program schedule and the demands of executive education and active consulting careers, the faculty was pushed to its limits.

And yet the demand for the B-School brand was insatiable. McArthur believed the school could extend its reach far beyond the campus borders through its publishing activities and the advent of a host of new technologies, from video to interactive CD-ROM to the Internet. There was a huge audience that, with neither the time nor the qualifications to get accepted to the B-School, still wanted access to its knowledge base. With natural line extensions, the B-School had been in the publishing business since 1922 with the vaunted *Harvard Business Review*. It had built lucrative businesses with both *HBR* reprints and sales of the thousands of case studies written and published by its faculty. In the mid-1980s, realizing that it was missing an obvious opportunity in not publishing the tomes of its widely respected faculty and other sought-after professionals and academics, the B-School founded its own book publishing arm.

Surprisingly, in this bastion of management wisdom, the publishing activities were highly disorganized and inefficiently run and yet were still generating $40 million in revenue by 1992. Businesses were scattered in fifteen locations around the campus, and McArthur grew frustrated. In 1992 he consolidated all these varied enterprises into one new business unit, Harvard Business School Publishing, and looked for strong growth within the unit. Despite several well-publicized political and organizational disputes, the publishing unit has coalesced into a dynamic and profitable business, affixing the B-School label on more than seventy-five hundred products and extending the brand into previously untapped market opportunities. New technologies are allowing faculty to replicate and disseminate themselves and their work in unprecedented ways.

Intent on transforming the way business is studied in the global market, Harvard now leverages its publishing activities as a substitute for putting students in seats. Its growing set of products, which includes the *HBR,* book publishing, case study reprints, video and interactive multimedia courseware, newsletters, and on-line reference materials for scholars, spreads the business gospel according to Harvard. The HBS Publishing Website has become a conduit for academics around the world to get instant access to HBS products.

"This is an extension of the school's mission," says Linda Doyle, president and chief executive of the unit, "to improve the practice of management. Since we can't bring everyone to the campus, we can extend the brand to the places where people work or to their homes."

The plans are ambitious. The school produced a three-part, fifteen-hour, interactive, CD-ROM-based course, for example, called "The Interactive Manager." The course, designed by the Harvard B-School professor Linda Hill, contains segments such as "Managing Change," "Leadership," and "Managing the Problem Performer." Built around the same case study method used in the B-School classroom, the interactive program contains video segments and audio- and text-based simulated encounters with employees. Designed to allow managers to self-direct their training experience at their own pace, the program contains advice from Professor Hill as to how to handle specific management dilemmas and *HBR* articles for follow-up reading. Companies like AT&T, Fidelity, Morgan Stanley Dean Witter, IBM, and Chase Manhattan Bank helped develop the material and have purchased the program for their internal management training programs.

In an attempt to stay abreast of fast-changing technology trends, such courses are already being offered via Intranets—private corporate networks on the internet that will spread access even faster and further. Doyle acknowledges that new technology will render past investments obsolete. "If anyone is going to make them obsolete, I want it to be us," she says. Still, she points out, the bulk of the unit's revenues emanate from its oldest businesses, the *HBR* and case studies.

The unit sells more than six million case studies each year, so dominating that market that Harvard's case studies have become the de facto standard for nearly all graduate-level business training that employs the case method. More than twenty-five hundred case studies have been digitally scanned and are now available on the HBS publishing unit's Website.

The *Harvard Business Review,* despite its well-publicized internal struggles and editorial defections in the early 1990s, has surged back with hardly a trace of tarnish on its world-class image, and there is still no viable competitor on the horizon. Its circulation and renewal rates are higher than ever, Doyle says, and it continues to serve as a champion for pushing the envelope of management theory. In a powerful way, the *HBR* is an educational program for the school rather than simply a publication. "Part of our mission is to take the most important ideas on the most important issues facing leaders and communicate them—be a publisher and editor in the marketplace of ideas," says Clark.

To that end, the book publishing unit has provided yet another powerful brand extension. Rather than continue to allow its star-studded faculty to be published elsewhere, the B-School decided to carry its own publishing banner. Now star faculty like Michael Porter and John Kotter are published by HBS Publishing, which competed with other publishing houses for their books. Like all true radical marketers, the publishing unit has leveraged its power and influence well, taking in non-Harvard authors, such as Gary Hamel and C. K. Prahalad, Charles Handy and Benjamin Zander, and teaming up to produce best-sellers.

Doyle says the book publishing unit, like other parts of HBS Publishing, is driven by factors other than economic incentives. Maintaining quality and integrity means publishing works with clearly limited audiences in order to improve and enhance the practice of management. And it means turning down the regular stream of inquiries for books that seek the Harvard label and offer best-selling potential. "We wouldn't touch *Dilbert*," Doyle says.

—— Avoiding the Slide into Mediocrity ——

Harvard Business School's leaders are acutely aware of the potential of technology-driven extensions of the brand. As electronic versions of courseware become more and more powerful and interactive, the ability to deliver Harvard Business School digitally will test the brand. The tension between wanting to extend the brand and diluting the brand remains a paramount concern. The B-School mantra is that it is a short slide from good to mediocre.

The publishing unit's revenues, in fact, are critical to the operation of the B-School, essentially making the difference between the school running at a profit rather than a loss, according to Doyle. (The school receives a huge endowment, which, despite its size, covers only 25 percent of its operating expenses, and therefore the school must still support itself as a profitable business.)

Dean Clark insists that reading *HBR* articles and using interactive multimedia courseware is still no substitute for attending Harvard. The campus and classroom experience remains unique, Clark says, and being part of the community, face-to-face with faculty, is unlikely to be replaced anytime soon by a virtual experience. Indeed, Clark claims there is evidence that the electronic medium tends to increase a student's desire for face-to-face engagement at the campus.

Still, the mystique associated with the HBS brand is at risk when the label is affixed to thousands of products and offered at the click of the mouse via the Internet. The integrity of the brand is at stake, and the B-School understands that. Faculty committees oversee all B-School ventures and provide the checks and balances for any questionable calls.

"Our challenge is to be able to expand our range without diluting the brand," Clark says. "But the risk on the other side, the risk of sitting still and doing nothing, is equally as great."

12

Boston Beer Company

Brewing Up a Marketing Success

*"Change is good, but you don't want
to lose what you really are."*
—*Jim Koch*

Success, perhaps more than any other single factor, can produce the ultimate challenge for radical marketers. A small but earnest entrant into a market, fueled by radical marketing, can fly fast and hard under the radar screen of its giant competitors and carve out a profitable niche before those bigger players ever take notice. The true test of a radical marketer's prowess may, in fact, come when it awakens the bear. In 1996 Jim Koch came face to face with the biggest bear.

Koch (pronounced "Cook") is the founder and CEO of Boston Beer Company, brewer of Samuel Adams Boston Lager and more than fifteen other "craft" brews. Craft or specialty beer refers to the all-malt beers brewed in small batches by hundreds of independent microbrewers. Koch is a sixth-generation brewer, Harvard Business School graduate, former manufacturing consultant, and quintessential radical marketer.

Since 1984 Koch has built a fast-growing, highly profitable company and carved out a much-envied niche. In pioneering the craft beer market, Koch and Sam Adams did nothing less than change the American beer landscape, if not in volume, then certainly in attitude. Samuel Adams, with its consistently high quality, premium price, smooth, rich taste, and national presence, gave handcrafted beer credibility and thus a place at the bar. Its success kicked off a frenzy of new beer offerings and a cornucopia of new flavors and seasonal brews. Handcrafted beer is now a $3 billion market, according to the Institute for Brewing Studies in Boulder, Colorado.

In his original business plan, Koch estimated that sales of five thousand barrels of beer annually would generate a profit and that it would take three to five years to achieve that volume. Boston Beer surpassed that mark in eight months.

Although Koch himself quite vocally disdains the concept of marketing—preferring to preach the gospel of face-to-face selling—Boston Beer nonetheless offers a raft of marketing lessons, many of which have since been adopted by even the biggest and most traditional of its competitors. Indeed, Sam Adams received the highest compliment possible for a radical marketer: the focused attention of the market leaders.

In the craft beer market, the $210 million Boston Beer Company is the dominant player, brewing more barrels annually than the next five competitors combined. Though Koch was not the first to commercialize a craft beer, he was the best, combining a fierce belief in his product, an inability to be scared off by the daunting odds against success, and a string of innovative selling concepts fueled mostly by his lack of financial resources.

Like other radical marketers, Koch owns the marketing function himself, has kept Boston Beer's marketing function small and flat, and has made face-to-face customer contact a staple of his company's marketing efforts. If, at the outset, his task seemed impossible, Koch viewed it as a business opportunity and employed innovative strategies to build a market and a loyal community.

Rather than build his own breweries and pour his minimal resources into bricks and mortar, for example, Koch rented space in existing breweries, such as Pittsburgh Brewing Company (makers of Iron City Beer) in Pittsburgh, where he could use his own ingredients and beer recipes but leverage the excess capacity of these breweries to create higher profits. This kind of "contract" brewing was unheard of among craft brewers, who believed that the dinner had to be cooked in one's own kitchen to be genuine.

Early on, Koch rented warehouse space in an old defunct Boston brewery, where he set up a small portion of his production. He later refurbished the brewery, set up research and development offices for new products, and started running tours for curious customers. The location, more useful for marketing than volume production, served to give the impression of Sam Adams as an old-fashioned Boston brew. But Koch understood intuitively that to get his product out in volume in front of potential customers, he could not get hung up on where the beer was brewed. If it was his recipe and his ingredients, and high quality was maintained, he could sell it proudly.

In little more than a decade, he built a ubiquitous brand with minimal advertising and promotion, a feat that would have taken larger competitors decades and hundreds of millions of marketing dollars to achieve. Quickly outgrowing Koch's initial dream of creating a successful local Boston beer, Samuel Adams is now a popular brand in all fifty states and overseas; a beer lover can walk into a bar almost anywhere and order a "Sam" and be presented with a bottle or glass of the rich, amber-colored lager. It is a brand-builder's dream come true.

In the U.S. beer market, however, where 192 million barrels were sold in 1997, craft beers make up a minuscule 6 percent of the market. Boston Beer's 1.25 million barrels—compared to Anheuser-Busch's 96 million barrels—gave it under 1 percent of the $50 billion market. In the craft beer market Boston Beer is the proverbial big fish in a small pond.

—— Rousing the Bear ——

Nevertheless, Boston Beer's success caught the attention of the $11 billion Anheuser-Busch in St. Louis and stirred up the kind of passion there usually reserved for its bigger competitors. In the domestic beer market, where growth had gone flatter than stale ale, Anheuser-Busch couldn't help but notice the craft beer segment, which was enjoying annual growth rates of 25 to 30 percent over the previous decade. And very visibly waving the craft brew flag at the top of the heap was Koch, an aggressive (some say arrogant) advocate for "better" beer—better, that is, than Budweiser.

Anheuser-Busch currently owns 45 percent of the U.S. beer market and has a publicly stated goal of achieving 60 percent of that market within the next decade. Hundreds of competitors were not able to survive the Anheuser-Busch juggernaut. According to Tom Dalldorf, publisher of the *Celebrator Beer News,* a popular industry publication, there were three thousand beer brewers in the United States at the turn of the century, a figure that fell to under fifty after giants like Anheuser-Busch and Miller "homogenized the American beer culture."

By the 1970s, hundreds of regional beers with loyal local followings had disappeared or been subsumed by one of the bigger players. The domestic "beer wars" evolved into a three-way battle between A-B, Philip Morris's Miller Brewing Company, and Coors. A beer lover's choice was simple: yellow beer or yellow beer light. Using brilliant traditional marketing fueled by expensive power advertising campaigns, Budweiser attained brand recognition on a par with the likes of Coca-Cola and Kodak. By the late 1970s and early 1980s, the big three, led by Budweiser, controlled the beer market. Its hallmark ad campaign from the 1960s—"When you say Bud, you've said it all"—could not have been more accurate.

But Budweiser in recent years had fallen prey to declining sales—dropping steadily for six straight years—and by 1997 was off 20 percent from its peak years. A-B executives spent heavily on advertising, with a signature series of Budweiser ads featuring frogs and other amphibians, in hopes of recouping market share. And they couldn't help but notice the fast growth in the craft beer segment.

Despite the David and Goliath scenario, A-B decided to take aim at the craft beer market, and Boston Beer in particular. Beer industry pundits believed A-B's motivation was not only to storm into this marketplace itself but to put further pressure on the remaining regional breweries, which depended heavily on contract brewing revenues. August Busch IV, the company's thirty-four-year-old heir apparent and vice president of brand management, told *Brandweek* magazine in April 1996 that in their quality surveys they found many consumers rating Sam Adams number one. Further, Busch said he felt that the microbrews, by creating false impressions about where the beer was brewed and by whom, had inflicted damage on the Budweiser brand. The bear was awake and angry.

"Our quality perception has been damaged by some of the smaller microbrewers," Busch said. "A very, very smart gentleman and very good marketer, Jim Koch, will go out and say small is good, that small, handcrafted batches are of better quality. . . . On premise, that is a very good conversation-generating platform that can damage us. We feel that it is the obligation of a brewer that will use crafty marketing along those lines to disclose the origin or the brewer of their products."

A-B cranked up its powerful public relations machinery and gained widespread media coverage by charging that the craft brewers, and Boston Beer Company in particular, were misleading consumers by contract-brewing their products in the facilities of regional beermakers like Stroh's. A segment on NBC's *Dateline* newsmagazine, promoted and aired during the 1996 World Series, was particularly damaging.

The *Dateline* reporter pointed out that Boston Beer Company marketed Samuel Adams as a beer "handcrafted in single batches" and brewed by Boston Beer Company in Boston, Massachusetts. The label on the bottle even invites the consumer to visit the small, traditional brewery in Boston.

"So we did," the reporter continued, "and found a small, brick building, a photo tribute to previous generations of Koch brewers, and just as you see in Sam Adams commercials, the small copper kettles and equipment used to brew the beers. But there's one small problem with this picture: At least 95 percent of all Sam Adams beer isn't brewed here . . . or anywhere even near Boston."

He went on to point out that the beer is contracted out to breweries in Pennsylvania, New York, and other locations. "That's right," he stated. "The Sam Adams you buy in the store was likely brewed in the same place as more humble and less expensive brands like Old Milwaukee, Stroh's, or Little Kings."

Koch, who had never from the outset of the company hidden the fact that Sam Adams was contract brewed, appeared on camera to state his case, but he appeared edgy and defensive, and from a public relations perspective, the appearance was a disaster. An A-B spokeswoman, appearing demure and well-reasoned, suggested that all the company wanted was truth in advertising and labeling. Despite the one-sided nature of the journalistically dubious segment, the broadcast inflicted tremendous damage, not just on Sam Adams but on the entire craft beer market. Craft beer sales, as well as Boston Beer's stock price, dropped significantly.

—— After the Bear ——

It was a costly lesson for a radical marketer. Koch had deftly generated remarkable media coverage from the earliest days of Boston Beer Company, using the press to create visibility that he could not afford to buy. Having been a media darling for so long, Koch was blindsided by the *Dateline* experience. He believes, in hindsight, that he made a tactical error in agreeing to appear on camera in the piece, claiming he underestimated the might of Anheuser-Busch's public relations capabilities.

Though no one believes the *Dateline* segment alone slowed down the entire market, it was a factor. In 1997, overcrowded with hundreds of products and the resurgence of competition from the imported beers, the craft beer market slowed to a crawl, and Jim Koch, having taken the company public in 1995, faced his toughest challenge. With his stock price mired below the IPO price and revenue growth disappearing, he had to call upon all his marketing guile to respond.

In true radical marketing fashion, Koch declined to fight on his competitor's terms. Though galled by the *Dateline* experience, he immediately saw the futility of getting into a pitched legal or media battle with a behemoth like Anheuser-Busch. Since Boston Beer Company is not yet fifteen years old, it isn't difficult for Koch and his sales and marketing people to remember their roots. Samuel Adams won because of a relentless mission to get the beer in front of consumers through aggressive grassroots selling.

Though the playing field has changed dramatically, Koch believes the path to the future is through the radical marketing past: hire only passionate missionaries to sell the beer, constantly revisit and rethink the marketing mix, concentrate on more and more focused and face-to-face selling, now aided by increased media spending but still aimed at finding the next beer drinker to join the community of Sam Adams loyalists. With just under 1 percent of the domestic beer market, Sam Adams has legions left to win over.

"Change is good, but you don't want to lose what you really are," Koch says. "It's true of other great brands: there is a core to who they really are that is immutable. If a beer drinker is comfortable with that core, he wants to know that it is not going to change, that Sam Adams isn't suddenly going to become hip and trendy or have reptiles and amphibians as spokespeople."

For Koch, who has turned away numerous offers to sell out, the challenge is to find revenue growth in an increasingly competitive market. Like other radical marketers, his visceral connection to his customer base gives him a deep understanding of where the road may be winding. Rather than retreating to a boardroom to lay out a strategic five-year plan, Koch returned to the roots of his success: the bars, restaurants, and liquor stores to talk with and observe his customers.

Though he has opted to spend more than $15 million on television advertising in select markets—a radical change for Boston Beer Company—his biggest expense is in putting more well-trained bodies on the street. He more than doubled his sales force in less than three years, adding more aggressive young salespeople to work sixteen-hour days and get close to the customers. Boston Beer Company has more than 175 salespeople in the field, the third-largest sales force in the entire beer industry, not far behind Miller Brewing, and far out of proportion for a company of its size.

"Essentially," Koch explains, "we've always believed we had a better beer, so the most important thing is to get it in front of consumers, get it into bars, restaurants, and stores in a visible way so that people would try it and be reminded of it."

Koch, whose aggressive business approach clearly rubbed many in the craft beer world the wrong way, found himself in an unenviable squeeze: reviled by the giants ahead of him and resented by many in the segment he dominated. If the *Dateline* episode served any positive purpose, it galvanized most of the specialty brewers behind Boston Beer. After the broadcast, editorial writers in beverage industry publications reminded craft brewers who the real "enemy" was, while praising Koch's contributions to the spread of better beer.

It also helped remind Koch that despite the company's 35 percent annual growth rate for thirteen years, fortunes can shift quickly and dramatically. The best radical marketers find ways to connect back to their past while not losing sight of the future.

"The obvious temptation is to say, 'We're there, now we need to look like the big guys, to do the things the big guys do,'" Koch says. "To me, that is a death strategy because they will always be able to be who they are better than we can be who they are.

"There's a tendency to overreact to the inevitable rhythms of what is a fairly organic relationship. People have grown up with Sam Adams, and some would say this is a whole new phase, so you have to abandon what made you successful and strike out in new directions. I don't see that. I believe, in fact, that we have to continue to do the things that made us successful."

To understand Koch's success, it is necessary to return to the beginning and track the evolution of the Boston Beer selling model. For Koch, the prescription for success was nothing less than a primer in radical marketing.

Brew What You Love and
—— the Money Will Follow ——

When Koch founded Boston Beer Company in 1984, he was a successful thirty-four-year-old manufacturing consultant earning $250,000 a year with the prestigious Boston Consulting Group. But like most radical marketers, Koch not only saw a business opportunity, he felt a calling. If he had chosen to stay in consulting, he would have represented the first generation in his family in 150 years to forgo a career as a brewer.

Koch, who attended Harvard as an undergraduate and later earned graduate degrees in business and law from Harvard as well, initially saw no future in brewing. But when the craft beer market began to blossom on the West Coast in the late 1970s and early 1980s, Koch became intrigued. He read with fascination about Fritz Maytag, an heir to the Maytag appliance fortune, who had purchased the Anchor Brewing Company in 1965 in San Francisco; after re-creating the steam-brewing tradition, he had reintroduced the practice of all-malt brewing in the Bay Area.

As the domination of the domestic beer market by Anheuser-Busch, Miller, and Coors solidified in the late 1970s, a small but determined legion of beer lovers had sprung up in California, Oregon, and Colorado and begun to brew their own mixtures of rich, flavorful, microbrewed beers. In 1977 the first microbrewery opened in Sonoma, California, and two years later federal legislation was passed allowing beer to be brewed at home, which set off a rush of interest in creating flavorful and innovative new beers. In 1982 another new law allowed the creation of "brewpubs"—restaurants that made and sold their own beer. A new industry was born.

In Boston, far from the heart of this brewing revolution, Koch felt the reverberations. Coming from an Ohio family steeped in brewing tradition, Koch had long been frustrated by the rush to uniformity of the U.S. beer market. His father and grandfather had both been brewmasters at small regional breweries near Cincinnati in the days before a few giant breweries consumed the industry. In creating a mass-produced beer aimed at the lowest common denominator, the giant brewers ignored the beer drinkers who wanted a more flavorful and interesting beer. Those folks had long paid a premium for imported beer, but to Koch, they were getting little for their money: a negligible amount of increased flavor and beer that was not fresh.

Like other radical marketers, Koch saw the opportunity, a hole in the market that he could fill with a fresh and flavorful premium beer. Koch likes to recollect how he wandered up into the attic of his father's home and, next to a stack of old *Road & Track* magazines, discovered a box of old family beer recipes that his father had saved from his great-great-grandfather's days in the business. One in particular caught his attention. It was a recipe his father had brewed in the 1960s using special German hops.

Intrigued, Koch brewed up a batch of the beer in the kitchen of his Newton, Massachusetts, home, steaming off the wallpaper as the beer boiled on the stove. The dark, rich flavor was striking. He knew immediately that he had a winner . . . if he could get the product into the market. Building a company to sell the beverage, however, was a different matter. His Harvard Business School background had taught him a simple but crucial lesson: a company could enter an existing market only if it offered a product that was either cheaper or better. Without one or the other, you were irrelevant. His own family, starting with his great-great-grandfather who owned a brewery in St. Louis, proved the point. Collectively, they'd owned thirteen breweries, and all had failed.

Koch, who had been an Outward Bound instructor for three years in the early 1970s, knew about survival techniques. The first lesson was obvious: don't go after the big boys like Budweiser or Miller. Instead, he believed he could target the import market and find Heineken or Beck's customers willing to try a better domestic beer, even if it was more expensive.

A common thread among radical marketers is the ability to see a market with crystal clarity while outside observers do not. Indeed, radical marketers tend to view the impossible as an opportunity. Koch understood immediately that he had a product so much better than what people were used to that it was capable, on its own, of creating customers and demand. Unlike the big brewers, he didn't need to compromise the product to get to a mass market. Instead, he could focus on that section of the market, the consumers who wanted a better glass of beer, and sell. Koch knew there was a market; he just didn't know how big that market was.

While still on the consulting firm's payroll, Koch quietly launched his new company. He put up $100,000 of his own money and raised another $140,000 from friends and relatives. With several as yet unnamed bottles of the brew stuffed into his briefcase alongside a few icepacks, Koch nervously strode into a neighborhood bar and began talking up his new beer to the man behind the counter. It turned out that the fellow was the bar back (someone who stacks glasses and fills the shelves), and he spoke no English. "He looked at me as if I had two heads," Koch recalled.

The manager came over, and Koch went into his spiel yet again. He pressed for the manager to taste the beer. After sniffing the brew and swallowing a few mouthfuls, the manager nodded and ordered twenty-five cases. Boston Beer Company was suddenly in business. For Koch, it was a cathartic moment, a dramatic illustration of the power of one-to-one selling. Marketing was a sham, he thought. All the fancy ad campaigns, demographic studies, and promotional efforts were useless if you weren't willing to meet your customer face to face and sell your product.

Koch wrote in *Inc.* magazine years later:

> When I got home that evening, the vision in my head was that it's really selling that drives most businesses: the direct interface between the product and the customer, the crucial feedback loop. And if more CEOs had to go out and sell their products, day in and day out, they'd pay more attention to what they are making. When you are out there selling, face-to-face with your customer, there's no place to hide.

A determined iconoclast, Koch dispels traditional marketing methods as "bullshit." Once, speaking at an entrepreneurs' dinner at the Library of Congress in Washington, Koch made the comparison: "sales is to marketing what sex is to masturbation. Marketing you can do all by yourself in a dark room. Sales involves communication with other people, and there's a real result to it." Rather than study marketing textbooks, Koch prefers to search through *The Odyssey* or T. S. Eliot's poems for consumer insights. He likes to recall that he took only one first-year marketing course at Harvard Business School, and that was because it was required. His consulting career focused solely on manufacturing, which he considers an advantage.

"When I started, the idea that you look at things through this rigid notion of demographics and market research never occurred to me," Koch states. "And I couldn't afford it anyway. Even to this day, I spend a lot of time in the markets, so I don't have to see focus groups to know who my customers are. I used to go to a bar at night and do a promotion and talk to twenty people. You do that a couple of hundred times, and you ought to have a good idea what your customers want."

To Koch, traditional marketing may work for the huge brands like Coca-Cola, Budweiser, or Crest toothpaste. But he believes that in most cases traditional marketing is a "smoke screen for an inability to really understand what is going on with the consumer." The idea of understanding the relationship with consumers through expensive marketing studies is not logical. Because it is such an inexact science, market research is more akin to educated guessing than real knowledge. "It's like going to an astrologist," he declares.

Though he disdained formal marketing, Koch's business plan unfolded with a series of innovative marketing maneuvers, often out of simple necessity. Though he longed to own his own brewery, and indeed later invested nearly $3 million in an aborted plan to build one, Koch's primary mission was to get Sam Adams into the glasses of customers. Beer, he reasoned, is relatively cheap to make, even with the choicest barley malt and hops. The brew is 95 percent water, and rather than slow himself down, as other craft brewers had done, by building his own brewery, Koch immediately decided to outsource his brewing to others.

Koch quickly caught flak from others in the nascent handcrafted beer industry who believed that unless a brewer used his own equipment, he didn't own the beer. Like other radical marketers, Koch believed with religious fervor in his product. The flavor, the quality, the consistency were the things customers cared about. Where the beer was brewed and by whom were irrelevant as far as he was concerned.

Absent the financial resources to hire consultants and invest in market research, Koch did his own unscientific polling of beer drinkers in search of a name for the lager. He was leaning toward New World Boston Lager but was persuaded to use the name Samuel Adams (a Boston icon and renowned patriot who was also a local brewer) after printing up mock labels and testing names with anyone willing to listen, including businesspeople seated next to him on planes. He surveyed more than one thousand people and tallied up the results, which clearly favored Samuel Adams. "I figured, here's a cheap way to do it, and what better place than a plane," Koch said in an interview in *Inc*. "It was my demographic—businesspeople, a lot of whom were interested in a better beer."

—— Stoking the Publicity Machine ——

Koch wanted a partner and spread the word. Several colleagues at Boston Consulting Group slipped their résumés onto his desk. "But they all looked like me," Koch said. Instead, in an inspired move, he hired his twenty-three-year-old secretary at Boston Consulting, Rhonda

Kallman, as employee number one. Kallman was young, attractive, and outgoing and worked as a bartender and waitress at night. She knew the Boston bar scene in a way the shy Koch did not and provided him with both an entrée and insight into his market without resorting to expensive market research. Kallman, four years out of secretarial school, knew how bars operated, who had the buying decision, what it would take to move the beer.

In classic start-up mode, Koch and Kallman filled every role. Koch taught himself to drive a forklift so he could move cases of beer from the warehouse to the delivery truck. Kallman would arrive at 6:30 every morning after late nights of pub crawling to load and deliver cases of beer. After a full day of selling, Koch would board a flight to Pittsburgh to oversee the overnight brewing, check into a Holiday Inn for a quick shower and change of clothes, and fly back to Boston for more sales calls.

After hiring Kallman, Koch turned next to a local public relations professional named Sally Jackson, who specialized in restaurant and hotel accounts in Boston, and offered her $36,000 a year to take on the nascent company's account. Jackson suggested that would be just enough to cover her fees but not expenses. Koch had no more cash to offer, so he gave her 2 percent equity in the company.

Jackson huddled with Koch and suggested they flip the usual public relations methodology. If she put together press kits and mailings and contacted journalists herself, they would have assumed that Boston Beer was a big company, not an earnest, two-person, bootstrap start-up worthy of attention. Instead, she had Koch call the media himself to tell his story. And rather than focus on the "Living" or "Food" sections of the print media, they aimed directly at the business pages, believing they could achieve dual results: publicity and notice among the core beer-drinking audience—twenty-one to forty-nine-year-old males, who also happened to be the same audience for the business press.

With his passion for his beer and a compelling story, Koch began to generate a steady stream of press for Boston Beer, starting with a story in *Business Week*. "My family was making beer when Eberhard Anheuser was selling soap," Koch crowed in that article. With Jackson helping him set the strategy, Koch became a proverbial media darling for the rest of the decade, generating stories in *People*, the *New York Times*, *Fortune*, the

Wall Street Journal, USA Today, Newsweek, Forbes, and dozens of other newspapers and magazines around the country. It was prototypical radical marketing: the story delivered free of charge to tens of millions of potential customers.

Six weeks after he founded the company, Koch, Kallman, and Jackson displayed Samuel Adams for the first time at an embryonic industry event called the Great American Beer Festival in Denver. The event began, according to Tom Dalldorf, as a party for craft beer makers with perhaps 30 breweries and 300 people in attendance. It has since become a major hallmark for the craft beer industry: in 1997 more than 35,000 attended the three-day festival, which featured 430 breweries and more than 1,400 different beers.

For Koch, the festival represented an unparalleled marketing opportunity. While few other breweries sent their chief executives, Koch was on hand to tell the Sam Adams story in detail. They poured countless samples of the beer and told whoever would listen about the prized ingredients and brewing techniques that created the brew. The professionalism and Koch's intensity paid off.

At the end of the show, a "people's choice" award for "best beer" was awarded, chosen by an unscientific balloting of the show's attendees. That first year, Samuel Adams won the award, and Koch was ecstatic. He had barely pasted the first labels on his beer bottles when suddenly he could boast the title of "Best Beer in America" as awarded by the Great American Beer Festival. No matter that the festival was itself a contrivance of the nascent craft beer industry and that no one outside the small enclave had heard of it. It was a badge of honor, instant credibility, that could be heavily marketed.

At the Denver airport the next morning, with their flight back to Boston delayed, Jackson spied an empty bank of pay telephones and went to work. On the first phone, she dialed the *Boston Globe* and convinced a reporter to interview Koch on the spot. While Koch chatted on one phone, Jackson dialed the next Boston media outlet and the next, until Koch had worked his way around the phone bank. In the taxi on the way home from Logan Airport the radio blared a story about the local beer that had been named "Best Beer in America."

Koch took full advantage of the award, displaying it on bottles of

Samuel Adams and on posters, banners, and other promotional materials. And having tasted victory that first year, Koch was determined to win again. "Jim coveted that award," Dalldorf said. "He made it his mission to get that award year after year." As it grew, Boston Beer arrived at the festival with an enthusiastic group of beer reps—half of whom were attractive young women—and poured bigger glasses of beer, held receptions for attendees, and marketed their story.

"Jim is the ultimate beer spinmeister," Dalldorf adds. "He set up the dynamics to make this a priority for his company. He did what any good marketer would do—take it and run with it." Samuel Adams won the award four years in a row, and then the festival, under pressure from the craft brewers, did away with the award. (Currently, a panel of expert judges do blind taste-testing to give out a series of gold medals. In the 1997 competition, Boston Beer won three gold medals.)

The aggressive marketing did not sit well with fellow craft brewers, and Koch gained an unwanted reputation within his own industry. In the laid-back West Coast world of craft beer, Koch was perceived as a calculating outsider who was capturing market share with a contract beer that some believed did not merit inclusion in the category. As his flame grew brighter and sales of Samuel Adams soared, many wished he would get his comeuppance.

But Koch had little time for petty infighting. He continued to innovate and build the brand. At night, his mind raced with possibilities. He viewed himself as a teacher with the task of educating the beer-drinking public about the potential of better tasting, higher-quality beer. Sales kept soaring, and profits began to pour in.

—— Freshness Counts ——

For Koch, the simplest but most profound realization in growing his company was to focus completely on just the key issues and not get derailed by less important ones. "For us, that meant two things," Koch says. "If we make great beer with every batch and work our asses off to sell it, we'll be all right. If we compromise on either one of those, we're screwed."

While on a trip to Germany to buy the special hops that go into Sam Adams beer, he decided to tackle the world's most demanding market, the birthplace of brewing, and try to sell in Germany. Because of its ingredients and brewing methods, Sam Adams passed the strict German purity laws that require that beer include only barley, yeast, water, and hops (without the adjunct ingredients like corn or rice that beers like Budweiser use). Sam Adams became the first American beer to be imported into Germany, a story that Koch took aggressively to the media.

And in 1987 Koch decided to market the advantage of contract brewing. He contracted with a brewery on the West Coast so that he could get fresh beer anywhere into the market within twenty-four hours. Because he refused to add preservatives to his brew, Koch knew the beer would not be as fresh after four or five months on a store shelf. In an aggressive marketing coup, Boston Beer became the first beer company to stamp a freshness date on its bottles with a promise that its beer would be in the marketplace within twenty-four hours of being brewed or the company would take it back. Bottles of Samuel Adams that passed the "sell by" date were also taken back. The company swallows more than $1 million worth of outdated beer each year, but the cost is well worth it. Indeed, so great was the response that virtually all the competition, including giants like Anheuser-Busch, have followed suit.

Koch is nothing if not relentless. Lacking the deep pockets of the major brewers, Koch took an alternative approach to advertising. He chose radio as his medium of choice because it was cheaper and more accessible to his target audience of twenty-something males. He saved money by writing and recording the ads himself, always pushing the envelope and adding a bite to his messages.

In one of the first radio spots, aired in 1987 during the centennial celebration of the Statue of Liberty, Koch told the audience: "When America asked Europe for its tired and its poor, we didn't mean their beer." He also mentioned competitors like Heineken and Beck's by name, pointing out that they added adjunct ingredients to their exported beer, thus rendering it unsellable in Germany. His needling drove the breweries to change the ingredients of their exports.

Koch loved the controversy, seeing that it attracted attention. He quotes David Ogilvy, the advertising guru, who once said, "You can't save souls in an empty church." His marketing, in fact, reflected his personality and the edge that he brought to his venture. Not only did Koch own the marketing function, he relished it and nurtured it and took every opportunity to sell his product. On December 31, 1992, when he climbed to the 23,068-foot summit of Mount Aconcagua in South America, the highest peak outside the Himalayas, Koch pulled out a bottle of Sam Adams beer and held it aloft. He knew on that day, with the Everest climbing season shut down for the winter, that he was higher than any human being on the planet. It was the kind of publicity stunt that Virgin's Richard Branson would be proud of. And Koch enthusiastically shared the story with the press upon his return.

You can't start a company like Boston Beer, Koch believes, without a willingness to break the rules and push the envelope. Among the more successful alternative marketing concepts he introduced was clever point-of-sale promotion to create awareness and visibility for his beer. He pioneered Samuel Adams hospitality nights at bars and beer dinners at fine restaurants in Boston and later around the country, a marketing ploy just recently emulated by his larger competitors.

In 1986 Koch introduced customized plastic menu stands and tent cards in bars and restaurants. For more than a decade, Boston Beer has taken the menus or beer lists for these establishments, printed them on Samuel Adams menu cards, and placed them on every bar and table they could reach. The company produces more than two million menu cards, and most of the major brewers have since copied Boston Beer. "In 1985 this was the only way anybody knew Sam Adams was available," says Rhonda Kallman.

—— Staying Close to the Customers ——

Kris Keidel, a thirty-year-old sales rep for Boston Beer, handles the company's home territory, the bars and restaurants around Boston. Her visits to her accounts never conclude until she distributes Sam Adams tent cards or menu stands around the bar or dining room. Her Jeep Cherokee is filled to overflowing with Sam Adams promotional material, from paper tent cards to giant banners that cost $40 each, which the company distributes liberally to its accounts.

According to Kallman, who oversees the expanding Boston Beer sales force, the reps are instructed that they must never leave an account without making some improvement on behalf of Sam Adams, be it distributing tent cards, helping to fix a faulty draft line, or leading an education session for the wait staff on a new Boston Beer offering. Keidel's mandate is to garner 30 percent of the on-premise craft beer space in any new account, a task that has become increasingly difficult as the category has exploded with entrants in the past few years. Even in its home territory, Samuel Adams is under pressure. "Lead with Lager" is the sales staff's rallying cry, a reminder that the original Sam Adams Boston Lager is the flagship, a brand that mustn't be bastardized.

Keidel is young, attractive, and aggressive; fully 40 percent of the Boston Beer sales reps are women. While the major brewers like Anheuser-Busch or Miller use distributors, Boston Beer prefers to sell direct to its accounts. At one Boston restaurant and pub, Keidel pushes to make sure a draft line for a new Boston Beer offering called Boston Cream Ale is working properly. She asks the manager to allow her to lead an educational session on the new brew for the wait staff and promises to return the next day to conduct it. The pub, a favorite spot for local college students and tourists, has a long, rectangular bar with an astounding eighteen draft lines for various beers and ales. Keidel has done her job here. Four lines belong to Boston Beer; just one offers Bud Light.

Indeed, Wall Street analysts who track the industry agree that Boston Beer has the best-trained, most-effective sales force. The sales reps must take a full week of training in selling techniques, account management, and more every three to four months. "Our sales force is our competitive advantage," Kallman says. This cadre of foot soldiers are like Mormon missionaries, says Tom Dalldorf of *Celebrator Beer News*. Smart, dedicated, and eager, they work sixteen-hour days, host beer nights, and keep detailed records of all their activities for Koch and Kallman to track.

"In a short time, Jim put craft beer all over the country, in every retailer and most taverns, because he understood beer making and marketing and executed very well," Dalldorf says. "The craft beer industry owes Jim Koch a debt of gratitude for teaching it how to sell beer. He made the craft beer market possible much earlier than it would have been if it had just been a bunch of hippies making beer and sharing it with locals."

—— Brand Extension with Brand Integrity ——

Boston Beer also understood the importance of extending the brand without diluting it. Soon after the initial success of its flagship Samuel Adams Boston Lager, the company began to experiment and introduce different flavors of beer, specifically pioneering a highly successful brand extension using seasonal brews. From Honey Porters to Cream Stout, from Octoberfest to Winter Lager, the company continues to extend its product line to create variety for a customer base that loves to experiment with new tastes.

In 1994 Koch pushed the limits by introducing the strongest beer in the world, a 35-proof, cognac-like drink called Triple Bock. The beer, which tastes more like a vintage port or sherry, sells for $4 a bottle, $100 a case, in small, 250-milliliter, cobalt blue bottles embossed with Samuel Adams's signature in 24-karat gold ink. Though Triple Bock has not yet earned a profit for Boston Beer, Koch is especially proud of the brew and even more outspoken about the company's need to make it. In a series of radio ads, he bragged about the fact that Triple Bock, because of its alcohol content, is illegal in nine states.

"You would never do a marketing study and discover that the world wants to buy a beer for $100 a case and be able to drink an ounce and a half at a time," Koch says. "If you surveyed a million beer drinkers and asked if they wanted a beer like this, nobody would.

"But that's not the issue. It was inevitable that we would make a beer like this, odd as that seems, because one of the things we are committed to doing is pushing the boundaries of beer. It's part of who we are as brewers. If you are serious about beer and committed to having fun and making challenging beers, then you do this."

The possibilities, for Koch, are endless. In 1995 he conceived of a "homebrew contest" in which individuals could submit their home-brewed beers and the winners would actually be bottled and sold by Boston Beer under the brand name Longshot. More than sixteen hundred beers were entered, and a panel of sixty-five expert judges picked three winners who received $5,000 in prize money and royalty rights for their beers.

Koch was not above creating subsidiaries to sell products he didn't feel fit the Samuel Adams mold. A Boston Beer brewmaster had urged Koch for several years to make an Oregon-style ale, with American hops and a distinct Northwest flavor. Koch relented, but rather than add to the Samuel Adams brand, he opened a subsidiary in Portland, Oregon, called Oregon Ale and Beer Company. Though the beer has been a popular seller in the region and in major national markets, its presence served to incense the close-knit Oregon brewing community, which took offense at Boston Beer's contract brewing methods and its audacity in claiming to be an Oregon craft beer.

—— Coping with Success ——

While Boston Beer became a lightning rod for both accolades and controversy as its fortunes grew, Jim Koch faced the radical marketer's inevitable dilemma. Dramatic growth has changed the marketplace and thus changed the rules. Boston Beer spent more than a decade creating a new attitude about beer in America, and that was matched by explosive growth in the industry. As Koch sees it, the company is no longer driven by rapid growth but by a slower, more steady expansion on the base that it has built.

"This is a niche, and a niche has boundaries," Koch says. "Those boundaries protect us from the big guys, but like other boundaries, they are limiting." Koch claims that he and Kallman knew all along that by targeting an audience that wanted better beer, the company would reach these limits sooner or later. "That's okay," Koch says. "I'd rather be the best choice for 1 percent of the market than the fifth-best choice for 90 percent of the market. Fifth-best in that case would be Stroh's."

But with a customer base for whom experimentation is a way of life, the clutter in the craft beer market has hurt Samuel Adams. Koch needed to find a way to lure the "triers" back into the fold while finding new customers to make loyal. Kallman felt that the company had reached a crossroads in the late 1990s and had to answer the question: So what? Everyone knows that Sam Adams is a quality beer and has been very successful. So what next?

Kallman believed that the brand needed repositioning with a new, younger audience. She noted that Koch has always been involved in every aspect of the company, from finance to brewing, and that having a company president with this amount of energy and insight is invaluable. But moving the brand forward on Koch's intuition alone no longer allowed for a cohesive marketing strategy.

What happened after that is an important lesson for radical marketers. Reluctantly, Koch softened his hard line against traditional marketing. After ten years without a formal marketing department, Koch, four years ago, hired a brand development vice president with a traditional beer marketing background and gave him the green light to expand the company's marketing activities. Koch agreed to a series of approaches that would have been unthinkable a decade ago, concepts he had long detested, such as market research studies, focus groups, extensive use of outside marketing consultants, and a $15 million budget for television and radio advertising. Basic tenets of radical marketing, like making sure the CEO owns the marketing function and keeping the marketing function small and flat, were abandoned in favor of these traditional approaches.

Not surprisingly, these traditional efforts failed. In 1998 the professional marketer left Boston Beer in frustration and under a dark cloud. He'd been successful building a marketing department, spending large sums on outside consultants, and hiring a high-powered advertising agency. But he'd failed to sell any beer. Koch, in attempting to embrace this more traditional route, encountered what large corporations run into with massive marketing departments: each subgroup of marketers tries to optimize their own piece of the equation, but this usually serves to undermine the overall identity of the brand.

Koch was appalled, for example, when the marketing department began creating packaging for various products with snowmen and sailboats and a promotion to give away a satellite dish. "This is not me. This is not Sam Adams," Koch declared. "What are we telling the consumer? Are we satellite dishes? Are we snowmen? We had radio ads with a guy slurping beer off the floor, another playing spoons. That is not us!"

Koch noted that when he did everything himself, the graphics were clunky, the advertising crude, but it was effective because it presented a clear, simple identity. And it was true to the brand.

Koch's intuition tells him that what the company's marketing needs "is to be more like us." To that end, he pulled back control and authorized that all marketing go through him once again. "I'm the only one who really understands what Sam Adams is. I created it," he says. "It's hard to get uniformity from committees. Committees are about compromise, and Sam Adams is not about compromises."

Radical marketers do not give up turf easily, and when they are burned, as Koch was, they tend to return to the tenets that brought them success. Koch now owns the marketing function again and has taken a philosophical approach to the heightened competition and difficult business environment. When Anheuser-Busch launched its public relations broadside in 1996, for example, Koch's response was to go out and buy the *Stars Wars* film trilogy and watch the entire three movies in one marathon session. He believed that the craft brewing industry's battle with A-B was analogous to that story: a group of rebels blow up the Death Star (the Death Star representing A-B's rampage to get everyone to drink Budweiser or Bud Light), but the bad guys (A-B) respond aggressively in the second movie, *The Empire Strikes Back.*

Koch was especially interested in the third movie. If there was a lesson, it would be learned here. For Koch, the travails of Luke Skywalker, having lost a hand in a battle with Darth Vader, represented the challenge Boston Beer faced. The force that helped create the initial success was not enough to reach a new, higher level; Luke was lost, detached from the Force, unable to focus on a clear path forward. The lesson, Koch concluded, was humility, a willingness to go back and learn and bring new skills to the battle.

"It was time to go back and be humble," Koch says. "We were not successful because of our inherent virtue. We were successful because we tapped into something. We led it and rode it at the same time. If, going forward, I am going to be in charge of this, I need to do some learning, to change and grow at the same time I make the right decisions about what is us. We cannot compromise on that."

Though he admits that his thinking is esoteric, he says the answers lie not in marketing texts but in metaphor. "If you want to understand this, you might as well go to the first four chapters of *The Odyssey* and find out what was in Telemachus's head when he set out to find his father. Or read Eliot's 'The Love Song of J. Alfred Prufrock' and find out what makes Prufrock unappealing to us. Yes, it's esoteric. But you are not going to figure out why people started smoking cigars again by thinking rationally. It's metaphorical. So you go to people whose stock in trade is metaphor, not marketing."

Koch's motto: refuse to seek conventional solutions. If you use conventional tools available to everyone, you will get answers available to everybody. Tools can be useful and provide information, and information can come from a lot of sources, but ultimately, says Koch, "the answers have to come from the part of you that is governed by spirit and metaphor and imagery and mythology. And your own passions. I deeply believe that's where the answers come from, particularly for something like Sam Adams."

13

Applying the Lessons of Radical Marketing to Traditional Marketing

"Consumers can still tell the difference
between pseudo-relationships and the
real thing. Sometimes they don't care
and sometimes they do."
—*Robert M. McMath*

One remaining question, and an important one, must be: Are the lessons of radical marketing suitable only for small, niche companies in their start-up phase, or are they applicable to more traditional marketers in mature, well-developed, advertising-intensive businesses? We believe that they are applicable, and that traditional marketers who do not consider adopting radical marketing techniques are both leaving themselves vulnerable to attack from aggressive radical marketers and missing out on opportunities to build new businesses.

There are indeed traditional marketers who pass the tattoo test. We call them "trad/rads," because they have managed to marry the best elements of the radical marketing model with the raw power of the traditional marketing approach to become industry leaders. Nike, for example, began as a quintessential radical marketer: a bunch of runners selling waffle-bottomed athletic shoes out of the back of a station wagon to other runners just like themselves. Now Nike is a $9 billion company that, in 1997, spent more than $150 million in advertising. But Phil Knight, Nike's CEO, still makes the marketing decisions. "Nike Towns" are a little bit about retailing and a lot about keeping in touch with customers. And "Ekins" (Nike spelled backwards), the young field sales force, are easily identifiable by their "swoosh" tattoos.

Budweiser is another trad/rad. Despite its huge size and mammoth marketing budget, there is passion in the Busch family, which has run the company for generations and pours a tiny taste of beer for every Busch baby on the day it is born. August Busch III, the CEO, has signaled the importance of marketing by naming his son and heir apparent to the top marketing post—although he himself stays actively and prominently involved. Even while openly attacking Sam Adams and the rest of the specialty beer market with a well-crafted public relations campaign, Budweiser adopted some of the very radical techniques Boston Beer first used against them. August Busch IV, the company's young marketing vice president, spends much of his time listening to customers in bars and restaurants. Bud has copied and successfully leveraged Boston Beer Company's' famous freshness-dating tactic and even launched a massive advertising campaign, sans amphibians, that extols Budweiser's commitment to quality. From Jim Koch's point of view, imitation is the sincerest form of flattery.

The unconvinced may still correctly argue that both Budweiser and Nike have very strong radical roots—most notably CEO owners instead of professional managers. The real question remains: Can truly professional marketers, and those without radical roots, become trad/rads?

A few years ago "lightbulb" jokes became popular. "How many psychiatrists," went one, "does it take to change a lightbulb?" The answer, of course, was: "One. But the lightbulb really has to want to change." The same may be true of traditional marketers. It takes only one, but they have to really want to change. Unfortunately, the track record of acceptance of radical marketing techniques by traditional marketers is not good. For every successful trad/rad such as Budweiser or Nike, there are many others who don't want to try to understand radical marketing.

You can look to Apple Computer, which turned from its radical marketing roots to traditional marketing by bringing in John Sculley from Pepsico as CEO in 1984. Sculley, the consummate traditional marketer, professionalized Apple and cleaned up its radical marketing approach. Apple's well-documented troubles have stemmed from a wide variety of factors, and it would be unfair to blame them all on the ham-fisted shift from successful radical marketing to unsuccessful professional marketing. But it is undeniable that formulaic traditional marketing could not save Apple, and not ironic at all that the company's board looked to Steve Jobs, Apple's cofounder and original radical marketer, to try to right the foundering ship. Indeed, if Sculley, one of the great traditional marketers of the last two decades, was unable to successfully replace radical marketing with the traditional alternative, that must say something about both.

──── The Snapple Fiasco ────

There are many cases of confident professional marketers stepping in with plans to clean up a radical marketing approach, only to find themselves a good distance from the success they hoped for. Take the case of Quaker Oats and Snapple.

In this instance, the confident CEO was William Smithburg of Quaker Oats. Smithburg's confidence was seemingly well founded. In 1983 Quaker bought Stokely's for $238 million, and with the company came a relatively small beverage brand called Gatorade. At the time, industry analysts scoffed and accused Quaker Oats of overpaying. However, Quaker Oats grew the Gatorade business from $100 million to $1.3 billion in less than a decade, making it the third largest beverage company in the United States. Quaker Oats' success was based on classic professional marketing. The company took an undermarketed, niche supermarket brand and poured in hundreds of millions of advertising and sponsorship dollars. They used their huge sales force to squeeze out shelf space in supermarkets and began introducing a stream of new products, systematically changing every one of the variables taught in marketing school—flavor, color, pack size, and so forth. Gatorade was a stunning success, at least in the United States, where there was little entrenched sport drink competition.

Thus, when Quaker Oats bought Snapple in November 1994 for a whopping $1.7 billion and analysts again accused them of overpaying,

Smithburg was unfazed. Earlier that year *Beverage World* magazine reported that both Pepsi and Coke had turned down the Snapple acquisition for $25 million did not bother Quaker Oats. Nor did it appear to ruffle the Chicago-based food giant that by the time it made its acquisition, the tea category, in which Snapple competed, had finally grown large enough to attract the attention of Pepsi and Coke, and both had introduced their own competitive products.

Quaker Oats believed that the same formula that had transformed Gatorade would work for Snapple. They were very, very wrong. It was a mistake that would cost Smithburg, his second-in-command Phil Marineau, and the first head of the new Snapple division, Don Uzzi, their jobs. More important, it cost Quaker Oats' shareholders dearly, as the Snapple division's sales fell from $700 million before the acquisition to around $500 million a year later; the division would drop more than $100 million in profits over the two years Quaker Oats ran the brand. With Smithburg's resignation under pressure in 1997, Quaker finally waved the white flag and sold Snapple to Triarc.

Again, as in the Sculley situation at Apple, it does not seem to be an issue of bad marketing. Quaker Oats was and is a reasonably successful consumer goods company. With over one-quarter of their revenues devoted to sales and marketing and a string of marketing coups such as Gatorade to their credit, Quaker Oats undoubtedly had a staff of seasoned and adroit professional marketers. Nor was it that these marketers just didn't understand the beverage business. Indeed, when Marineau left Quaker Oats, he was quickly snapped up—first by Dean Foods and soon thereafter by Pepsi, where he has been installed as CEO Roger Enrico's heir apparent. Rather, the issue was apparently one of *different* marketing. All the changes Quaker Oats made—to the advertising, to the product line, to the distribution channels—simply didn't work.

The Snapple story has been well chronicled by many, from *Direct Marketing* magazine to the *New York Times*. The company's founding was the stuff of entrepreneurial lore. Three childhood friends decided in 1972 to raise $30,000 to form a company to distribute 100 percent natural fruit juices in New York City. Six years later, they created their own brand, Snapple, and began producing the product themselves. By 1987 they had introduced natural sodas and natural teas and moved beyond their northeastern base to the West Coast. When Quaker Oats bought them, they had fifty plants, dominated the fast-growing natural tea category, and had begun making their mark internationally.

They had done so with a classic radical marketing approach. Snapple and its customers had that strong empathy, almost love, that is common between radical marketers and their customers. Snapple even *exceeded* the tattoo test. *Direct Marketing* reported that not only were Snapple tattoos common at the second Woodstock festival, but one New Jersey couple used Snapple as their newborn son's middle name.

Quaker Oats was not impressed. Perhaps the first warning of the company's utter disregard for Snapple's radical formula was the fact that they immediately reduced the Snapple staff from 270 to two dozen. But more important, they also changed the distribution system. According to *Forbes*, Quaker Oats did not realize until after the acquisition that Snapple employed a completely different distribution system from that used by Gatorade. Radically different.

Rather than use a well-organized network of tractor-trailers delivering pallets of Gatorade to huge grocery chain warehouses, Snapple reached the stores via a small army of three hundred independent distributors in panel vans. One of Quaker Oats' first moves was to take the high volume and very important supermarket accounts away from the Snapple distributors and give them to the huge, sophisticated, and computerized Gatorade distribution system. In turn, Quaker Oats offered Snapple distributors the right to sell Gatorade to their small accounts. For these small businesspeople, the exchange was financially disastrous. Their rabid enthusiasm for twelve-hour days of peddling Snapple to everyone from Safeway to street vendors soon waned. To serve the supermarket customers better, Quaker Oats also cut the product line from fifty to thirty-five flavors and introduced a number of new packages—multipacks, plastic bottles. All of these changes were very logical and professionally sound, and all struck at the very heart of the pact that Snapple had with its employees and its consumer base.

Soon Snapple volumes began falling—the result of this series of disastrous changes to the distribution system—and Quaker Oats quickly lost patience. Pre-Quaker, virtually all of Snapple's marketing and product development had been done by these fanatical customers, who wrote and called constantly—suggesting everything from marketing ideas to flavors. *Direct Marketing's* managing editor, Greg Gattuso, said, "Fans give Snapple enough market research to keep most marketing research departments busy for years, demanding, among other things, more caffeine-free drinks, more diet drinks, bigger bottles, twelve-packs, and less glue on the labels."

Rather than employ a slick pitchman like Gatorade's Michael Jordan, Snapple used Wendy Kaufman, an order department administrator. She wasn't very polished, but she was undeniably genuine. While she became famous as "Wendy the Snapple Lady" on a series of cheaply produced television commercials in which she answers letters from real-life fans, she had, in fact, started out *really* answering letters. For many years, she opened every letter herself until the volume became too great. According to Maryanne Farrell, Snapple's national marketing director, the marketing strategy was based on "consumer love of the product."

Indeed, leveraging this customer closeness was an essential part of what Snapple was, even in the early days after the Quaker Oats takeover. In 1995 Dave Elzinga, Snapple's group marketing manager, said, "Nearly all our advertising is based on our response to the over 3,000 fan letters, videotapes, and crafts we receive every week." Early on, Quaker Oats utilized Snapple's 250,000-name customer database and, from a handwritten customer suggestion, sponsored a successful Snapple convention. It attracted fans from all over the country.

But the Snapple advertising approach soon gave way to a more polished and traditional approach. The result was a very unsuccessful ad campaign. Not only did Snapple's existing customers not get it, apparently no one else did either. The Spike Lee–created campaign, "Threedom Is Freedom," was, according to the professional marketer Smithburg, intended to broaden Snapple's appeal without losing its "funky" image. It is a textbook case, were one needed, of the dangers of substituting a patronizing, superficial view of the consumer for a genuine one.

Not only did the message change, but so did the medium. Like most radical marketers, pre–Quaker Oats Snapple was a surgical strike advertiser. Its ad budget for 1993 was $30 million, the same percentage it had been for the previous twelve years. Rather than take the broad-brush approach of advertising on broadcast television, Snapple primarily used more targeted media, such as cable, and advertised on radio shows like Howard Stern's and Rush Limbaugh's. For Quaker Oats, which spent ten times as much in relative terms to advertise a product as did Snapple, this approach was inadequate. As soon as Quaker Oats took over, Howard and Rush were out because they were too controversial. Mainstream network was in. Ad expenditures quickly doubled. Out with surgical strike, in with adblast.

Again, it would be overly simplistic to blame Snapple's woes totally on the change from radical to traditional marketing. After all, to be fair, Snapple was experiencing growing pains before Quaker Oats bought it, and these were part of the reason for selling out. However, the change in marketing formula certainly played a part. The hubris of Quaker Oats certainly compounded the problems. Nor, as *Forbes* implied, was the Snapple marketing formula a secret before the takeover.

In May 1994, Bruce Oman of *Beverage World* wrote a thoughtful analysis of Snapple's "unconventional wisdom." Indeed, *Beverage World* named Snapple its 1993 "brand of the year." Everyone in the industry knew why Snapple worked and understood its formula for success. Quaker Oats' marketing elite simply dismissed that knowledge out of hand.

Perhaps the most insightful postmortem on the whole Snapple affair was written by Robert M. McMath in the delightfully named *American Demographics* column "What Were They Thinking?" He relates the Snapple story to another one he witnessed firsthand early in his career. "During the '50s Goddard's silver polishes established relationships with its customers. The [advertising] campaign wasn't big and splashy, but deliberate. . . . Sales doubled year after year until S. C. Johnson took over and applied its brand of marketing savvy—mass production, pallet load shipments, and big thinking. Goddard's polishes are still on the market, but a shadow of their former selves." He goes on to say, "Consumers can still tell the difference between pseudo-relationships and the real thing. Sometimes they don't care and sometimes they do."

As an epilogue, Glenn Collins of the *New York Times* reports that Triarc, Snapple's new owner, has reversed the policy that took the supermarkets away from the distributors, cut Quaker's lengthy new product development time back from one year to a few months, and rehired Wendy. He concludes, "So far, beverage experts say, Triarc appears to have put Snapple back on track."

──── The Saturn Scenario ────

The Snapple case would seem to suggest that it is simply impossible for professional marketers to get their heads around radical marketing or for radical marketing to work on a large scale. In fact, neither is the case, and the proof comes from a most unlikely source.

In 1994 *Business Week* reported on a remarkable event. On June 24 and 25, forty-four thousand Saturn automobiles descended on Spring Hill, Tennessee, home of the first Saturn plant in the United States. *Brandweek* later reported that and yet another one hundred thousand participated in local events. The thirty thousand people who showed up in Spring Hill were met by two thousand of the plant's eighty-seven hundred workers, driving shuttle buses, manning display booths, and directing visitors to the tent where they could get a Saturn tattoo. (The tattoos were temporary and could be washed off. After all, this is a family sedan, not a Harley "hog.") According to Don Hudler of Saturn, visitors came from as far away as Alaska, Hawaii, and Taiwan to attend.

Most of us can understand why one hundred thousand people would travel to Daytona Beach or Austin or Milwaukee to show off their motorcycles. It is a bit more difficult to understand why thirty thousand people would drive across America to attend a barbecue honoring a midsized American car made by General Motors—and to be honest, a somewhat nondescript little car at that.

According to David Aaker, the Berkeley professor who has made the most thorough study of the Saturn phenomenon, the story began on January 7, 1985, when GM Chairman Roger Smith announced GM's intention to develop and build cars "manufactured in the U.S. that are world leaders in quality, cost, and customer satisfaction." The car debuted five years later in 1990.

By 1992, only two years after the launch and despite a relatively small dealer network, Saturn had become the tenth-highest-selling brand out of over two hundred sold in the United States, and the fourth highest if fleet and cash rebate sales were excluded. Two different industry studies proclaimed Saturn to have the most valued dealer franchises in the United States, second only to Lexus. Awareness of the car among the American public jumped from 1 percent at launch to 79 percent one year later. Over 95 percent of Saturn owners said they would enthusiastically recommend the Saturn to others. This was higher than the percentage registered by Lexus and even Mercedes. In other words, Saturn was the GM success story of the decade, and one of the great brand-building success stories of all time. It is all the more amazing because it is an American success, and one created by General Motors, a conservative and traditional company. Indeed, Saturn is a radical marketing superstar created by the quintessential traditional marketing machine—sort of.

Aaker attributes Saturn's success to two factors. First, reasonably enough, Saturn is a good car. "Too often there is the illusion that brands can be created by advertising, without a product and service that really deliver quality and value—that image is a 'problem' of advertising," Aaker writes. "The reality is that the product drives the image. The Edsel of the 1950's would have been a symbol of quality today if Edsel had built quality products that first year. Some very good advertising and marketing were wasted because of a shoddy product."

Saturn was a wonderfully unique product proposition—for the first time, *Automotive News* reported, someone had promised the world a totally recyclable car. And not only was the Saturn product good, but the Saturn Company stood behind it. The company offered a money-back guarantee. They were obsessively quick to rectify any mistake, real or perceived. Indeed, they received tremendous mileage, both in their commercials and through word of mouth, by quickly recalling defective cars and even having an engineer fly to a remote location to fix a defective seat.

But the second factor was radical marketing. The Saturn marketing plan was simple. According to a key team member from the Hal Riney advertising agency, who helped launch the car, "We started out with two guiding principles. First, we intended to sell the 'software,' not just the car. By software we meant the whole car-buying experience. Second, we never resorted to car-talk in our communications. We insisted on speaking to people intelligently and in a straightforward way. It clearly helped that we were in California, far from the influence of Detroit-think."

As Aaker noted, by settling in California, the Saturn team was on the front lines of the Japanese invasion, closely connected to consumers, rather than being insulated in Detroit, one of the few places in America still dominated by American cars.

The key to Saturn's marketing is that Saturn has concentrated on the customer relationship and on building loyalty to the brand. Saturn's slogan, "A different kind of company, a different kind of car," is far more than just lip service. The company has convincingly demonstrated many of the characteristics of radical marketers—loving your customers and staying close to them, hiring as if your life depends on it, committing to the long term, and, most radically for a car brand, using a mix of grassroots and traditional advertising to communicate with customers.

Saturn's defining moment perhaps was the 1993 recall: the company realized that all 350,000 cars built before April 1993 had a wire that was improperly grounded. Rather than the customer disaster it could have been, the recall became a tremendous coup. First, Saturn recalled the cars voluntarily rather than in response to a government mandate. Fifty percent were repaired in two weeks. A competitor's government-mandated recall repair rate reached only 33 percent after twelve months, Aaker points out. Most important, the Saturn dealers turned the recall into a celebration, brilliantly using it as a marketing event and excuse to spend time with customers, taking them to baseball games, throwing barbecues, and washing the cars after repairing them. For Saturn customers, rather than being a chore, the recall was a reaffirmation of the brand promise, perfect proof of the Saturn brand commitment to them over the short and long term.

Another particularly interesting component of the Saturn story was how Saturn used marketing and advertising. *Ad Age* reports that Saturn chose Hal Riney as its agency twenty-nine months before launch, to give Riney time to become fully steeped in understanding the customer and what Saturn was trying to communicate. This worked spectacularly well, so well, in fact, that Riney in time became the de facto guardian of the brand and champion of the consumer. Interestingly,

Riney was not even originally one of the fifty agencies that applied for the account. Indeed, Riney had questions about joining up. In the words of Don Hudler, then vice president for sales and marketing for Saturn, "He wanted to know if we were for real." Riney knew that the $100 million ad budget planned for Saturn's start-up, although a staggering sum by radical standards, is not a very large budget to sustain a car nameplate, much less to launch one.

Indeed, the only reason the budget was sufficient was because, again, Saturn used radical marketing techniques to generate huge word of mouth. Saturn also used relatively less advertising as a total proportion of the communication mix. The company has proved to be the most adroit user of public relations of any of the major car companies. This was "absolutely not accidental," according to Hudler.

But despite the relatively modest budget and high use of other communications tools, advertising was an important part of the mix. And in Hal Riney, Saturn found a marketing partner who very quickly understood its role and the automaker's strategy. In fact, Hal Riney was not charged with selling the car. Rather, the agency was charged with creating a meaningful conversation with a particular set of customers—those who do not enjoy the haggling and the "Boy, you're really a tough cookie and I'll have to talk to my manager to approve this deal" games endemic to new-car purchase. Riney quickly understood, and because they were involved with all communications—from national advertising to local dealer ads to internal employee communications—were able to create a natural, unaffected, and consistent voice for the entire organization. In one well-publicized example, Riney vetoed a dealer plan to give away a car because it wasn't Saturn style. Instead, they substituted a contest where current and prospective Saturn owners could win a trip to Spring Hill to help build their car.

Riney also was instrumental in convincing Saturn to eschew the classic GM and Toyota formula of hokey car names such as Cressida and Lumina. Instead, Saturn used simple, clean model numbers. The decision was both pragmatic (to avoid splitting an already small budget between product and company) and principled—Saturn was all about straightforward communication, not hype.

As important as all these contributions were, though, Riney's greatest

contribution may be in the ads themselves. Riney's ads have shown customers, real customers, telling stories. That these were real people, not
actors, was groundbreaking enough, but even more surprising was the
fact that Riney refused to show only customers selected from the center
of the mass market. Instead of just using male baby boomers, Riney
showed a mix of people—for example, an older woman who uses her
Saturn to pick up friends for bingo. By daring not to aim for the center
of the mass market and speaking to consumers without hype and
hoopla, Riney and Saturn used advertising to build an astounding consumer connection. One ex-Riney staffer says she has seen only one other
visceral connection with consumers as powerful as the one Saturn created—in her old days at Apple.

Knowledgeable marketers have been stunned at Saturn's success. The
Brandweek columnist John Bissell called "Saturnstock," the company's
Woodstock-like festival, "remarkable." He marveled, "Even more
incredible is that this coup was hatched by General Motors, that bastion
of traditional and conservative marketing." Correctly, he understood
that the real importance of the Saturn success was that instead of the traditional approach of targeting non-users and begging them to try the
product in hopes that some of them might like it, Saturn targeted existing users, trying to build loyalty and counting on these customers to
attract new ones. Saturn was the first car marketer to understand and act
on the Bain & Company finding that 80 percent of profits come from
existing customers but only 20 percent of marketing expenditures go
against them. He quotes David Sholes of Rapp Collins Worldwide:
"They succeeded in *doing* something we all want to do." Hudler believes
one of the most important Saturn innovations was realizing that "the
primary audience for advertising is the owner base, the dealer network,
and the employees. If you can get them on board, they'll create the word
of mouth."

Raymond Serafin, then of *Ad Age* and now with DMB&B, echoed
a similar conclusion. "Saturn is a rousing marketing success," he wrote,
"a textbook case of how to build a brand through a single-minded
focus on how customers relate to the product and the company behind
it. All done despite a weak economy and competition from more that
forty other brands."

—— Are There Lessons Here? ——

Will Saturn's success provide an example for other traditional marketers? Some are skeptical. Many have openly rejected the Saturn formula. General Motors clearly chose to continue its reliance on traditional advertising. A subsequent article in *Ad Age* refuted Saturn's success and noted that there is "still no substitute for traditional ads. Carmakers know how to cultivate 'their' sort of buyers, and ads trigger a response." In fact, perhaps they *don't* know how to cultivate these buyers. In early 1998, GM's share of the U.S. market dropped below 30 percent for the first time in decades, although it has since rebounded.

In some respects, it is, of course, natural to find some resistance to the Saturn approach in a magazine devoted to advertising. But even those with less vested interests have been reluctant to accept the more radical approach. In a 1994 article in *Sales and Marketing Management*, Jack Falvey summed up the counterview by arguing, "Attempting to attract customers . . . and buying customer satisfaction ratings with love and liberal customer service budgets can't be sustained." He concludes that there is "no need to invent a 'pretty good' alternative." This conclusion is stunning: an utter rejection of the car success story of the 1990s by a seasoned professional.

Even Aaker is not sanguine. "There is considerable resentment within General Motors that Saturn has received resources that were needed elsewhere and a tendency to attribute the Saturn success to money rather than to how the money was spent. It is not easy to change any organization, and GM is not just any organization. There is a real question as to whether they can develop the motivation and ability to change." One insider grumbles, "Truth be told, if you multiply its one profitable year by ten or so, it still would not recover its investment." They also point out that Saturn is no longer based in California but has been moved to Detroit.

We are more optimistic than Professor Aaker and other skeptics. Marketing, and in particular advertising, is strangely conservative for an industry built around innovation and creativity. It has clung to one organizational model, brand management, for sixty-eight years, and to an archaic and obviously inadequate agency compensation system for even longer. Innovation, when it comes, invariably comes slowly and against great resistance. Sadly enough, despite a great deal of talk, most of the breakthrough marketing innovations of the last two decades are still fringe ideas in the mainstream marketing world—database-driven "inside-out" marketing, "one-to-one" customer loyalty programs, and so forth.

Nonetheless, there is change.

Slowly but surely, the best traditional marketers are becoming radicalized. Although few would label themselves radical, Iams' Tom MacLeod and Virgin's David Tait are converts nonetheless. Many consultants are convincing their clients to break out of the old drift-net approach to customer acquisition. And the clients are listening.

Examples of little revolutions are everywhere. Nestlé, the world's largest food company, made former frozen food salesman Peter Brabeck-Letmathe CEO not long after he radically changed the company's marketing strategy. Several years ago, as vice president of strategic business, Brabeck-Letmathe created the Casa Buitoni Club, Nestlé's bold experiment to establish one-to-one communication in a quintessential "mass market." Launched in the United Kingdom, the Casa Buitoni Club was a strategic initiative to build a community of users around Nestlé's pasta brand, Buitoni. Nestlé assembled huge databases of people who loved Italian cooking and established robust dialogues with these customers. As *Ad Age* reported in January 1998, "Club members were encouraged to turn to Buitoni as a helpful expert for advice on all aspects of Italian cooking. Moreover, they were invited to participate in recipe and new product development." Nor is it stopping here. Brabeck-Letmathe has the same goal for Nestlé's other businesses: "to know our consumer in much more detail." Nestlé is now rolling out similar initiatives across other products and countries.

Casa Buitoni Club, next to Saturn, is probably the most ambitious radical marketing experiment ever carried out by a classical mass marketer. But it is not the only one. R. J. Reynolds and Philip Morris have also built huge databases of their most loyal customers and developed special programs. BellSouth has experimented with new, segment-focused organizations. And those trained at Saturn are now back in the GM mainstream, in key marketing positions from Detroit to Tokyo, all with an understanding of what can be done and with a radical gleam in their eye. Don Hudler, who would also probably squirm under the label "marketing revolutionary," believes that radical marketing will stick. "Yes," he says, "Saturn will become more like GM. But it will cut both ways. Saturn will have an impact on GM as well." He points out that even though he has an office in Detroit, he also has one in Spring Hill.

And if *GM* can spawn a radical marketer like Saturn . . . just think what you could do.

Epilogue

Despite the spotlight we have placed on the ten companies in this book, it is clear that these are hardly the only radical marketers at work today. In truth, the movement to the radical edge is well entrenched and spreading rapidly. The chief constraint on broadening our list has not been any lack of candidates but rather the time and resources necessary to research and develop the cases.

The original list was based primarily on the experience of the authors, generated naturally in the course of their consulting and journalism careers. But as we searched more systematically through secondary sources, we came across numerous possibilities: Printmark International, Yahoo, Safeskin, Sonic Toothbrush, Southwest Airlines, Amgen, the Mayo Clinic, Broker Restaurants, IDG Books, Amazon.com, Consumer Financial Services, Waremart Foods, Bank of Boulder, and Redmond Products. What is particularly striking is the sheer diversity of the group, spanning industries from health care to high-tech to retailing to financial services. Nor was there any regional concentration, as in the high-tech industries; radical marketers are cheerfully building successful brands from Boston to the Bay Area, and from San Antonio, Texas, to Rochester, Minnesota.

Another source of radical marketers, and an unexpected one, were the executives and academics with whom we tested the book's premises. Virtually everyone was able to nominate yet more candidates. An insurance executive suggested New Balance Athletic Shoes; a London-based consultant brought Billy Graham to our attention and pointed out the differences between his Crusade and those of more traditional marketers like the 700 Club; an executive recruiter told us of the fast-growing consulting firm Cambridge Technology Partners, where the head of marketing is an ex-commodities trader and speechwriter turned brand builder par excellence. Ben Shapiro, a consultant and former marketing professor at Harvard Business School, made a case for Dell Computer Corporation. It seemed as if everyone knew at least one radical marketer. Our conclusion: there are enough radical marketers around to provide material for two books, or even three.

In a world with increasingly aware consumers, skyrocketing media costs, and ubiquitous traditional marketing formulas, it is harder than ever to be heard above the noise and gain competitive advantage using those old formulas. Indeed, what we now call radical will more than likely one day represent the mainstream. And that will be a good thing, because marketing, at its best, is a dialogue with consumers, filled with creativity and passion, that makes a lasting and visceral connection.

Acknowledgments

No book happens in a vacuum. Contributors, both large and small, are numerous, invaluable and inspiring. The authors would like to thank Joel Kurtzman, who served as the catalyst for this research and published the articles in *Strategy & Business* that lead to this book. We also want to thank Laureen Rowland, our editor and relentlessly enthusiastic champion at HarperBusiness. Indeed, the entire team at HarperBusiness was uniformly supportive and deserves acknowledgment—Adrian Zackheim, Jodi Anderson, Michele Jacob, Amy Lambo, and the incomparable Lisa Berkowitz.

We also offer our gratitude to Jackie Collette, Sally Jackson, Loretto Crane, Bryan Brown, Garreth Jones, Joyce Gadra, Chris Romoser, Rick Secor, Peter Land, Mark Fredrickson, Dennis McNally, Guy Washington, George Harrar, Linda Harrar, Janie Morse, Barry Adler, Leonard Gingold, Lorie Savel, Mark Borges, Bob Buday, Sung Park, Lisa Figlioli, Richard Rifkin, Bill Haney, Chris Lederer, Ray Serafin, Rich Gould, Brian Fischer, and John Colasanti for their direct contribution to this effort. Steve Greyser, Ben Shapiro, David Newkirk, Milind Lele, and Prafulla Gupta helped us frame our definition of traditional marketing and hone the contrasts with radical marketing. Barbara Martz offered sage counsel and encouragement throughout the process.

Many of the professionals of Booz-Allen & Hamilton are acknowledged by name throughout this book. However, Sam would also like to offer a broader thanks to all of his former colleagues and to the firm itself for the extraordinary environment which encouraged him to push his thinking on the topic of radical marketing.

Finally, Glenn would like to thank his family for their remarkable love and support. Sam offers thanks and more to Liz Upsall. And she knows why.

Index

D

E

F

G

N

O

P

About the Authors

Sam Hill is co-founder of the Helios Consulting Group, which helps top management solve complex marketing problems. He has almost twenty years of experience working on marketing issues for leading corporations around the world. Before Helios, he was partner with and chief marketing officer of Booz-Allen & Hamilton and vice-chairman of DMB&B, a top twenty global advertising agency. He has contributed to *Harvard Business Review, Strategy & Business, Fortune,* and the *Financial Times.* He lives with his wife and two children in Winnetka, Illinois.

Glenn Rifkin is a veteran business journalist who has written extensively for the *New York Times.* He is the co-author of *The Ultimate Entrepreneur: The Story of Ken Olsen and Digital Equipment Corporation* and has also contributed to the *Harvard Business Review, Fast Company,* the *Boston Globe, Forbes ASAP,* and *Strategy & Business.* He is currently a senior editor with Knowledge Universe Publishing. He lives with his son in Acton, Massachusetts.